M000020883

Bend

WHEN LIFE DARES YOU TO *break*

Dig deep—
Bend on!
Beth

Beth Lueders

41Ten & Co.

"There is a well-known quote by an unknown author that says, 'Whenever you find yourself doubting how far you can go, just remember how far you've come.' *Bend* will engage you in riveting stories of people who have experienced overwhelming challenges in their lives. In so doing, you may reflect on your own life and recognize that like them you have the strength and endurance to bend as well."

—**Jean Driscoll,** eight-time winner of the Boston Marathon— Women's Wheelchair Division, U.S. Olympic & Paralympic Hall of Fame member, motivational speaker, author

"We understand how painful it is to get news that things are not going to turn out as you hoped. *Bend* features individuals and families like us who have learned to dig deep and believe beyond the immediate circumstances to come through stronger than we ever imagined."

—**Rick and Melissa Hinnant,** founders of Grace & Lace, noteworthy *Shark* Tank entrepreneurs, philanthropists

"As a seasoned investigator and explorer, I appreciate Beth's commitment to asking the tough questions and digging deeper to discover how any of us can carve a comeback from disruptive adversity. Brave. Intriguing. Insightful. *Bend* is a must-read for anyone determined to rise above and press onward."

—**Bob Cornuke,** biblical explorer, president of B.A.S.E Institute, author, speaker

"*Bend* is a timely book about bending, rather than breaking, in times of adversity. Beth, a sincere and sensitive writer, introduces us to unsung heroes and heroines who knew how to 'bend' when facing difficulty. Their varied stories, presented in detail, send a message we need now. Beth is a compassionate witness to the strength of the human spirit and the vast mercy of God."

—**Marcy Heidish,** award-winning author and poet, National Endowment for The Arts recipient, university literature professor

"In her timeless narrative style, honed by thousands of hours of writing about grief and suffering, Beth takes on one of the great assumptions of our time: heartbreak. Using real and riveting stories from a broad spectrum of trials and tribulations, Beth weaves together her case's hopeful possibility: we bend but don't break. Beth opines that God has put something unbreakable inside each of us. At times haunting and at times inspiring, *Bend* is the perfect book for anyone looking to reframe their own struggles and grief and discover their own innate ability to bend."

—**Justin Foster,** Root + River cofounder, speaker

"We've all faced times when we've felt like quitting. Masterfully written, *Bend* is one captivating book that will not let you give up. *Bend* is a definite page-turner, and it resonates with my own passion to inspire others to just take the next one step . . . then the next. Beth bravely shows us that what happens to us does not need to define us."

—**Ginger Martin,** CEO American National Bank, Oakland Park, Florida

"*Bend* reminds me of what Martin Luther once said: 'God can use a crooked stick to write a straight line.' The book is full of the real life stories of those who experienced bending beyond their limits but were not broken. *Bend* is a source of inspiration to look beyond any difficult life circumstances, discover the beauty, and look to God, who is right there with you through it all. This book instills a newfound gratitude and appreciation for life and an unspoken commission to live with purpose and resolve. To know that in this life you will face trials, temptations, and obstacles of various kinds— you yourself WILL BEND . . . but you don't have to break. And if you feel broken, you CAN be restored."

—**Daniel Gil,** professional Ninja athlete, finalist on *American Ninja Warrior,* motivational speaker

*To Dad, Mom, Jeanette,
and all cancer warriors.*

*Your lives courageously inspire
us all to keep bending.*

© 2020 by Beth Lueders
All rights reserved. Printed in the United States of America.
Published by 41Ten & Co.
Hello@BethLueders.com

No part of this book may be reproduced, stored in a retrieval system, or transmitted in any form without prior written permission of the author and publisher except in the case of brief quotations within critical articles and reviews.

Library of Congress Cataloging-in-Publication Data
Lueders, Beth
ISBN: 978-1-7351712-0-3
ISBN (e-book): 978-1-7351712-1-0
Library of Congress Control Number: 2020910283

Book design by Sylke Mears Lacy
Cover design by Joy A. Miller, Five J's Design

The Scriptures quoted are from the NET Bible® http://netbible.com copyright © 1996, 2019 used with permission from Biblical Studies Press, L.L.C. All rights reserved.

Scripture taken from the NEW AMERICAN STANDARD BIBLE®, Copyright © 1960, 1962, 1963, 1968, 1971, 1972, 1973, 1975, 1977, 1995 by The Lockman Foundation. Used by permission.

Scriptures taken from the Holy Bible, New International Version®, NIV®. Copyright © 1973, 1978, 1984, 2011 by Biblica, Inc.™ Used by permission of Zondervan. All rights reserved worldwide. www.zondervan.com The "NIV" and "New International Version" are trademarks registered in the United States Patent and Trademark Office by Biblica, Inc.™

Scripture quotations are taken from the Holy Bible, New Living Translation, copyright © 1996, 2004, 2007, 2013, 2015 by Tyndale House Foundation. Used by permission of Tyndale House Publishers, Inc., Carol Stream, Illinois 60188. All rights reserved.

Scripture quotations are taken from The Living Bible copyright © 1971. Used by permission of Tyndale House Publishers, a Division of Tyndale House Ministries, Carol Stream, Illinois 60188. All rights reserved.

Scripture taken from The Message. Copyright © 1993, 1994, 1995, 1996, 2000, 2001, 2002. Used by permission of NavPress Publishing Group.

Scripture quotations marked TPT are from The Passion Translation®. Copyright © 2017, 2018 by Passion & Fire Ministries, Inc. Used by permission. All rights reserved. ThePassionTranslation.com.

Printed in the United States of America
2020—First Edition

10 9 8 7 6 5 4 3 2 1

Contents

Introduction

Every day you are invited to observe the world unfurl in spectacular bending. Flowers raise their bowed heads to the nectar of the sun. Trees sway to the cadence of the wind. Mothers nestle newborns close for sustenance. Athletes arch and extend their sinewy muscles.

Bending is permanently dyed in the fabric of all of creation, and you and I are the crowning luster of bending. We are inherently designed to resist the curl, fold, and collapse when life dares to break us. We are created to stretch and buck against invasive pressures . . . no matter what. We are fashioned by the Creator to bend when the really tough things invade and we want to slump inward and give up.

Yet *Bend* will not let you give up. I will not let you give up. You see, in the following pages you will meet courageous everyday sojourners like you who have faced their own brink of, "I just can't do this anymore," and they hung on. They dug deep. They refused to quit. They bent. And beauty surprised them in the bending.

Everyone has a bending point. Do you know yours? Perhaps you're close to buckling under right now. Or you're weary from another pressure, another disappointment. Maybe your marriage has soured. Or you didn't get the job. Maybe you're lost in grief. Perhaps you're scraping the bottom financially. If so, welcome to your bending point.

In engineering, bending stress occurs when an object loaded with external forces begins to flex. Too much pressure and the object cracks or collapses. In your life, a bending point is that experience where steadiness meets disruption. A bending point takes you to the edge where doubt can drag you into discouragement, or despair leaves you for dead. When you feel your life is falling apart—or, you simply have nothing left—this is you bending.

Bend delves into the mystery of what keeps you, me, and any of us going. You make the best of days getting messy. Maybe you shape your resolve with gutsy drive and determination. Or you secure yourself to the moorings of faith. Perhaps you do both. Or you struggle to do any of the above.

As I type these words, I pause. My head slumps into my hands and tears trickle down my cheeks. I understand the angst of bending until you feel you'll SNAP. I get the pleading for pain to stop, for the emotional crushing to end.

More than I care to recount, the headaches, the twisting muscles, and the I-can't-move-my-neck days have knotted me into a brittle jumble, threatening to shatter my hope into jagged shards. I, too, am learning anew to bend and come more alive when I do.

For decades as a journalist, I've been on a quest to discover how anyone can find something of promise in the toughest of days. I pursue how faith uncovers loveliness. Along the way I wonder, do we *really* need God to right ourselves again?

I've zigzagged the planet to glean deeper richness from the people I interview. Seasoned farmers. Celebrated Olympians. Shunned prostitutes. Dying AIDS patients. Famed vocalists. I investigate and brush against the memories and experiences that people tend to cloak. In my conversations with both the exuberant and the grieving, I listen and wait with well-spaced timing between the hard-to-ask questions.

Writing this book bends me. My journalism school professors never prepared me for interviewing a witch. How do you tactfully ask if someone sacrifices animals? My professors warned me to stay objective and not enter into the story, but how could I not cry with Wayne and Gwen? Over regulated twenty-minute phone calls, I became friends with a prisoner serving a life sentence. How hard could I press him about his felony murder conviction?

There is a delicate art to avoid piercing the reservoir of tears that will gush forth when I ask: *How did you feel when* . . . ? Whoosh. *What was the most difficult part about* . . . ? Whoosh. *How are you doing these days*? Whoosh.

If we were lingering over a cup of coffee right now, I would gently ask: so how are you doing lately? After you let your story trickle out or whoosh forth, I'd hush my tendency to probe and simply voice out that you are stronger than you think. Keep bending, my friend.

Part of becoming stronger through bending is we listen to the perplexity in our thoughts. Thoughts that may echo these candid queries:

How could you, God?

Why would you, God?

Why me?

What were you thinking, God?

Questions. We all have them. Our questions invite us to cross-examine the superficial answers. How do we endure when setbacks compress, even nearly suffocate us, until we black out emotionally?

In *Bend*, I'm on a quest to discover what role faith plays in coming back through pain and adversity. Do we *really* need God to right ourselves again?

In my younger years I remember singing, "He's got the whole world in his hands," but I sometimes wonder if God has dropped a few people along the way.

You'll meet the tenacious individuals in the pages ahead and ask your own questions about life daring to break us. Together, we'll discover there is more to your story . . . there is more to mine. There is more to every bending point.

One

Just Before Sunrise

"The sunrise never failed us yet."
—Celia Thaxter

SOMETIMES I FEEL AS IF I'm the unseen narrator in a play who hovers just close enough to the characters to almost hear their inner thoughts. I follow the serpentine path of individuals who await a not-always-happy ending.

There is no script for what I witness. It's as if audience members whisper muffled questions that their programs don't explain. In scene after scene of the drama we call Life, I've come to learn that some questions have no quick-response answers. Like, *How could God allow one puny man to fuel a world war and the death of millions?*

There has to be more to the story, more to the curtain risings and intermissions we ourselves encounter. Together we lean into the unknowns of how Life earns a two-bit applause or an exuberant standing ovation.

Slowly baking to death withers your hope before it stops your heart.

Imagine yourself crammed in a sweltering attic hiding from Nazis. Your optimism faints as the thick August air tightens to wring your body of sweat. Trapped in this sweltering chokehold, you gasp to breathe fully. But in the trenches of the Holocaust, breathing is never a daily guarantee.

As one of Führer Adolf Hitler's targeted castaways of Jews, Gypsies, and other undesirables, if you survive to see another dawn—and dare to inhale deeply—the stench of brutality rushes to sour your soul.

During Germany's World War II domination, Wladyslaw (Walter) Plywacki refused to let anyone, especially the Nazi monsters, taint his soul or count him as a genocide statistic. Incarcerated at age eleven in an urban concentration camp within his home city of Lodz, Poland, Walter witnesses more than any child, any human, should see.

Poverty. Disease. Starvation. Each of these forces shrivels the captives into emaciated shells, shuffling in their misery until they drop. Walter vows not to be one of the thousands dying around him.

By May 1, 1940, Hitler's troops corral some one hundred sixty thousand Lodz Jews into a few city blocks and seal them off from the world. Over the next two years, "the ghetto" swells with another forty thousand Jews and Gypsies arrested throughout Europe.

Walter's pharmacist father, Maks, runs one of the two Nazi-permitted ghetto pharmacies but is limited to dispense little beyond aspirin. Maks, a resolute and steady family man, bears whip and saber welts on his back—scars of his youth as a Socialist who demonstrated against the Tsarist government.

One of the few Jewish officers in the Polish cavalry, Maks is a Polish patriot and agnostic who revels in debating theology with young Walter, pressing his son to read the likes of St. Augustine and Pascal. Walter's mother, Renia, black-haired and petite, exudes vibrant energy especially in her love for dance.

Although Renia struggles to make ghetto food ration cards stretch, on a good day, to provide them each six hundred calories in thin soup, moldy bread, and rotted potatoes, she never lets the Nazis dull her vitality.

"I accepted that I lived in a jungle. That's how I survived,"

Walter recalls of his family's nearly four and a half years in the Lodz ghetto. "Older people expected humaneness from humans and these adults died like flies. The ghetto was like a holding yard for the slaughterhouse. People were being beaten to death on the street while the German soldiers surrounded the scene, grinning in pleasurable cruelty."

Pleasurable cruelty only partially captures the ruthless nature of the Third Reich, whose abuse compels some Lodz prisoners to group together in suicide to avoid the inevitable. The first ghetto winter of 1940–1941, Walter's aunt and uncle die of typhoid, orphaning cousin William (born Wlodzimierz Fialko) who is six months younger.

Walter's parents adopt William who is gravely ill from typhoid himself. When some non-Jewish military friends smuggle in bootleg drugs to Maks, William edges his way back to health and the two boys quickly bond as true brothers.

Appointed to run a ghetto orphanage, paternal aunt Felicja sneaks Walter and William into the orphanage a few days at a time to nourish them with extra food. Of the occasional orphanage respites, Walter later explains, "Even in hell, if you're protected by the powers that be, you feel a slightly cooler flame."

In the ghetto's forced-labor factories, young Walter becomes a carpentry apprentice, then rewinds motors and generators at an electrical shop. "We tried our level best to stay together," Walter adds, "and tried to stay ahead of the horror."

With the escalation of "relocating" European Jews to killing centers in the summer of 1944, Walter, William, Maks, and Renia escape and hole up in an abandoned house just inside the ghetto's fenced perimeter. Walter soon realizes they are only one noise away from alerting the German forces of the hideaway.

When the Nazis conduct escapee checks several times a week at the house, Walter and his family scramble into the scorching loft to flatten their bodies between the massive wooden beams.

"You didn't dare to say a word, or fart or sneeze, because the Germans would open the attic door and shine a searchlight,"

Walter recalls of those terrifying raids. The Plywackis use surrounding fields as a latrine and only venture out at night. Walter scavenges the Lodz streets and other vacant houses for food scraps and once discovers a cow carcass. He slices off the animal's hind leg and lugs it back to the family.

"We just moved the worms away from the remnants and ate everything, including the bone marrow," Walter discloses, pointing out the difference between hunger and life-ending starvation. "When you're starving, you'll eat anything."

※

Eat anything? I've been invited to eat insects and monkey meat in other cultures, but maggots on decomposing beef? Oh, to be desperate with that kind of hunger. I do know the gnaw of wanting to eat *something*, though I started avoiding the clichéd "I'm starving" words soon after the specialist threaded a stretching device down my esophagus the first time in 2007. I've lost count of these procedures after six.

Every day, food and I spin in a cha-cha of conflict. No corn. No wheat. No onions. No shellfish. No caffeine. *Ad nauseam.* It's awkward to feel like a ravenous wolf peering down an entire grocery store aisle to discover there's nothing you can eat on either side of the shelves. It's an unwanted lifestyle change that's hard pressed me at times to just eat mashed potatoes. But it's far from starvation. Not like Walter and his family. At least I can forage in well-stocked supermarkets. What keeps one from breaking when you can't even forage?

It's long puzzled me how emaciated Holocaust captives could bend when life commanded, "Break . . . now!" How could they make it on watery soup and a few bread scraps? The morning after I interview Walter, I somehow instinctively dilute my oatmeal with extra water. With each bite, I pause to think about sustaining energy on runny gruel or skimpy vegetable soup.

Some have said Walter looks like the kindly protagonist Carl in the endearing Pixar movie *Up*, down to the broad, flat cheeks and grayish-white hair. Walter smiles more than Carl, but as I listen to Walter's recollections, I wonder how he avoids the frozen grump look of widower Carl.

Sometimes I'm not sure if Walter's recalling the horrific events of the Holocaust causes tears to slide from his eyes or whether it's just his temperamental aging tear ducts. Despite the inconvenience, Walter dabs his eyes with tissues, reminding me of my Dad's ever-ready white handkerchief. It's amazing to think that my own father, just five years older than Walter, was fighting as an U.S. service-man for Walter's release. Yet almost entirely cut off from the rest of the world, the Polish teen was engaged in his own hand-to-hand combat of bravery and grit.

What was coming is unimaginable to most of us.

"The Nazis were grabbing people and throwing them onto the train to Auschwitz, to the gas," Walter continues with his war memories. "Nobody told us anything, but my brother had contacts with the Polish underground, so I sort of knew what was coming."

What was coming is unimaginable to most of us. After nearly a month hemmed in at the abandoned house, Walter's family slumps past their bending point.

"We had to surrender," Walter clarifies with a pensive lull. "The heat pressure inside that attic was awful. It was probably 130 degrees. The psychological pressure was even worse."

Rather than succumb to the stifling heat or let the Nazis pounce, the Plywacki four trudge to the ghetto's assembly point where the final seventy-four thousand Lodz ghetto Jews are herded onto railroad cars to the Auschwitz death camp complex. Forty members of the extended Plywacki family are already dead.

Walter and his parents and brother crowd with about one hundred fifty others into a freight car designed to fit only forty humans. "There was a small open window, about one and a half feet by two feet, with barbed wire across it," Walter details as if back inside the swaying cattle car. "I would stand on my tiptoes to smell the fresh air from the outside, holding hands with a little girl from Czechoslovakia, an adopted daughter of my cousin."

The innocence of youth shatters before their eyes. Over the five sweltering days trapped in the train with no water and scant food, about thirty of the captives collapse and die. "My father stopped people from screaming. We thought screaming would bring the guards," Walter remembers of that fateful August, just days after his fifteenth birthday.

Arriving at Auschwitz II-Birkenau in the pre-dawn darkness, the panic is forever etched in Walter's memory. "The German soldiers commanded, 'Out! Out!'" Walter's voice rises, his bearded jaw tensing at repeating the Nazis' demands to me. "We were surrounded by lights, gunshots, screams, and the stench of burning meat. The Nazis ordered, 'Women left! Men right!'"

Walter resists running to his mother because he heard via the Polish underground resistance buzz that any woman with a child is guaranteed the gas chamber. Instead, he watches her disappear into a mass of other women separated from their families.

Once processed in the quarantine camp barracks a few hours later, Maks sees a lady yards away in the women's camp who knows the family. Maks motions to her, asking about Renia.

The friend simply places her hand in a slashing motion to her throat.

Renia was already gassed.

"The gas chamber was not humane. It took twenty minutes. I still feel guilty for not having said good-bye to my mother, but that was the only rational thing to do," Walter explains, dabbing his eyes. "The prisoners who were helping the Germans with the crematorium and the gas chambers were asked by new prisoners, 'How do we get out of here?' The helpers would point to the sky and reply, 'Through the crematoria chimney.'"

Jam-packing their grief inside so it never fizzes to the surface, Maks, William, and Walter wait—clutching the minutes before their own murders. Sweat pools, fear twists. Time roils and tumbles toward the afterlife, but the three are spared. Once released into the men's camp, the boys hear a rumor about twins getting extra food.

"Being so hungry, William and I lied that we were fraternal twins," Walter divulges, "and so we wound up in a holding pen for Joseph Mengele's crazy medical experiments." But two days later, a Polish block supervisor in Mengele's testing barracks whisks Walter and William away from the Angel of Death's agonizing and often-lethal genetic research.

Walter emphasizes that the overseer, himself a non-Jewish prisoner, risked his own death by torture to save the Jewish teens. Four months later in another extermination camp, two Polish Gentile nurses free Walter from being a guinea pig in a Nazi malaria experiment.

I wonder, is it simply a coincidence that Walter twice escapes laboratory maiming and death? Are Walter's holding-cell rescues the luck of the universe or are these rescuers human angels of mercy on earth?

With the average life expectancy in Auschwitz only two weeks, Maks, William, and Walter beat the odds. After about six weeks, they are herded into another freight car with about ninety others. Withstanding three days without even a sip of water, the inmates arrive at Germany's Landsberg-Kaufering IV concentration camp and the three Plywacki men are pressed into forced labor for the Nazis.

Walter harvests potatoes and helps construct concrete buildings. Other inmates whisper advice to join inter-prison transports to avoid becoming too familiar to camp guards, who callously kill Jews rather than get attached to them.

In early November, Walter and his father and William move to the Kaufering XI concentration camp and assist in building a fighter-plane landing strip. When someone sabotages the project, the three are part of human cargo shipped to the Riederloh punishment camp. As if survival in any extermination camp is not punishment enough.

Photo by Dorease Rioux

"The punishment? The guards were discouraged from shooting us. We were supposed to die by beating and starvation," Walter announces, his hands forming fists. "We were there two months, and only two hundred out of two thousand of us survived. You learned to eat roots of grass—anything you could find."

Walter is directed to be a Riederloh camp runner who relays messages between the guards and the German Reich protective echelon, the *Schutzstaffel* (SS). Through his runner duties, Walter befriends the Nazis' vicious guard dogs. "The SS officers were always hoping to see me torn apart by the dogs, but the dogs were nicer than their masters," Walter satisfactorily smirks. "And the dogs let me take their bones, which I ate. I shared them."

Walter reaches for his own canine companion, Widget, a yellow Labrador retriever who is a softy at heart in her own right. Aging in body, Walter's spirit is as spunky as in the days of defying his Nazi captors, hardened with their caustic berating, and hell-bent on the demise of millions of those deemed inferior. Every prisoner edged on a tightrope to the grave.

I'm curious to see Walter's tattooed Holocaust prison serial number, but he explains that later in the war the Nazis saved money on ink and simply sewed numbers on prison uniforms. Walter recites 112406 faster than many of us can recite our Social Security number. I can't imagine being branded like a ranch animal, your flesh pierced and bleeding, as you stumble away from the yells of "Next!"

Walter sees the dreadfulness register across my face.

"I accepted my death, but I was ready to fight for life," he pensively continues. "About a year before our first concentration camp at Auschwitz, my father started teaching me, 'It's okay to lick the Nazis' boots to keep your life. But if you think the Nazis are going to kill you, attack them and die in hot blood.' I was prepared to attack the Nazis, rather than let them treat me like a cow."

Yet Walter credits part of his resilience to his father's life-saving counsel to not overreact to the Nazis' harsh treatment. Maks himself models this resolute you-can't-break-me attitude, until finally at Riederloh, the continual starvation betrays Maks' brain.

Maks is now almost catatonic, with little hope. But one day with Walter watching, Maks rallies to verbally insult the Riederloh commandant to his face, over and over. In response, the officer repeatedly slams a shovel across Maks' head.

Pleading for the commander to stop, Walter's intervention shatters at the edges, falling helplessly into the Nazi's rage. Barely conscious in the barracks for the dying, Maks imparts his last words to his son, a mission that empowers both boys to not quit before their German overlords. "Make sure William stays alive." Maks dies two days later at age fifty-one.

Now completely orphaned, Walter stoically cinches his circle of protection around his little brother. In mid-January 1945, the Plywacki boys volunteer for a transfer to the Dachau I concentration camp where the malnutrition gnaws holes in Walter's legs and William drags his brother to a camp clinic. Here, Walter is slated for experimental malaria treatments.

"In the so-called hospital, two Polish male nurses who were Christians, or at least not Jewish, were bringing me all kinds of good food," Walter warmly recalls. "After about a week, they smuggled a corpse into my bed and smuggled me out into the camp and back with William. The nurses rescued me. I don't know why. I never saw them again."

Once again Death bungles its job with Walter. The forced labor supervisors add the boys' names to a list of inmates being shipped to Luftnachrichten Kaserne concentration camp and this proves another fortuitous move.

When the teens transfer to the Luftnachrichten Kaserne camp, the Nazis kill everyone else remaining in the boys' quarantine barracks at Dachau I. Could this near miss of extermination be another random act of kindness, a harmonious celestial happenstance, or is someone looking out for Walter and William?

As I contemplate the boys' fierce endurance, I find my copy of *The Book Thief*, the richly absorbing account of one community in Nazi Germany. Young Liesel Meninger reminds me of Walter, a refreshing contrast of innocence and iron will meld into persistence. Death narrates this bestseller with these brooding words:

It's probably fair to say that in all the years of Hitler's reign, no person was able to serve the Führer as loyally as me... I have endless ability to be in the right place at the right time. The consequence of this that I'm always finding humans at their best and worst. I see their ugly and their beauty, and I wonder how the same thing can be both. Still, they have one thing I envy. Humans, if nothing else, have the good sense to die.[1]

Walter has the good sense *not* to die and hand the Nazis more twisted satisfaction.

For two weeks at Luftnachrichten Kaserne, Walter and William assemble ME-236 jet fighters. Next stop: the Burgau concentration camp to build more jet fighters for a month.

I couldn't help interrupting Walter's recollection of this labor. I curiously blurt, "So you were assembling the very planes that were attacking your country?"

With his unflappable ease, Walter settles my puzzlement of what it is like to build the enemy's weapons.

"It kept me alive."

Enough said.

After a mid-March transfer to the Türkheim concentration camp, Walter literally marches out the front gate one day carrying a huge wooden beam, as if he is delivering it straight to a Nazi construction site nearby. William is to do the same an hour later, but is detained by guards. In the meantime, sly Walter begs for old bread in a local village and steals two pairs of leather boots before carrying the same beam back through the camp's front gate.

Hope dripping from their hearts every step. Plunk. Plop. Plunk.

The boots keep the boys' feet from extreme frostbite for the next part of their imprisonment—a death march back to Dachau. It is now early April 1945 and the Allied forces battle closer. Walter and William exhibit man-sized grit for fifteen-year-olds.

The SS soldiers unflinchingly shoot gaunt prisoners who can't keep pace on the five-day march. Or the Nazi forces just kill the captives on a whim. Bam! You think you can drink water from that stream? Bam! With each murder, the survivors' courage ices over. The slush of despair sinking in their spirits.

I find no words when I picture these battered Holocaust inmates with starving limbs, bristling against torture on the move. Hope dripping from their hearts every step.

Plunk. Plop. Plunk.

"What was it that kept you from completely losing heart? What kept you pressing through?" I ask Walter as he describes the brutal shuffle to Dachau. "I'm a tough son of a bitch," he quickly retorts, then corrects himself. "Was. Standing up to the abuse becomes a habit. It was a choice every time."

As Walter and William and the remnant of hostages stagger into the Dachau II (Karlsfeld) concentration camp, they smell the stench of hundreds of dead inmates heaved into train cars across from the camp. The image of piled bodies swirls in Walter's mind. Each of the remains is someone's loved one tossed away like garbage.

Walter and William realize they'll soon join the human carcasses if they don't outsmart their incarcerators one last time. The booms and rattles of Allied air and ground assaults embolden the boys' plan.

As best as they can guess, it's pre-dawn April 15. With all-or-nothing courage, the boys shimmy through the camp's electrified barbed-wire fence that is shorted out by Allied bombs. They cunningly escape while the German soldiers cower in underground bunkers. No Allied forces free the brave Plywacki brothers. In the dull trace of dawning light, they free themselves.

"We crawled our way across a potato field while it was gray, just before sunrise," Walter declares with fresh energy in his voice. "A German machine gun was shooting at us, but some Allied units started shooting back. We eventually just stood up and ran like hell into an abandoned anti-aircraft battery."

The panicked Nazis had already hightailed it and left a treasure trove—a bubbling pot of corn beef-vegetable stew on the stove. "Later on in life, I ate twice at five-star restaurants, but those meals were no comparison to that pottage," Walter shares with a contented grin.

With euphoric gulps and quick chews, the boys ravenously immerse themselves in their first savory food in five years. Covered with lice, fleas, and grime, Walter and William douse themselves in DDT powder and dress in clean German military uniforms with their dingy, striped prisoner jackets on the outside so as not to be mistaken for Nazi soldiers. Securing steel military helmets and grabbing pistols and hand grenades, the unwavering brothers prowl toward the Allied lines.

A band of American soldiers apprehend the boys along the way and lead them to a U.S. military field quarters. Through an American soldier who speaks Polish, Walter and William explain they just escaped from the Nazis. After a half-decade as Holocaust internees, the Plywacki brothers are finally free. The American men accept the Polish boys as part of their U.S. band of brothers.

"All of a sudden, I'm the safest guy in Germany in an American uniform, holding an American gun. I vomited twice after my first American breakfast. But within two or three weeks I was complaining with the other GIs about the quality of steak from the mess hall," Walter admits with a chuckle. "William and I became U.S. Army mascots in cut-down American uniforms. We shined boots and hauled trash. The guys were like fathers. They were all combat veterans who faced death like we did."

We take a break so I can help Walter replace his kernel of a hearing aid battery. He confides that his fingertips are clunky, thickened with scar tissue—a gift from the Holocaust winters. Walter sprinkles our conversations with the expletive-seasoned "GI English" he learned from his American compadres, but he is visibly more relaxed after recounting his survival of one the most brutal massacres ever recorded on the planet.

We've established a trusting rapport and I long to probe past the facts. I ask, "Did you grieve more for your parents later when you were safe?"

"Oh, yes, I grieved," Walter sighs, his eyes still tearing. "Yet when people were asking me to say a Jewish prayer for the dead, the Kaddish, I refused because I felt my parents were too good for prayers. When I went back to the camps with my eldest daughter, I finally said

Kaddish. I don't know exactly why, because I'm an atheist." I'm intrigued by his candor. "You're of Jewish decent," I pause. "So where was God in all the Holocaust for you?"

"God is sh*t," Walter answers, his cut-and-dried words forcing a slight wince inside me. "But you accept that and you grab your way through it or else you die. In the concentration camps, there was not much of a choice. I didn't feel abandoned. I felt alone. This was my normal."

"Did you ever feel like you would get out?" I inquire, drawn to Walter's raw honesty.

"I knew I was going to get out. Otherwise, it was not worth it. But I lived hour to hour. If you don't do that, you die," Walter assertively adds. "If you expect good things, you die. Expecting good kills you. Older people died like flies because they expected good things."

I wonder if Walter still carries a part of letting expectancy die so his own gutsiness doesn't die. After out-daring his captors in nine concentrations camps, I wonder if any remnants of expectancy or even hope poked through those tortuous years of his 1940 to 1945.

Walter summarizes his post-Holocaust time working for the U.S. Army across Europe. Then he recounts how he stows away on a ship to New York City, similar to the on-the-run life of Leonardo DiCapro in *Catch Me If You Can*. Once in America, the eighteen-year-old Walter tests his resourceful mettle on an assortment of jobs: printer's apprentice, U.S. Air Force radio school instructor, lumberjack, TV repairman, welder.

Walter etches his way into the U.S. history books in May 1953 when he, aided by the American Civil Liberties Union, wins the right for all atheists to bypass pledging to God in American courts. At his U.S. citizenship ceremony in 1955, Walter pledges the Oath of Allegiance without the familiar "so help me God" and officially changes his name from Wladyslaw Plywacki to Walter Plywaski.

Walter dates Louise and they marry his sophomore year at Oregon State University. After graduation in 1957, he establishes a successful career as an electrical design engineer. The couple moves to Boulder, Colorado, in 1962, where Walter joins the National Atmospheric and Oceanic Administration. Their marriage ends in 1981, but Walter proudly applauds the family they raised and the grandkids who visit in the summers.

"I have three daughters, five grandchildren," Walter lightly boasts with a twinkle in his eyes. "And a middle finger for the Germans eight times." After seven decades, the Polish emigrant still shows his feistiness.

In 2013, Poland awards Walter with its prestigious Knight's Cross of Merit for his "disseminating historical awareness on Polish and Jewish fates in the occupied Poland." I read about the government's

Walter proudly displaying his Knight's Cross of Merit award

honor and run across an online *Intermountain Jewish News* article about Walter.

For me, this is the most delicate part to report about the tenacious boy from central Poland.

"Once in Auschwitz, we were on lockdown in the barracks. And we hear high-pitched screams coming from somewhere outside," Walter details in the interview. "The Kapo comes in and tells us that the Nazis are burning children seven and under alive. Whether that was true or not, I cannot say. But I accepted it as truth. So for me, the voice of G-d at Auschwitz was the scream of a burning child."[2]

Walter's words hauntingly thud against my own reasoning, my own faith. The voice of God is the scream of a burning child? What horror! Please tell me there is more to God than this. What about the delightful laughter of billions of children throughout history? Doesn't this jovial side to the voice of God resonate louder than the shrieks of the death camps?

I nudge a little deeper about emotionally processing the abhorrence of the Holocaust. "I had nightmares even more horrible than reality. PTSD," Walter says slowly. "I started drinking too heavily to keep the nightmares off, so I became an outpatient at Walter Reed, and that helped a lot. Now I speak in front of schools and so on, and almost always I tell the audience at the end, 'Thank you very much for being my group therapy.'"

Revisiting the persecution from his own childhood reminds Walter he is free to breathe deeply, lingering in the present. "Do William and you ever talk about the past?" I inquire.

"William can't. He sometimes tells people he was born in Portland. I talk about the Holocaust, and it relieves me. Keeps the dogs of war away," Walter answers, clutching a chew toy delivery from Widget. "Actually, I've never had a very bad day after the war. I always compare life to what I've already been through."

William holds a doctorate in high-energy nuclear physics, and in retirement runs a bed and breakfast on his Florida sailboat, but predominantly resides in the foothills of Boulder, where Walter's own home was destroyed by a 2010 wildfire. Almost all of Walter's possessions—including his family photographs and twelve hundred books—were charred beyond recognition, eerily like hundreds of thousands of bodies in the Holocaust ovens.

Today ninety-one-year-old Walter and Widget share the Boulder home of Margaret, an accountant friend who keeps an eye on the remarkable man who likes to sleep late in his upstairs quarters and sharpen his intellect on the latest political commentaries.

"I would much rather say I am a Holocaust victor than a Holocaust survivor," affirms the once scrappy teen who emerged from the grip of his executioners weighing only ninety pounds. "Disregard the fear and just keep going. It's not heroic. You do what you have to do."

I scan my interview notes one final time. "What kept you from collapsing past your bending point? Is there a secret to that?"

"My father gave me his genes and his ideas," Walter reflects as the fading sun dims the living room. "The other part was good luck in running into human humans. Earning freedom was mainly luck, 90 percent."

Walter Plywaski is one of the world's perpetual survivors, or as I've come to know him. A victor. A realist. A friend.

❧

As I walk down Walter's driveway, my friend who joined me for the interview starts sobbing. I see her heaving shoulders. I unlock my vehicle, we slip inside. We've already said good-bye, but I glance to see if Walter lingers on his steps. He's back in the house.

The dam of my own tears splits open. I back out of the driveway, head down the block, and pull over.

We both weep and swallow hard for air. Through her broken gasps, my friend tells of giving Walter a parting embrace and they locked eyes as if peering into each other's souls, craving deeper meaning. Past the heartless Nazis, past the near suffocation in the attic, past the confinement of malice and murder.

"God bless you," my friend assured Walter. "I can accept that," the tenacious victor managed to speak. "As long as it's not forced on me."

I Wonder Was God noticeably absent in the Nazi-crazed years or was his presence just harder to detect at times?

My questions without quick-response answers continue: *Why does God tenderly make someone and bring them into this world with a disabling affliction?* There has to be more to the story.

I know friends who have answers to my question, but before I talk with them, Walter emails. He sends the link to the indelible documentary of the Auschwitz concentration camp, produced by Steven Spielberg and narrated by Meryl Streep. I wish I had Meryl's reassuring voice, her steady pacing as she recounts the Nazis' calculated exterminations.

With two minutes left in the fifteen-minute film, the camera pans to an overflowing heap of discarded shoes. Visitors at the Auschwitz-Birkenau Memorial and Museum draw within inches of the tossed-away footwear—an estimated forty-three thousand pairs collected post-war at this Polish camp alone.

I pause the video, tracing my eyes across the shapes and sizes of these remnants of leather and plastic. Entire families and neighborhoods once claimed these shoes as their own. I'm numbed by the immensity of innocence and loss.

Into each pair of pumps, loafers, and boots, a living someone slid her slender toes or pressed his thick heel. Someone ambled and skipped in the unassuming footwear. Soft, padded baby feet wiggled in the booties.

Halfway across the world, I know three girls with shoes who cannot walk in them.

Dig deeper. *Bend.*
Additional insights and reflections on page 237.

Two

Because She's Mine

*"I wish that for just one time, you
could stand inside my shoes, and just
for one moment, I could be you."*

—Bob Dylan

SARAH WAITS MOTIONLESS in her bedroom and I start yammering to her. Politely, Sarah's mother, Jodi Hammerstrom, reminds me that her twenty-one-year-old daughter cannot hear. At times my vocabulary around families of children with disabilities grows limited. What do you say that doesn't sound trite or fumbling?

In spite of my bit clumsy introduction, Sarah lights up with her characteristic smile and studies me with her kind brown eyes. I step gingerly over her blue oxygen hose snaking thirty feet to the front den's oxygen tank.

In the kitchen, I can't miss the empty IV bag hanging from a pole—a remnant from Sarah's recent pneumonia and the extra need for fluids. I'm sure to Jodi the IV bag and oxygen hose are normal fixtures in a day-to-day routine for a daughter who turned blue and purple during her last round of struggling to breathe. The things I take for granted in my world expands by the second. Breathing. Talking. Walking. Typing.

As we drive the mile and a half to the Cost Cutters, Jodi points out a number of the new houses and vacant lots in the foothills neighborhood affected by the June 2012 blazing wildfire. The inferno destroyed nearly 350 homes in Colorado Springs, Colorado, and scorched bare twenty-nine square miles into the mountains.

"They've rebuilt," Jodi matter-of-factly explains as we drive through her neighborhood. "They sold and moved . . . They've rebuilt."

A few minutes later, a seasoned hair stylist wets Sarah's dark brown, wispy waves with a spray bottle while Jodi steadies Sarah's head. Snip. Comb. Snip. The white scissors are just a shade lighter than Sarah's delicate, porcelain skin.

Sarah grows quiet and I wonder what she thinks. *Don't cut it so short! Hey, you got some water in my ear.* Although Sarah can't hear the upbeat "Sweet Home Alabama" booming from the crackling sound system, she's not missing much.

"Nice boots!" one of the stylists behind the counter compliments the mailman as he delivers a stash of correspondence in his bulky galoshes. "Shoes go right inside," he shoots right back as he heads out into the February slush.

Jodi pays for Sarah's cut and we brave the brisk air, leaving wheelchair marks and shoeprints in the sloppy snow. The van wends back up the hillside past a desolate house lot. I notice the street name and associate it with the only two people killed in the 2012 wildfire. The elderly couple died only seven houses from the Hammerstroms—a little over a block away. Jodi points out the husband and wife's birdfeeder still standing in the leveled backyard, untouched by the flames.

Is this a metaphor for life that forges on after unwanted news sears its way into a family? Your daughter will be significantly limited the rest of her life. But. She will bring you unexpected joy.

For a moment, I retreat into my thoughts to imagine parenting a special needs child. I lean into the unfailing nurture of Jodi and two other friends with daughters born with significant physical challenges. I script an internal monologue:

> You adore her. You smile over the grins and I-recognize-you head nods. You're good at focusing on the silver linings of your daughter being alive, but the realities are still reality.

She cannot pick up a spoon to eat, pull on jeans, put on makeup, or talk on a cell phone. No texting, no selfies, no giggling about boys. No chirping, "I love you, Mom!"

Day in and day out, you feed her, bathe her, dress her . . . and hope. Still your precious daughter inches a bit out of reach, disappearing into each disease complication and no one quite understands the overload of your heart.

You come to expect the lumbering silences. The people keeping an awkward distance because they just don't know what to say, how to engage without sounding patronizing or pitying. People are fearful about what they don't understand, while you're the perpetual coach. "It's okay. She can't hear you, but you can take her hand."

I've been one of the people who clumsily offers a look of compassion to children in wheelchairs while so wanting to budge the verbal wedge between us. While some children unable to speak grunt loudly in excitement, I know better than to raise my voice in return, as if volume will narrow our communication gap.

Gratefully, families of special needs children extend me unearnd graciousness as I try to learn what it is really like to give and hope and hope and give for a child with multiple health needs. How do the parents continue to hold up when a growing daughter is entirely dependent for everything from a drink of water to a nose scratch?

I invite Jodi, Dawn Mugele, and Leith McHugh for lunch at my house to talk at length about caregiving for their girls. The three mothers connected years ago through a special needs school program and Jodi's husband.

The three women met regularly at a restaurant, and eventually a handful of other mothers of children with disabilities joined them. The women talked shop of medical insurance, waivers, guardianship—something you think you might someday need with elderly parents not your five-year-old.

Together, the moms bolstered each other in their unpredictable pilgrimage. Over time, the mom's group naturally drifted apart, so lunch at my house is a mini reunion of sorts for Jodi, Dawn, and Leith. Munching on grilled chicken salad, balanced with mini chocolate cakes and fresh strawberries, we fall into an earnest exchange about when life bends us into something we never expected. I am intrigued by these women's undying commitment to their girls.

Photo by Anne Emmons

(left to right) **Leith, Dawn, Jodi, and Sarah**

Dawn and Katie Mugele

August 10, 1992, thirty-seven weeks into her first pregnancy, Dawn Mugele scooches off the sonogram table, slips on her shoes, and casually tells her obstetrician and the radiology tech, "Well, looks like everything is there." Looking back now, Dawn recalls their blank faces and uneasy silence. The phone call at home an hour later unloaded the news of a possible problem with the baby's brain.

The next day Dawn and her husband, Erik, find themselves the center of unwanted attention in a room full of doctors, interns, and teaching hospital students at Denver's Fitzsimons Army Medical Center.

"Well, that doesn't look good," the doctor conducting the high-tech sonogram interjects. "There's something really wrong here." The disturbing words unleash a gush of tears from Dawn. The doctor reaches for her hand and invites Erik to join them from the back of the room. The introverted father-to-be stays motionless in his own disbelief.

Directed to empty her bladder before an internal sonogram, Dawn stumbles to the bathroom and bawls, her wretched cries echoing beyond the door, prompting Erik to check on his distraught wife.

The next day, Dawn is induced and delivers six-pound, fourteen-ounce Katie Marie. The extent of Katie's birth abnormalities are still weighty for Dawn to explain. The cytomegalovirus (CMV) affected the ventricles or back part of Katie's brain.

"Katie's first three years were really hard. She had colic right off the bat. She had brain surgery at six days old. She had hydrocephalus, so they were relieving that. She had craniosynostosis, which is your brain fusing together too early, so at nine months they went in and took out her skull from here to here," Dawn motions on her own head the ear-to-ear skin incision surgeons made to cut her baby's skull from base to mid-front.

"I was living at a hospital and it was just not a good life. I felt alone. Every day it felt like I could just puke," Dawn explains, resting her half-eaten strawberry on her plate. "It was extra challenging if you got a nurse that you didn't like or was mean. I actually left the hospital late one night wrestling with, *I can't do this anymore. This nurse is making me so angry! I'm going to kill a nurse tonight.*"

The first three years, Katie averaged a stay every three months in the hospital for some major concern. Often during these hospitalizations, the Mugeles thought this life was over for their oldest child.

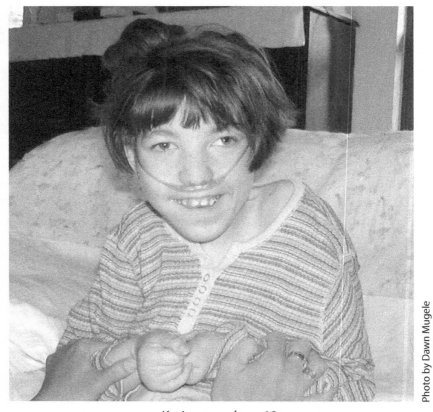

Katie around age 12

Katie's medical diagnoses increased: she was deaf and blind and endured a seizure disorder, cerebral palsy, scoliosis, kyphosis (a pronounced rounding of the back), chronic lung disease, and low platelets. Katie also had osteopenia, known as low bone density, causing multiple fractures over the years. A hefty list of medications accompanied the diseases.

"If mosquitoes bit Katie, they died. That's how much medication was in her system. And that's the stuff you're putting in your kid!" Dawn exclaims. "The doctors said Katie could die from her seizures, so we put her on a specific hormone for six weeks. The seizures slowed, but she was so drugged up, it was like wheeling around a fifty-pound doll rather than your child. That just felt wrong."

We shake our heads and empathize with Dawn. Leith comforts Dawn and the group by offering, "The decisions that we had to make for our daughters' care, parents shouldn't have to make.

The doctors expected Katie to live to eighteen months. She far surpassed that and lived to age fifteen. Much has changed since losing Katie on December 28, 2007, but for Erik, Dawn, and their two younger children, it's getting easier to talk about their beloved daughter and sister.

Dawn finds it especially easy to talk among other parents who've endured the uneven days of disability. Uneven days are the well-worn path for these mothers I've come to hold in highest regard. Leith delves in next, sharing about her daughter Hadley.

Leith and Hadley McHugh

At first the audiologist thinks newborn Hadley Rae McHugh has fluid in her ears. Born November 23, 1998, Leith and Aaron's youngest seems just a little different than her three-year-old brother. Diagnosed with a hearing deficit at ten days old, Hadley meets her pediatrician at two months. Hadley is tiny and switched to enriched baby formula. At four months, the doctor orders an MRI of Hadley's head, which had not grown since birth.

The scans are completed on a Wednesday, and with still no word over the weekend, the young parents assure themselves with "no news is good news." Monday they both wake up with an internal dread about Hadley. Leith persistently calls the pediatrician's office six times that day and finally speaks directly with the doctor who asks the McHughs to come to his office at 4:30 to "talk about your daughter's future."

Folding Aaron's white T-shirts, Leith plunks down the phone and hurls herself on the futon couch in their unfinished basement. Deep agony surges, forcing a mournful wail and wrenching stomach knots. Shaking, Leith dials Aaron at work screaming, "It's her BRAIN! It's her BRAIN!"

With shell-shocked Leith and Aaron in his office, the doctor tearfully describes the worst-case scenario and the best-case scenario for Hadley's condition called cerebellar hypoplasia. Part of the back, lower section of the newborn's brain is underdeveloped and missing.

Like Katie, Hadley grows into a young girl with deafness, seizures, and osteopenia. The osteopenia fractures Hadley's femur three times and her tibia once.

With limited vision and the function of about a three-month-old

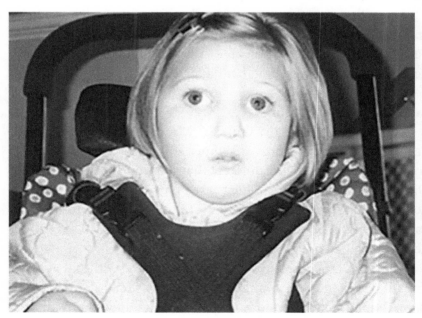

Hadley at age 4

Photo by Leith McHugh

38

baby, Hadley also struggles with ongoing skin wounds and complications from her gastrointestinal tube. Oxygen, central vein catheter, therapies, surgeries, eye patches, and hand and feet braces are all interventions to keep Hadley comfortable and stable. In 2007, before Hadley turns ten, Leith shares a post: "Our life is FULL, beautiful, and hard all mixed into one. Haddie is about like a two- to four-month-old baby for the most part. We do believe that she can see, hear, and understand far more than we are aware of. She knows us, for sure."

With all Hadley's roller coaster health flare-ups, by 2009, after Hadley's hospitalization from pneumonia, the family senses she is ready to die at home. "The kids line up down our street to say good-bye," Leith recalls, "and two days later she opens her little eyes!"

Mom, Dad, brother Holden, and younger sister, Averi, refer to Hadley's near passing as her "dress rehearsal for heaven." With a delicate tension of holding Hadley's life loosely and wanting to clutch her closer, the family continues to love on Hadley with kisses under her earlobes and pats on her diapered behind.

Resilient Hadley Rae brings such joy, and family and friends gratefully celebrate her twelfth birthday. Just two months later on January 28, 2011, Hadley graduates from dress rehearsals and closes her final act on Earth.

As Leith and Dawn look back on raising gone-too-soon daughters, I wonder if losing a child is like an out of body experience—grief draining your vitality, leaving you suspended above a normal routine. Adrift in an endless fog. What gave these mothers courage to come back to Earth . . . eventually? How did hope tether them?

Existing in that mystical space between living with and living without your child is uninvited and unkempt, a scruffy mess at times. Definitely not something which parents sign up for in advance.

Jodi and Sarah Hammerstrom

We're in a relaxed circle now in the living room with Dawn and Jodi on the tan corduroy love seat and Leith in the matching chair to my right. I want to know what Jodi is thinking as she listens to these other mothers describe disability's frayed edges.

"I see my friends going off on a weekend; they don't have the reponsibilities. They are kind of footloose and fancy free with their children grown and moving on. I still have a twenty-one-year-old baby at home," Jodi begins. "Sarah requires more than a baby, as far as caring for her and knowing how to lift her, knowing how to feed her. She weighs about eighty-five pounds."

Like the other girls, Sarah is deaf, but the cytomegalovirus (CMV) that attacked during delivery in April 1992 caused cerebral palsy, leading to severe scoliosis. A spastic quadriplegic who is susceptible to lung infections, Sarah has endured her number of surgeries too: a metal plate in her right hand to help straighten it, two hip repairs, and the removal of the top of her left femur bone.

"Sarah is really a good eight to ten inches difference from one leg to the other, which makes it awkward getting her out of her chair," Jodi explains. "I've grown to accept my calling in life as being Sarah's mom and caregiver, but I feel like everybody is moving on and I'm being left behind. It creates within me this envy and jealousy. You start to get angry at some of these people that you love and it's not their fault."

Leith instinctively picks up on the frustration and alienation. "Your other friends want to help and want to understand, but they don't get it. When someone hasn't walked the special needs road, you don't know how to respond," Leith adds in. "You respond out of the best thing that you know to say. People are uncomfortable with your traumatic story, and they don't know what to do with it. They back-pedal and start saying things, 'You must be very special. God picks special people to care for special kids.'"

Both Jodi and Dawn knowingly respond, sharing a couple of stories of awkward moments with strangers, in particular, who don't

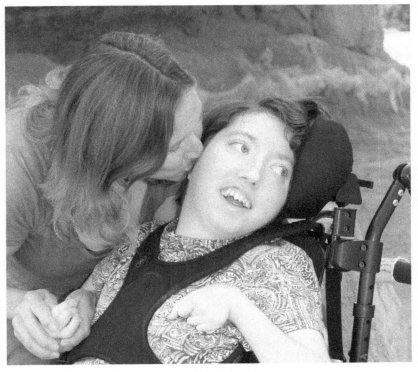

Jodi and Sarah

know what to say when they encounter a child strapped almost motionless in a fully loaded electric wheelchair.

"I sometimes take those opportunities to educate people," Jodi continues, taking another sip of her coffee. "I just try to be gracious, especially with little kids or people who are afraid of Sarah. I try to explain, 'She's just like you, she wants to be friends.'"

Sarah has made friends at the Goodwill developmental disabilities day program she participates in Monday through Friday. At home, Jodi longs to keep consistency with trained certified nursing assistants who regularly help Sarah. "You feel like your life is always dependent upon other people for your relief," Jodi points out, rubbing her aching arthritic hand.

All three mothers know their share of exhaustion and being

pushed far beyond what they ever thought they could handle. We've covered the generalities of living with a child's severe limitations and the conversation shifts below the surface. I risk a more direct question: In caring for your special needs child, what is it like to feel you've reached your quitting point?

"Right after Katie was born, I was so angry. Why me? Why do I have to have this hard stuff? Everybody else was having babies and they were beautiful and healthy and whole," Dawn voices calmly yet firmly. "I was so angry at God, and I truly did not believe he was a good God at that point. Like the song 'God Is So Good,' I was like, 'No, he's not! I'm done!'

For three years we had smiled and said, 'Look at us. We can do this. God is so good.'

"I remember being in church and feeling like nobody here knows I'm falling apart. My eyes were burning laser daggers at the pastor as I was thinking, *You have no clue what you're talking about. I'm about to fall apart right here, blow up in the service. I was churning inside. If he says one more thing about I know you're going through trials, I'll . . . .* He had no clue that I wanted to wring his neck."

Leith presses the fork around the last crumbles of cake on her plate. "I get the emotions of feeling you are given more than you can handle," she empathizes. "Hadley was throwing up what looked like black coffee grounds and screaming. For three years we had smiled and said, 'Look at us. We can do this. God is so good. Look at us. We're doing this.'"

I ask Leith to clarify their tenacity. "Did you feel internally that God is good, or you just said that to get yourself through?"

I kind of believed it, but in those moments it's hard to think that God is really good. My anger literally unleashed, and I sat on the carpeted floor and I beat the crap out of the floor, over and over. I just couldn't stop," Leith confides, searching her eyes across my taupe carpet. "When I finally pulled my hand up, I was like, 'Ah-h-h-h-h-h!!!' The doctor called it a boxer's fracture."

Two years later, Hads was screaming for a month and wouldn't stop. Something was wrong and the McHughs had her checked with numerous scans. But every day, almost all day, they sedated her with Valium.

"Finally, we took her to the hospital and said, 'We are not leaving until you tell us what is the matter with her,'" Leith recalls. "We found out it was gastritis, which is treatable, yet really painful. But before we made it to the hospital, I punched and punched the big Day-Timer on my desk and broke my hand again."

Dawn recalls Leith lashing out against Hadley's pain and the family's agony. "I remember you sent out an email that said, 'I'm taking Hads to the hospital, but pray for me. I just broke my hand again.'"

Leith grimaces just thinking about her literal fistfight with Anger. "I swore I would never do that again, but it was all just beyond me."

Although anger is something that can seethe in Jodi when she's extra tired or lacking a caregiver break, Jodi tells us she's learning to sidestep a knockdown with anger and resentment.

"How do you love a child like this who is crying all the time and miserable and unpleasant?" Jodi poses. "Sarah was that way for the first couple of years and I would say to my husband Doug, 'Why us? Why is God bringing this into our life? What did we do? Did I do something wrong? Is God punishing me?'"

While Jodi voiced her whys, Doug would remind his wife that Christians are not exempt from adversity and heartache. Eventually, Jodi began to accept the whys, turning her main question to: How do I parent Sarah well?

Why? Why? It's woven into our DNA to ask in trials: Why? Or, why now? In grade school, I was the kid who'd raise my hand and ask "why?" when a teacher shared a particularly puzzling point. By high school, I learned to not bother. But now past fifty, I feel free to ask "why?" but not always expect a full answer in my lifetime.

The frankness of Dawn, Leith, and Jodi reminds me of the angst and inquisition in *Rabbit Hole,* the Pulitzer-prize winning play brought to film. In the 2010 movie, Becca (Nicole Kidman) and Howie (Aaron Eckhart) are parents whose four-year-old son is killed by a car when he runs into the street chasing his dog.

I walked out of the movie theater exhaling a long "that was intense!" sigh and applauded the raw depth of a grieving family muddling through to find their equilibrium. Jodi's "why" comments start a replay in my head of the scene when Becca and Howie are at a grief support group listening to another couple reminisce about losing their little girl.

"You just have to remind each other that it's just part of God's plan and we can't know why. Only God can know why," the distraught father methodically explains, his voice breaking.

"God had to take her," the wife jumps in. "He needed another angel." Locked in a pondering stare, the husband faintly parrots back his wife's words, "He needed another angel."

Becca quickly interjects. "Why didn't he just make one? Another angel. I mean he's God after all! Why didn't he just make another angel? . . . Huh?"

Becca firmly quizzes the couple, the tension almost calcifying in the room. Her voice noticeably narrows to a whisper, "Just putting it out there."[1]

Becca's "why" question reveals both brilliance and curiosity. Why doesn't God make his own new angels instead of taking our precious ones decades before we'd like? It's almost a question I can hear Leith and Dawn or Walter Plywaski asking.

Jodi, Leith, and Dawn talk confidently about God's hand on their lives. So I want to know how their faith buoys them when the waves crash in. Didn't they ever just want to give up hope?

"I often feel broken, weary, weak, tired, and discouraged. I am still carrying the weight and burden of a disabled child," Jodi acknowledges. "I haven't felt successful or brave, but I feel like I've been faithful. I hope that somehow I am changing, growing, and being strengthened for the better."

Leith applauds her friend. "You've gotten Sarah through almost twenty-two years. That is incredible!"

As Jodi soaks in the encouragement, Leith asks her own question of Jodi. "Is it hard to be with us?"

"No, because I know you know where I'm coming from. Truthfully, sometimes, I'm almost envious of the fact that you don't have to do this anymore," Jodi notes a bit hesitantly. "You have the mourning and the loss, and it almost sounds weird, but I often wonder how I am going to respond the day that Sarah dies. And I almost long for it. I long for the day that she will be whole, and she won't be in pain, that she will be understood."

The words continue to tumble for Jodi, as if she as locked them inside years ago and lost the key. "I feel so inadequate in taking care of Sarah sometimes. It's almost like I pray that the Lord would take her home before I can't take care of her anymore. So it's weird to pray that your daughter would die—because I know you two have daughters who have died—and it doesn't seem right."

Dawn turns to connect with Jodi's eyes. "We prayed the same thing. We prayed that either God would heal Katie here on Earth or take her to heaven and heal her there," Dawn reassures. "Even in Katie's thirty hours or so with pneumonia before she died, I remember telling Katie that I didn't want her to do this anymore. And I struggled thinking, *I don't want to do this anymore.*"

Dawn traces back to the rawness of her surrender. "It was too much. I couldn't continue. Even right before I turned around in the living room and found out that Katie was gone, I had just said, 'I don't want to go get antibiotics one more time.'"

❧

I shuffle on the edge of understanding these mothers' groans of the heart over letting a loved one go. My mind flashes to my standing helpless beside my mother lying eerily still in Critical Care, unresponsive after a massive stroke. Alone in the hospital parking lot, I slumped into the car's steering wheel. "I can't do this!" I lamented. "I can't do this!"

I've cringed over the raspy, lumbering breaths from my father's double pneumonia in his final skirmish with metastatic cancer. And in the agony, I repeatedly begged, "Just take him, God! Just take him!" But I've never hovered over a daughter writhing in pain, who was unable to point to the hurt or scream out, "Help me, Mommy!"

Jodi nudges me back to our conversation with her perspective on the smudgy line of wanting someone to live yet wanting them free from affliction. "Doug thinks that someday pneumonia or the flu will probably take Sarah. She's been generally healthy, which I'm thankful for, because I hate it when she gets sick," Jodi adds. "It's horrible to watch her struggle and not be able to breathe. So it's times like that when you're wondering, 'Lord, can't you just take her?'"

Dawn and Leith again offer a knowing nod. "A few weeks before Hads died, she had another infection brewing in her leg. I stood in her closet and told God, 'I really don't think I can do this much longer. I can't do another infected leg with another wound bath for another six months,' Leith shares. 'I can't keep doing it, and I don't know what that means. I'm not going to kill my daughter, and I don't want her to die. And, I can't keep doing this.'"

Leith's declaration of "and" thuds against my own emotions with pivotal meaning. These moms are not alone in the angst of wanting their child to move on from earthbound disability yet feeling horrified at even imagining life without her. In the international bestseller *Ghost Boy*, the mother of Martin Pistorius faces similar hounding in her spirit.

What seemed an ordinary sore throat turned her energetic twelve-year-old son into a mute quadriplegic. Martin recalls one fateful night hearing his parents fight again over placing him in a full-time care facility. Martin's father storms off and his mother collapses into a sobbing heap on the floor.

> She was wringing her hands, moaning, and I could feel the raw grief flowing out of her. . . . Mum looked up at me. Her eyes were filled with tears. 'You must die,' she said slowly as she looked at me. 'You have to die.' The rest of the world felt so far away when she said those words, and I stared blankly as she got up and left me in the silent room. I wanted to do as she bid me that day. I longed to leave my life because hearing those words was more than I could bear. As time passed, I gradually learned to understand my mother's desperation, because as I sat in the care home and listened to other parents talk, I discovered many others felt just as tormented as she did.[2]

What about the darkness and desperation? When a parent is tormented by her child's disability, does faith in God have any advantage over no faith at all? How has spiritual and emotional bending instead of splintering beneath their caregiving load helped Dawn, Leith, and Jodi cope differently?

I took a detour for a few years. I was anti-God.

"All three of us had a solid relationship with God before our girls were born," Dawn stresses, her mug nearly empty of tea. "Throughout our daughters' lives we all had faith. . . ." Leith leans forward to interject, almost propelling herself out of the cozy chair.

"And I took a detour for a few years. I was anti-God," Leith takes a concentrated breath, letting her vulnerability surface even more. "When my anger hit. It hit hard. I was drinking a lot. I wanted to have an affair. I was in another world. Literally, all I could pray for probably two or three years was, 'F you! Amen. You're not a good dad.' The thing that sent me over the edge was Hads' leaking G-tube."

The hospital staff fumbling to fix Hadley's leaking gastrointestinal feeding tube strong-armed Leith to her max. As the hospital team worked to put in a new tube, Hadley's stomach acid kept oozing out, burning her skin. Plus, the eight-year-old was frantically crying from failed needle pokes to find a vein.

"I finally couldn't handle it. I handled her suffering to that point pretty much with, 'We've just got to get through this,' but that time in the hospital sent me over the edge," Leith explains, her jaw tightening at the memory.

"With a room full of men—Aaron's friends were all there—Hads is looking at me with pleading eyes, screaming, and I can't make her understand that this is going to help in the end. But these grown men had to excuse themselves. They couldn't watch it any more. And that particular time I raged at God, 'You are a bad dad! I get allowing some suffering, but this is torture and torment. This is horrible. You could stop this like that, and you're not doing it.'"

Ugh. Leith confesses the honest words so many of us feel but never allow to skid across our tongue. "You could stop this, God." In my thirty-some years of interviewing people in nearly twenty countries, I have never heard anyone call God a "bad dad." I know he's heard far worse.

Leith describes stumbling so close to The Edge, that precipice marred with jagged spires threatening to rip her clean through with exasperation and fury. Leith's three-year tailspin eventually turns on its axis when Aaron wakes up one morning and drives his wife straight to the doctor.

Her diagnosis? Depression and anxiety mixed with low vitamin D. Blend in erupting issues from her own childhood and Leith was more than primed for medication and counseling.

Would she really have ditched God forever? Really called it quits with the Almighty? For good?

"I knew in my gut that he was still the big guy. I still had some kind of respect or something," Leith pauses before opening the spigot of her internal wrestling. "I didn't turn my heart away; I turned my eyes away. My heart was saying to God, 'I know ultimately, I'm not going to walk away from you, but damned if I trust you.'"

Does it get much more honest than a long-time Christian saying she doesn't trust God? What could draw her back from the spiritual shattering, the almost irreparable fracture of confidence in her Creator?

"I have a really, really, really good man, and it was painfully hard for him when I was a mess. Aaron was scared that my mental health wouldn't come back," Leith discloses before nestling back in my living room chair.

"It was hard with my other two kids who'd ask, 'Why isn't Mommy going to church?' And I'd respond, 'Mommy's just going to stay home with Hadley,'" Leith explains. "We'd figure a way to brush them off each time, because they were little enough that we couldn't explain, 'Mom's pissed at God.'"

Leith is forthright about some friends being supportive of her nomadic awakening and others not so much. "It made people really uncomfortable that I was in the place I was in. As I was getting well emotionally, I went with Aaron to a worship concert and something in the music that night started a gradual shift in me. I didn't jump right back into trusting and believing—it was slow, slow, slow. I wanted others to know, 'Just let me be in the space I'm in, because I'm not going to go do something crazy destructive. I just need space in my heart.'"

Space in her heart. I understand the elbowing of emotions, crowding and clumping until your insides choke with the heaviness. "So do we really need God to right ourselves and begin again?" I ask.

"Yes, I think we do," Dawn explains, her voice picking up vibrancy. "I'm so glad we weren't left in the place where we were still so angry with God. I hated feeling that."

❧

I get a bit misty from the intensity of hearing how these mothers held it together day after day watching their girls work at being alive. A relative calm during the night or naptime blaringly interrupted by the feeding tube alarm. Saying "I'd love to, but . . . ." to social occasions. Stifling the dreams of a worry-free ski trip or vacation.

No "let's get a dress for the prom." No "let's plan for your wedding." No motherly reminders of, "Someday when you have kids of your own."

I pose a question of perspective to these women who now feel like in-the-trenches-of-life sisters to me. "What would you say to other parents who are going through similar care of a special needs child?"

Jodi is quick to share that as much as she adores her family, they do not fully understand the pressure of trying to figure out Sarah. "It doesn't really register with them, if at three in the morning, I think Sarah is too hot or too cold and I have to get up and put an extra blanket on her. It's a mother thing," Jodi notes with an evenness in her voice. "But even in the midst of feeling alone, I feel like the Lord is still there with me and he understands. I feel like I'm doing my work unto him, not unto other people. Who cares if I'm changing another poopy diaper? Who cares if I'm cleaning up puke? The Lord always does."

There is something steadying about these mothers pressing close to God whom they know sees their unceasing love and concern. That the God who fashioned Katie, Hadley, and Sarah in the womb fully understands the inside worlds of these girls where thoughts ruminate and swirl but never leave in words.

"We love having Sarah at home. Our kids, Lauren and Jonathan, are so good with Sarah. She adds so much joy to our life and she's got a great sense of humor. Yet I do have issues with my health, with arthritis," Jodi says turning her hands palms up. "My body is weakening, so you begin the process of wondering what to do with Sarah. I wouldn't feel guilty if I had to put Sarah somewhere; I would just feel sick. I hate the idea of having somebody else take care of her. I am not at that point, but maybe someday."

That someday never arrived for Dawn and Leith, but they understand the buckling against the idea of relinquishing their child to someone else's attentive nurture.

"And nobody else is going to care for her because she's mine," Dawn remembers of her protection over Katie. In the numbing first days after losing Katie, Dawn lost herself in cleaning out Katie's room and clothes. The family sold the van, but daughter Anika wanted to keep her sister's shower chair.

Leith's family reserved Hadley's room basically untouched for eighteen months until Leith's mother planned to visit and requested to stay in Hadley's room. Leith removed Hadley's sheets and washed them. Teen son Holden took it the hardest that Mom washed his sister's sheets.

The laundering of Hadley's bedding reminds me of Becca in *Rabbit Hole* painstakingly removing her son's drawings off the refrigerator and placing some of his clothes in the washing machine. Becca stares blankly into the agitating washer, swishing around the shirts and pants. It's as if the grieving mother longs to wash away her sorrow yet is caught in the unspoken terror that she'll erase her child's memory in the process.

Nothing will dissolve the memory of Katie and Hadley, and Jodi knows the same is true for Sarah, if she dies before the rest of the family. Jodi needs to pick up Sarah from her day program, so I ask a wrap-up set of questions about discovering hope through adversity and getting to the place where you are okay with being a full-time caregiving parent.

"I find meaning in adversity comes from a deep, strong confidence that God is in control of every detail of life. He was in control of the virus that destroyed Sarah's brain," Jodi points out. "Because God is sovereign over viruses, that gives me a peace and confidence to know that Sarah was not an accident. Sarah wasn't an oops. She wasn't a mistake. Sarah was planned by God and he finds pleasure in his special child, Sarah. It is not always easy, but it is an honor to be chosen to care for Sarah."

I am humbled by these mothers' life-tested convictions and their candor of feeling at times adrift, seeking to numb the grief in alcohol or sleeping binges. Fearful of making surprising and regretful choices: the embrace of another man, the walking away from faith . . . forever.

"There are times when I still struggle with that question of suffering, but now in hindsight, I can look back and say Katie was the

(left to right) Jodi, Dawn, Sarah, and Leith

Photo by Anne Emmons

biggest blessing ever in our lives," Dawn reflects. "I also have a hope that God has a plan that we don't get at all. There is the hope that I am going to see Katie again, and there's excitement of I can't wait to see what she's like. We will definitely have some massive conversations."

I am one who would like to hear those catch-up conversations between a mom and her daughter who was never able to form a full word. This thought draws me inward to my own limitations from a rare muscle metabolism disorder. I too was born with a genetic disease, but my troubling symptoms didn't start until my late forties. Children born with this mitochondrial condition seldom live into their teen years.

On my worst days, my calf and feet muscles contort, leaving me hunched over, pounding my fists into my spasming flesh. But these excruciating episodes usually subside within an hour or two. I may not be able to walk normally for a day or so, but I do regain my footing. Gratefully, with medication and daily monitoring, these tormenting times only flare a few times a year now.

My chronic malady feels so ant-like when I think of Katie, Hadley, and Sarah's health, yet I can relate to their mother's wrestling with God over the physical and emotional agony. And I wonder: Would a milli-fraction of a difference in my DNA have left me never speaking, confined to my parents pushing me around in a wheelchair? Or perhaps destined to an early death myself?

Jodi's even-keeled perspective lends answers and steadiness to my own suppositions.

"The ultimate question is how do you accept that God is in control of all things, even though it looks like it's bad. That's where faith comes in. It's a mystery that we don't understand why God allows certain things to happen, but over the years I've discovered that there are blessings in disguise," Jodi summarizes. "You can go through life being bitter at God or be honest with him and say, 'I don't understand this. This is hard. But I'm going to trust you and wait to see how the story unfolds. This life is all temporary and such a blip in the midst of the big picture of living.'"

A number of months later, I visit Jodi and Sarah at their home and for Sarah's Saturday morning haircut. After we return from the salon, Jodi unloads Sarah' wheelchair from the van and I follow them inside through the garage. I step alongside a pile of shoes and boots bunched in the mudroom. Missing are shoes for Sarah—the girl and now young woman who doesn't lace up running shoes or slip on flip-flops for the mall.

Although Sarah, like Katie and Hadley, will not leave shoeprints in the slush or toe prints in mud, each creates countless footprints on countless hearts.

One young care volunteer who learned to administer Katie's feeding tube and adjust her oxygen levels posted online the day Katie died: ". . . it's hard to imagine life without her. But Katie walked for the first time today! The first words she ever spoke were to her Father. Pretty freakin' awesome, huh?"

I know three girls with shoes . . . who could not walk in them on Earth, but can in heaven.

I Wonder Not everyone arrives in this world in mint condition. What benefit do these babies bring to those of us born healthy?

54

Dig deeper. *Bend.*
Additional insights and reflections on page 240.

Three

More Than Skin Deep

"Achievement has no color."
—Abraham Lincoln

R-E-S-P-E-C-T. (JUST A LITTLE BIT. Just a little bit.) Aretha Franklin, the Queen of Soul, reverberated R-E-S-P-E-C-T deep in our musical psyche, but for a handful of black athletes, R-E-S-P-E-C-T took six and a half decades to knock one out of the park in an ultimate grand slam.

Born in the 1920s under the shadow of Colorado's Pikes Peak, these boys turned young men lived in the moderately tamed West, where most folks inherited skin the same color as a mountaintop in mid-winter. White. Pale white. Creamy white.

The history records extol the hardy black prospectors and miners who ventured to the southern Colorado region eager to cash in on the lure of the Gold Rush of 1858 and beyond. By 1871, when former Union Army General William Jackson Palmer founded Colorado Springs, the tide turned for greater equality for people of color. General Palmer, an industrialist and philanthropist, declared that the city's schools would be open to all ethnicity of students to earn a solid education together.

Soon African-American families worked their way to the growing Victorian spa resort town at the base of Pikes Peak, America's Mountain, and established an industrious community of shop owners, newspaper publishers, craftsmen, ranchers, and more.

What General Palmer intended as a blended city of brotherly love in time edged into a territorial divide of us vs. them.

According to the book, *The Invisible People of the Pikes Peak Region: An Afro-American Chronicle*, by the late 1860s black children were excluded from extracurricular activities, athletics, and clubs. Within a decade, black individuals were banned from eating at white restaurants and usually not permitted as staying guests in white hotels. Segregation seeped in like oil on rags that burned on a Ku Klux Klan thirty-foot cross at the top of Pikes Peak in July 1923.

Three years after this semi-clandestine Klan induction ceremony of thirty new members, Joe Morgan was born in Colorado Springs. In February 1928, his newborn brother Justus arrived. A year and three months later, baby Sylvester Smith entered the world in the city 6,035 feet above sea level.

Not long ago, I was honored to meet with all three gentlemen, now in their nineties. Together we retraced their boyhood through adult years living in Colorado Springs and how they hit a home run in the struggle for racial equality long before civil rights heated up in the South. Their longtime friend, Lucy Bell, orchestrated my meeting with the elder statesmen, and I am deeply grateful. As a retired teacher, Lucy is a premier historian and writer on what it was like to grow up black in segregated Colorado Springs.

Joe, Justus, and Sylvester can readily recall what it was really like to live in a community where just your skin color earned you D-I-S-R-E-S-P-E-C-T. (More than just a little bit.)

Fortunately, after World War II, many residents of Colorado Springs pushed for an end to racial discrimination and urged equal opportunities for whites and nonwhites throughout society. Yet by the mid-40s, when the Morgan brothers and Sylvester were in their teens, their dirt-roads hometown with its predominately white population of around 45,000, still erected barriers for black citizens.

The boys could only swim on Wednesday, "Black Folks Day," at the public pool in Monument Valley Park. The pool was drained and scrubbed every Wednesday night for white patrons to start with fresh water on Thursday. Half of the playground at Prospect Lake, a popular city recreation spot was off limits to nonwhites. If coloreds wanted to swim in Prospect Lake, they had to swim on the side without a lifeguard and not use the bathhouse facilities.

If the boys wanted to attend a movie, they were instructed to sit only in the balcony or maybe a back row if the theater wasn't crowded. Restaurants throughout Colorado Springs denied table service to blacks and directed them to eat in the kitchen or get take-out orders, often picking up their food at the back door.

Joe and Justus remember being denied service at Woolworths after attending a movie. The next day they returned to the five-and-dime with friends and insisted on being served. The staff poured salt into the black patrons' milkshakes and onto their sandwiches. Joe, Justus, and the others refused to pay for the tainted menu items and called police. The cops tasted the food and drink and concurred that they wouldn't pay for the spoiled orders either and let the young diners go free.

"We weren't allowed to go play at the Boys Club or the YMCA or those types of public places either," Sylvester tells me during our interview at the Hillside Community Center, in an older section of the city where he grew up.

Justus remembers the disappointment of being turned away from entering the YMCA. "We just wanted to be like other boys and participate in sports," he says with a hint of sadness in his soft voice.

At Colorado Springs High School, now Palmer High, the teens faced further injustice in sports. Blacks were not permitted to participate in organized contact sports like football or basketball. One or two exceptional black athletes occasionally were allowed to compete on these teams. Justus, a mighty fine left-handed pitcher was allowed to pitch for their high school team and the American Legion team. But most black youth, like Joe and Sylvester, only played baseball with their neighborhood friends.

Justus and his American Legion teammate Sonny (James) Bell, a standout right-handed pitcher, determined to rally a team of local black youngsters and give them an opportunity to excel on a baseball team outside of street ball.

The all-black team threw out their first pitch in 1948 under the name, Brown Bombers, borrowed from world heavyweight boxing champion Joe Louis, the Brown Bomber. The team's original name, Clouds of Joy, was quickly abandoned for the more masculine Bombers name. The boys were enlivened when Jackie Robinson joined the Brooklyn Dodgers in 1947 and broke the color barrier in Major League Baseball. The bases were loaded for a cultural shift warming up in the bullpen of American athletics.

Yet for the young and hopeful Brown Bombers of southern Colorado, their team lacked even basic equipment. They found broken bats and nailed and taped them together. Some secured uniforms, but their jerseys sported different sponsors on the back. Focused and eager to play ball, the guys shrugged off their ragtag athletic wear.

Lauded as the "best pitchers in the state," Justus and Sonny proved a lefty-righty pitching dynamo. Joe commanded first base, often wowing the crowds with his spectacular leaping catches and landing gracefully in a full-split stretch. Centerfielder Sylvester proved precision fielding and a strong arm. Sam Dunlap scooped up line drives at second and outfielder/shortstop Larry Moss whipped in hits. Oliver Bell (Lucy's husband and Sonny's cousin) also played shortstop and belted most of the home runs. Catcher Jesse Vaughan kept the pitchers at their best.

Other 1949 and 1950 Brown Bombers included Clarence Banks, Cecil Bass, Marvin Brooks, C.W. Brown, Ellis Clements, John Morgan (Joe's twin brother), John Moss, James Smith, and Jimmy Wheeler. Les Franklin and Henry Morgan contributed as eager bat boys. A cadre of family and friends stood with the team too.

The Bombers traveled out of town on a rickety, old school bus that frequently broke down. Sylvester remembers one particular bus trip to Trinidad, 130 miles south of Colorado Springs, along the New Mexico border.

"It was so hot down there, such a hot place to play," Sylvester recounts, wiping at his forehead like he was back in the steaming heat again. "Since the Trinidad team charged admission, we'd get a little stipend, but it wasn't much. The bus had a tendency to break down on these away games. We never had to stay out or anything, but we had to wait and cool down the bus."

(back row, left to right)
A.B Turner (coach and manager), Clarence Banks, James Smith, Joe Morgan, John Morgan, Larry Moss, and John Moss.
(front row, left to right)
James Wheeler, Sonny Bell, Ellis Clements, Justus Morgan, C.W. Brown, Cecil Bass and Marvin Brooks

Justus joins in with his own recollections of the less-than-reliable transportation to and from games. "We got a flat tire going down to Cañon City and had to use those manual pumps trying to fill that tire," Justus adds. "It was kind of comical when you think about it."

Although the men can chuckle today about their inefficient bus rides, their treatment by opposing teams and ball field crowds was no laughing matter. Overt racism seethed more on road games to towns like Burlington, Grand Junction, and Limon. No motel throughout the state would let them stay. Instead, the team had to endure these long-distance away games in one day. The 300-plus-mile Grand Junction trip consumed at least twelve hours on the road.

"After our games, we hopped back on the bus and headed back home," Joe added matter-of-factly. "No restaurants, no place to sleep. But that's the way it was."

The name-calling against the Bombers congealed with thick intensity. "Strike that coon out" and "we don't want no niggers in our town" sneered rowdy fans. Sometimes, the sheriff would apologize for the obnoxious individuals while escorting them out of the park.

They flexed their muscles and opened their minds to believe they were worth more than childish insults and second-class treatment.

The Bombers kept bending and coming back when their limited opportunities and the cruelty of others could have driven them to despair. Instead, they flexed their muscles and opened their minds to believe they were worth more than childish insults and second-class treatment.

At one game out east of Colorado Springs, at Rush or maybe Calhan, the team's finicky bus clunked to a halt a few miles outside of town. Some of the players ran ahead to let their opponents know the Bombers were on their way. But the crowds were fairly hostile to the Colorado Springs team. Rumor has it that some townsfolk let black cats loose on the field before the game as a sign of crude humor. Even with the fan opposition and a lumpy cow pasture for an outfield, the

Bombers readily thrashed the rural team.

During some games, the pestering moved beyond racial slurs from the stands or the opposing team's dugout. Pitches whizzed close to the Brown Bombers' heads. Cleats aimed for the black players' shins. On occasion a bat "accidentally" slipped during a hitter's follow-through and sailed straight for the Bombers' pitcher.

"We faced hardships. You know, when you're sixteen, seventeen, or eighteen years old and playing a game, it would affect you differently than if you were twenty-five," Joes shares of the continual jeering at his team. "We always thought we had to be twice as good to make the team. Seeing people walking into restaurants that we couldn't go in and being around things like that has a little effect on your mind."

Sylvester breaks in on Joe's thoughts. "We were called all those slur names and stuff." Justus is quick to add his perspective, "I didn't pay attention to it."

If the childhood chant of "sticks and stones may break my bones but words will never hurt me" is true, then the Brown Bombers' class act of holding their tongues and letting their athleticism do the talking showed opponents a thing or two about manners and common decency.

Sylvester looks back on leaving early in the morning to drive south to play a couple of town teams and then playing prisoners at the Colorado State Penitentiary in Cañon City. "There are some good ball players in prison," notes Justus. "I don't think we ever beat them."

A highlight of the prison games was how the inmates showed kindness to the Brown Bombers. "The joy of going to the prison was us getting our equipment from them," Sylvester says. "They'd give us their old balls and bats. We didn't have but two or three bats, and they were all taped up. If the prison bats were broken, they would give them to us. Then they'd feed us good."

Joe remembers the penitentiary game when their team was treated to a plentiful and hearty noontime meal. The Bombers suspected an ulterior motive too late as they walked out to the prison's big yard feeling stuffed and sluggish. At one point, two inmates broke into a fistfight that delayed the game. Once their food lethargy wore off, the Bombers rallied from behind to tie the game at 9-9 in the ninth inning. But no extra innings were allowed. The prisoners' allotted recreation time was up and the game declared over.

In addition to the inmates gifting their old equipment, others were benevolent to the black players too. Ed and Fannie Mae Duncan, the owners of Colorado Springs' famed Cotton Club, and their family, sponsored the team. Ed served as the team's manager.

The Duncans' backing gave the players a major upgrade in matching uniforms and shiny black or brown bats. If the bats were not already these dark colors, the players would paint the wood black or brown.

The Duncans' budding restaurant, and later nightclub, was named after the Cotton Club in Harlem. Ed and Fannie Mae's business was the first in largely segregated Colorado Springs to allow patrons of all races.

Of course, feisty Fannie Mae did not back down from the police chief's original order that she serve only black customers age 21 and above. In her rebuff of Chief "Dad" Bruce's decree about creating a "mixing" culture at the club, Fannie shared spunky words. "I check 'em for age," she declared with a bit of confident sass. "I didn't know I had to check 'em for color." Soon Chief Bruce became a Duncan ally.

For twenty years, the bustling jazz club on West Colorado Avenue at Sahwatch Street featured popular black musicians including Louis Armstrong, Duke Ellington, B.B. King, Count Basie, and Mahalia Jackson to name a few. Flip Wilson, a soldier at nearby Fort Carson Army post, credits the Cotton Club with his start in stand-up comedy.

People of varying social backgrounds and skin color crammed into the legendary integrated nightspot to dine and dance freely together. While the city's higher-brow hotels and social clubs remained open only to whites, Fannie Mae placed a black-and-white sign in the Cotton Club's window, "EVERYBODY WELCOME." If only the rest of the city and sports fan were as accommodating.

With the Duncans as mentors, it's no wonder the Brown Bombers stood unfazed by those who lashed out at their skin color and stellar athletic abilities. Most home games for the Bombers were played in Monument Valley Park on weekend afternoons, where the crowds, at times, reached five hundred fans. After a home game, the Bombers and dedicated fans would celebrate their victories over hamburgers, chili, and milkshakes at the Duncan family's restaurant.

Perhaps the Brown Bombers' sweetest revenge in being discounted and disrespected: they won the city league championship. Twice. Their first championship in 1949 created quite a buzz.

The local newspaper, *The Gazette*, printed this about the momentous game: "A wild and rugged evening which saw two members of the losing team tossed out of the ballgame marked the Brown Bombers 9-6 victory over the Still Bros.-Jackson Gas team for the championship of the city league. Major popoff session of the evening occasioned action by members of the Police Department to quell an incipient riot."[1]

Joe, Justus, Sylvester and their teammates earned their second league championship at the start of the 1950s when the black population in Colorado Springs was numbered at 1,176 or 2.5 percent of the entire community of 45,472. Definitely a minority in a white-dominated region, the Brown Bombers defied their detractors, excelled at their sport, and turned their backs on growing bitter at being ridiculed and overlooked.

"Baseball and sports were an outing for us. I think the highlight for me was having the opportunity to travel," Sylvester says fondly of his days with the Bombers. For a few minutes the nonagenarians reminisce about their years on the field while my mind does a high floater back to when I played softball in grade school and a town team in high school. We were a rural community of all-white kids playing against other area towns of all-white kids. Badmouthing and bullying existed, but not over our skin color.

The only black people I ever saw in my county before college were some Nigerian immigrants who lived in Omaha and drove down to buy goats from a local farmer. I wouldn't call our Midwest farming community racist; we just did not have exposure to different ethnicities much beyond our predominately German ancestry.

Outside of my Caucasian upbringing, I have a number of darker-skinned friends, and I spent a summer living in Congo back in 1983. Yet, I will never come close to experiencing such mean-spirited epithets as the young Brown Bombers.

"Remember when pro ball was cut down, and all the Major League players were out at the Air Force base and we had the opportunity to play against some of them?" Sylvester asks his longtime buddies, shifting my focus to the incredible men around me at the table. "And the one, the Yankee, the second baseman was here, but he stayed in trouble all the time."

"Billy Martin," Joe quickly recalls of the scrappy infielder whose pro baseball career later included his being a five-time manager of the Yankees.

"Yeah, he was a character," Sylvester notes with a slight shake of his head. "The pros treated you better than the rest," Joe says of the Bombers' opportunity to test their skills against some of the country's finest baseball professionals. Joe, Justus, and Sylvester recall some of the playing conditions they faced that the pros did not, like playing at night with only two small lights to illuminate the field. The teams could barely see the ball once it left the bat.

Those were the days of Justus throwing backdoor sliders and Joe and Sylvester flashing down some leather on plays. Once the Brown Bombers graduated from high school and won their second championship, the city league's popularity waned. Softball and the minor-league Colorado Springs Sky Sox team edged to the forefront of the city's sports fascination.

Besides, the Bomber players were now young men looking to make their way in a world that was beginning to thaw to icy race relations. In 1943, Joe and his twin brother, John, were drafted into World War II and sent to U.S. Army basic training at Fort Jackson in South Carolina. The Army was segregated, separating blacks and whites into separate platoons and housing quarters.

Most black troops were relegated to labor and service units, but Joe marked typing skills on his application form and was assigned to administrative office work. When the War Department encouraged sports teams as part of training programs, Joe joined the black basketball team and later the all-black baseball team. The talented athlete was then invited to play on the Army base's white team. As the only black player on the team, Joe enjoyed the practice games, but was up for discharge before the season actually started. The Colorado native had seen enough of the South and did not re-up.

Photo by Robert Parham

(left to right) Sylvester, Joe, and Justus

As the Korean War kicked in, Justus and Sylvester also joined the Army and served stateside for a couple of years. "I would have stayed in the service, but I couldn't handle that black and white army," says Sylvester of the troops segregated by color. Justus interjects with his own recollection of the Army, "I was in an all-black unit. We had white officers over us, the high ranking. I almost had to serve overseas, but I'm grateful that the war ended."

Back in Colorado Springs, the Army's Fort Carson brought positive change to the Pikes Peak region. The arrival of seventy-eight black troops to Fort Carson in 1942 and later an all-black tank destroyer battalion added fresh diversity to the post and community. After their brief military stretches, Joe, Justus, and Sylvester moved back to the place of their birth. They married and started families.

"If Fort Carson never came to the city as a military unit, it probably would've meant nothing for us," Justus explains. "We came out of high school and there wasn't anything here much for jobs except for custodian work, shining shoes, washing dishes, and waiting tables. I'm not saying those are not honorable jobs, but many of our people had to move out of town so they could make a better living."

Elder Joe adds his praise for the Army post too. "One of the best things that happened was World War II," Joe states. "I hate to say it, but Fort Carson came here and lots of jobs opened up, civil service jobs, administrative type work. It was the best thing that ever happened for work opportunities."

Joe worked his way into a steady thirty-seven-year career with the U.S. Postal Service and stayed involved with baseball as a well-respected local umpire who was admired for his fairness. In 1970, he was the first black umpire for Colorado's high school state tournament. The former Bomber first baseman was inducted into the Colorado Springs Sports Hall of Fame in 2004.

Brother Justus and Sylvester pioneered as two of the first black warehouse supervisors at Fort Carson. In 1967, Justus pursued his father's footsteps and became a reverend at Morgan Memorial Chapel Church of God in Christ. Rev. Justus continues to preach there today.

After his civilian work at Fort Carson, Sylvester transitioned to a twenty-six-year career at the Colorado Springs Fine Art Center as a security guard and escort to kids' groups who visited the art museum. The gregarious Sylvester also mentored youth in the community for years.

Other determined and talented Bomber players fared well too. Oliver Bell, a star athlete at the University of Northern Colorado, became a notable physical education instructor for School District 11. Sam Dunlap worked his way to a supervisor with Denver Equipment Co. and was the first black baseball coach for School District 11 and a well-respected youth mentor and community liaison.

> *"You laugh to keep from crying. That's how you keep going."*

Rev. Jesse Vaughan, Sr. also became a pastor and helped establish the Emmanuel Missionary Baptist Church and served as a Colorado Springs Police Department chaplain. Rev. Jesse retired after forty years of civil service at the Army's Fort Carson. Almost all of these brave souls are gone now, so I am grateful that Joe, Justus, and Sylvester were well enough to meet.

I ask the former baseball champs what has kept them going over the years. Justus takes a lighter approach with his response, "You laugh to keep from crying. That's how you keep going." His eyes perk up at the thought of humor helping them all through. Sylvester credits their resiliency to the parents and teachers who kept them in line.

"If I had my life to live over, I'd like to live in Colorado Springs, because at least we got a good education. Other people across the United States and the South, they were catching hell. But we got a good education," Sylvester stresses. "Seemed like the white teachers would push us academically, especially down there at Lowell Elementary. I went to South Junior, and we got a good education there too. But to do that, our parents had to be behind us. And mine would come down to the school with a stick."

"We had discipline, that's for sure," Justus adds before recounting the time he and some junior high-age friends would sneak into the Colorado College football games. "We'd go over the barbed wire and tear our britches. We didn't have enough sense to realize the security guys were watching us the whole time. They met us after the halftime and put us in the paddy wagon and drove us downtown to the police department. I remember whoever was in charge took us back to a cell. He didn't lock us in there; he just slammed the door. That made me say, 'This isn't for me!'"

That was a wise observation for the youngster who has been a pastor for more than fifty years. When I ask Rev. Justus how his faith has helped him weather all kinds of tough lessons of racial taunting and more for nine decades, he gets a twinkle in his eye and thinks back to the beginning seedlings of his personal faith and attending the church his daddy founded.

"I was about five or six and I had a little box that I would stand on at the street corner and say, "Repent!" I would walk up the street with the box and visit a couple who used to babysit me. And I would tell the husband, Mr. Gray, 'You better repent, because you're going to hell.' That's not something I should have been telling him," Justus chuckles, "but he graciously accepted what I said. Over the years, my faith has been a great strength to me to help weather any storms and trials and such a great opportunity to know more about the Lord Jesus. I wouldn't exchange my faith. It's been the better part of my life."

Knowing God was on their side brought tenacity to many of the Bombers when opponents and crowds turned mouthy and mean. "When they took the Bible out of the schools, that's one of the worst things they could have done. And the Pledge of Allegiance too. There's a lack of discipline with kids today," Sylvester declares. "You find discipline, like in my church. I have been in that St. John Baptist Church since I was four years old. When we were coming up, discipline would come through the parents. They'd just look at you. And you knew you were wrong."

With parents to help their boys turn into stellar baseball champions and later upstanding citizens, it's no wonder the Bombers didn't insist on broader recognition for their part in injecting greater racial fairness in their city and state. The team continually rose above their shabby equipment and uniforms and an onslaught of derogatory sneering and ridicule.

They dared to dig deeper and kept bending.

Brown Bomber Colorado Springs Sports Hall of Fame Inductees,
(left to right)
Rev. Jesse Vaughn, Joe, Justus, Sylvester, and Sam Dunlop

Photo by Rob Miskowitch

On Tuesday night, October 28, 2014—sixty-five years in the making—the legendary Brown Bombers were enshrined in the Colorado Springs Sports Hall of Fame. Five of the surviving Bombers at that time, Joe, Justus, Sylvester, Jesse, and Sam, lined up in the Class of 2014 spotlight at the Broadmoor World Arena, a venue of the world-renowned The Broadmoor resort. The historic luxury hotel was established in the early 1900s when segregation was extending roots in Colorado Springs. Back when the Bombers were playing ball, the only way they would have stepped inside the legendary five-star hotel was to work as the help.

But the young boys turned elder statesmen took the high road in their attitude, words, and actions. Six and a half decades later that high road led them to high honors.

When Sylvester was notified that the Brown Bombers earned their way into the Sports Hall of Fame, his emotions swelled, "This is one of the greatest things that ever happened to me. We've gone through so much over the years. I guess I got a little sobby. It's a big deal."

After letting their athleticism speak louder than words back in 1949 and 1950, the Brown Bombers were finally rewarded with much-deserved accolades. These days people are calling Joe, Justus, Sylvester, and their Bomber teammates mentors, heroes, and icons.

R-E-S-P-E-C-T. (More than a little bit. More than a little bit.)

I Wonder It's been said we are all created equal. Does the Creator play favorites with skin color?

Dig deeper. *Bend.*
Additional insights and reflections on page 242.

Four

Semper Fidelis, "Always Faithful"

*"On the seventh day God rested—
Marines filled sandbags."*
—Unknown

DING-G-G DONG-G-G. The doorbell both startles and elates Nina Deeds. "Oh my, gosh," she squeals. "Is that Josh?" Nina rushes to the front door and flails it open. But immediately, she slams it shut.

Nooooo, nooo, Nina frantically wails to herself. *THAT is NOT my husband! THAT is NOT my Josh!*

On the afternoon of May 17, 2003, Marine Corporal Joshua Deeds returns from his three-month deployment in the Middle East to find his wife and the mother of their two-day-old firstborn greeting him like a disturbing stranger.

"I was startled just by the look in his eye. I was expecting Josh, but he had this stern, empty look," Nina recalls years later. "It was more intense than the staring-past-me look that he had returning from boot camp. This time Josh's innocence and excitement for life was gone. I wondered if he was safe to be with us."

What happened to Josh behind enemy lines? What was so horrific that altered him so drastically and nearly crushed the life out of him? And almost shattered his marriage?

I live in a community surrounded by a fortified military presence—

the United States Air Force Academy, and to the south the Army's Fort Carson, Peterson Air Force Base, Schriever Air Force Base, the North American Aerospace Defense Command (NORAD), and U.S. Space Command.

Thousands of active-duty military and retired veterans live in my city, some right next door. But until I met Josh Deeds, I had no realistic comprehension of the wrenching ordeal many service men and women encounter. Some military soldiers sacrifice by giving their very lives for our country and others keep sacrificing every time the sun comes up. Josh Deeds is one of these soldiers.

The U.S. Marine Corps released their slogan in 1977, the year Josh was born. "Marines. The few. The proud." Growing up on the outer edge of Huntington, West Virginia, young Josh learns to hunt, fish, and fit in with the Appalachian-proud folks of his home state. The same picturesque Mountain State that claims John Denver's hit "Take Me Home Country Roads" as it's official state song.

"Take me home, West Virginia," could be Josh's heart song at age sixteen when his mother and stepfather move the family to Memphis for his stepdad's air traffic controller training. The societal differences prove too much for Josh, who longs for re-planting his roots back in Shenandoah River country. After a few months of living in Tennessee, Josh moves back home to live with his grandmother.

The teenager pours a foundation for his independent, self-reliant spirit and becoming a no-nonsense kind of guy. Staying in his familiar surroundings also helps him step around his early days of abuse at the hand of his mother.

"My mother was seen as a pariah. She was a drug addict and alcoholic, and she would beat my little brother and me with the buckle end of a belt," Josh shares, his stouthearted voice cracking slightly. "I kept thinking, *God, why are you letting this happen? Please protect me from this.*"

The incongruence of what was really happening at home and hiding family secrets within their church pushes Josh to mistrusting faith. Eventually as a teen, Josh separates himself from going to church with his grandmother and concentrates on his Reserve Officer Training Corps (ROTC) opportunities in high school. At age eighteen, Josh drops out of school and starts traveling the country with a company that cleans department store carpets and flooring. He also turns to drinking and smoking to numb out some of his painful past.

"By age twenty, I was drinking and smoking a lot, and finally said, 'I can't do this forever,'" Josh reflects. "So I go back to Huntington, quit my job, and decide to join the Army."

The Army recruiter pays for a round-trip bus ticket to Memphis so Josh can say good-bye to his mother. When Josh arrives in Memphis, he stops by the sporting goods store where his mom works as the assistant manager.

"I see a young lady and hear, 'Oh, Debbie, he's so cute,'" Josh says, grinning at the memory of that day. "That was it. I knew at that moment that I didn't want to pursue the Army anymore—I wanted to pursue her."

The "her" is Nina, a store employee who has heard about Josh from his mother. Even though Nina is almost seventeen and in a two-year relationship with another guy, it is truly love at first sight for both Nina and Josh.

Josh calls his Army recruiter that same day and breaks his verbal commitment to join America's oldest military branch. Next, he lands a luggage salesman job two stores from where Nina and his mom work. Josh and Nina start dating and quickly grow serious.

Realizing that he doesn't want to sell luggage for the rest of his life, Josh reconsiders the Army. In downtown Memphis, all the military recruiting offices are next to each other. As Josh heads to the Army office, the Marines sign catches his eye.

"I thought, *I'm pretty sure I can do that.* I remembered my grandfather who served in the Marines during the Korean War," Josh says. "So I went inside the Marines recruiting office, and they gave me a test. I scored very high, off the charts."

The Marines want Josh to be an aircraft mechanic, but Nina

encourages Josh to fight for what he really wants to be: a Marine Police Officer. Josh signs his enlistment papers in April 1999 and proposes to Nina in August. In November, he leaves for boot camp in San Diego. For the next thirteen weeks, Nina receives only three short phone calls from her on-a-mission fiancé.

"We take purpose-led recruits and build them into victory-driven Marines—transforming the most willing into the most capable."
—Marines.com

After three months of grueling training regimens and screaming drill instructors, Josh graduates from the Marine Recruit Training Depot on February 11, 2000. A week later on February 18, he marries Nina back in Memphis. A month later, Josh is sent to the military police school academy at the USMC Detachment in Missouri, apart from his new bride for four months.

The Deeds buy a black Volkswagen Jetta, cramming all their possessions in their 5-speed compact and drive across country to Josh's first official Marine police assignment at Camp Pendleton, about forty miles north of San Diego. The twenty-three-year-old Marine settles into his duties with the military police.

In June 2002, Josh receives a stop-loss order, which means he must stay in the Marines until the order lifts. There is a projected stop-loss enforcement of eighteen months. Josh considers applying to local police departments before he leaves the Marines, but the stop-loss order changes his forward-thinking plans.

Instead, six months later in December 2002, his unit is issued a standing order to be deployed for buildup within sixty days. Nina keeps busy as a preschool teacher on base and says good-bye to parent after parent who deploys. Fear and nightmares creep in for her, while Josh hunkers down, preparing for the inevitable.

A few weeks later, Josh learns their unit is now under a warning order and must be ready to deploy within seven days. Life spins wildly for the young couple.

Photo by Jerry Daniel

"It was shocking! Nina was pregnant with our first son, and we didn't see this coming at all," Josh clearly remembers. "On January 23, Nina kissed me good-bye and I left."

Josh and his all-male unit fly twenty hours, vacillating between hyped emotions of excitement and anxiety. "We didn't have a clue where we were going," Josh recalls. "We didn't have a clue when we'd be back."

Their families had no clue either. Rumors drifted among Josh's fellow soldiers on whether they were heading to Iran, Iraq, or Syria. Others felt certain with the current war in Afghanistan they were headed there.

Wherever these battle-ready Marines would press their boots on the ground, they were already used to bending and bending until they nearly broke.

"It wasn't until we landed that we realized where we were headed. In the airport, we looked around and saw "Welcome to Kuwait City." I knew then. 'Oh, man, we're going to Iraq!'"

"I can't believe your leadership didn't tell you anything," I exclaim to Josh.

"They couldn't, because the president hadn't even talked about our military going into Iraq until March of 2003," Nina interjects. "This was in January."

"This was an initial buildup," Josh adds, coughing and steadying his voice for what lies ahead in our nearly three hours together.

"So what was going through your head then?" I ask Josh. "You're in the airport and you see the sign."

"Honestly, I was kind of excited because I remember in the Marine Corps boot camp studying the Hundred-Hour War, the Gulf War, where we rolled into Kuwait and we just pushed Iraq out," Josh explains. "We rolled over Iraq in less than a week."

My insights on America's most recent battles are a bit hazy, so I just let Josh fill me in. He seems fervently determined to walk me through his introduction to combat, and I am both eager and hesitant.

I've always been that way about war movies. I am intrigued by the profound impact on world history and the kick-butt intensity, but sometimes I literally close my eyes and cover my ears so I don't have to witness the on-screen blood and gore. But I know what Josh shares next is not a Hollywood rendition of actual wartime reality.

"So we just landed and I'm thinking, *If we're going to Iraq, this is the best war possible. We're going to roll over everybody, and we're going to go home in a month,*" Josh elaborates. "Even my police officer supervisors from Pendleton said, 'Yeah, you're going to pick up rank really quickly because you'll be a combat veteran, you'll have fought in a foreign war. Your life is going to be easy after that.' Boy, did I not know how difficult life would soon be. Nobody knew."

Nobody knew. Josh and Nina turn to each other with a look that I can barely put into words. They lock eyes for a moment, and it's as if the world decides to stop spinning. What was Josh about to reveal?

"I volunteered for a group of guys that would gather intelligence, and if I had to do it over again, I would have never volunteered, honestly," Josh compels the words to tumble out. "Because we were behind enemy lines the majority of the time. We had no support from American forces anywhere."

Plopped down in unknown territory, then behind enemy lines with no support from anywhere? I hold in my guttural groan. Here is where Josh and I exchange a rapid-fire dialogue. Nina remains silent, but I notice her tears begging to spill out.

Josh joins five other guys, three of whom had served together in previous conflicts. Part of their mission is to observe, and part is snatch-and-grabs to find out what people know.

Nina remains silent, but I notice her tears begging to spill out.

Me: And who was the enemy?

Josh: Everyone. Men, women, and children.

Me: This was a highly covert mission. That had to be scary.

Josh: You knew that you could die at every given moment of every given day. Imagine living as if your whole life is happening sixty times a minute, sixty minutes an hour, twenty-four hours a day.

Me: How do you prepare for something like that?

Josh: Ever since I was young, I was able to pick up any weapon and hit a bull's eye no matter the distance. I knew that every Marine is a rifleman, and we all practiced making great rifle shots, but it never really clicked with me that I would qualify for this role. And that's what I did. I was the guy who was supposed to make the great shots to protect my team.

Some of the guys in our team were lifelong, and they were

way off the ragged-edge deep end. I had to rely on these guys for my life, but I would never trust them around my family or friends. Ever.

While Josh is abruptly immersed in covert operations in Iraq, Nina contends with a barrage of fears. After not hearing from Josh for about six weeks, she feels panicked and drives to the base's crisis center.

"It was surreal being there. The commanding officer's wife of Josh's unit he left with confirmed that Josh was safe," Nina recalls, looking back on her gut-wrenching separation from Josh during most of her first pregnancy. "Josh was working as a base MP, so when he deployed he was supposed to be guarding aircraft. Or, so I thought at that time. I spent every night praying and begging God to protect Josh and bring him home for our son."

Me: In this time of intelligence gathering, how long was that?

Josh: Three months.

Me: So if there were some impending target in the way, you were the one that would just take it out?

Josh: Yes. Didn't matter if it was an adult, a child, man, woman.

Me: But you were told what to do.

Josh: No. I made judgment calls. We were told by our commanding officer that whatever judgment call we make is never going to be questioned. I was coming from a background as a police officer and doing my best to do the right thing at all times. But this job of not knowing what exactly you're going to be doing was the biggest shock. A moral injury. One day you're upholding all laws, and literally a week later you're breaking all laws.

Me: And you can't talk about it.

Josh: And you can't talk about any of it. I had the option to stay with the group after the war, but I knew that if I had stayed there, there would be no way I would ever come back mentally.

A lot of guys say it's a switch you can flip, but for that type of work, there is no switch you can flip. Once you turn it on, it's on forever.

"It is instilled in your body that you can't be afraid of anything anymore. . . . Once you're a Marine, there's no turning back."
—Marines.com

Whiz. Crack. Bang. January 23 to May 13, Marine corporal Josh Deeds unknowingly becomes one of America's military snipers continually on the move deep in enemy territory.

While Josh is already locked in unspeakable hostilities for his country, the Iraq War officially launches on March 19, with the U.S. and coalition forces bombing Bagdad, Iraq's capital. Dictator Saddam Hussein and his military reportedly possess or are building weapons of mass destruction. On May 1, President George W. Bush declares the end of the three-week major combat operations.

For 109 days in Iraq, essentially cut off from the rest of the world, terror surges within Josh. He knows that at any second he might be the one on the receiving end of a rifle, a knife, an explosive device, a nerve agent.

Josh glances down at the table for an instant, and Nina breaks in, "And he never served with these guys ever again."

Josh returns to the States two months ahead of the rest of his deployment unit. Even Josh's own commanding officer has no idea what Josh did overseas and why he is returning with another unit. The colonel simply asks his wife to pick up Josh at the airport on May 15 and drive him home. Home is now base housing on Castle Street, where Nina slams the door in his face before her mother quickly nudges her to let him in.

Josh looks back on that greeting and their strained marriage going forward. "Nina later told me, 'I had to come to realize that the guy who'd left in January 2003 never came back. Who came back was completely different,'" Josh slowly voices. "I looked the same, but I wasn't the same guy."

After falling in love in Memphis, Josh and Nina dreamed of raising a family. Nina miscarried in 2002, but they were grateful to see baby Joshua arrive the next spring. With Josh newly back from Iraq, they determine to be all in on parenting their newborn.

Josh reports back to police duties at Camp Pendleton and Nina stays at home to care for baby Joshua, then their second son, Jackson. Jackson is born in October 2004, almost eighteen months after Josh returns from Iraq.

"I was blessed to be able to stay home with the kids, yet Josh was constantly working extra hours and doing everything he possibly could to not be at home," Nina recalls of their early years as parents. "We were basically living two different lives."

Why? Josh longs to be a father and build a close-knit family he never experienced, yet he is marching in the wrong direction.

"I didn't realize it at the time, but I had the early onset symptoms of severe PTSD (post-traumatic stress disorder) and severe TBI (traumatic brain injury)," Josh confirms. "I didn't have medical tests or ask for help. There were no evaluations at the time."

Flying under the radar post-deployment, Josh mans up like a loyal Marine and doesn't let on about his symptoms and pain. He punches autopilot and stays at work eighteen to twenty hours a day.

"I was continually angry and struggled to sleep. I did not know how to deal with normal life anymore. At work I could be involved with the most stressful situations and be completely calm and love it," Josh explains. "But as soon as I came home, and I heard a baby cry, or I needed to go to the grocery store, or I needed to get gas or pay a bill, I would just freak out. I couldn't handle it. I didn't want to realize what I'd become."

❧

What *did* Josh become? A hyper-sensitive cyborg incapable of tender emotions? A deeply conflicted husband and father? A military hero cast off as a loner?

On top of his physical injuries, Josh has no one to talk to about what really happened in the war. Even Josh's own buddies he was deployed with wondered where he was and what he did during the three months. Back in the States, when he will not say, they basically ostracize him.

"I would never answer questions," Josh recounts of his post-war conversations. "I was told to never answer questions and don't tell anybody what you did."

In the months and years after Iraq, even with Nina, Josh just cannot open up. When Josh tries to let Nina in a bit, she fears she will have horrible nightmares. When she is pregnant with Jackson, she does not want the emotional stress to harm their baby.

In February 2006, Josh receives orders to join 1 Marine Expeditionary Force, counterintelligence, to deploy back to Iraq and complete a similar mission.

"I knew that if I went back, I would never come back mentally or emotionally. I didn't want to put my family through that. I'd heard horror stories by then about guys coming back and killing their whole family and themselves," Josh shares. "The type of work we did is not for normal people. It's not for people that want to have families. You can do that work, but you cannot have a family, period."

Nina adds to Josh's explanation. "Not with your personality," she states, placing her hand on his arm. "There are certain personalities that can, but once Josh buys into something, that's it."

Josh asks for his order to be switched, and fortunately, another position in Japan opens up at the same time. In July 2006, the family moves to Iwakuni, Japan, where Josh is appointed the U.S. Customs and Immigration Chief at Marine Corps Air Station Iwakuni, the base where the Japanese planned the Pearl Harbor attack. Still a part of U.S. military law enforcement, Josh reports to the Marine general but ultimately to Japan's prime minister as the person enforcing

Japan's immigration and customs laws on the U.S. military base.

"I didn't realize how bad my PTSD and TBIs had become. I knew and my wife knew that I had a mouth on me. If somebody gave me a stupid order, I would argue with it," Josh states, his face approaching a frown. "I never got charged because I knew all the laws. I knew how far I could go before I was insubordinate."

Again, Nina adds a bit more to the facts. "But you got put in the corner," she says. "They put Josh off to the side to work independently, not around other Marines. That's why he was in Customs."

After three years in Japan, where their daughter, Jillian, is born in March 2007, the Deeds rotate back to Camp Pendleton so Josh can become an infantry instructor. During training, however, Josh badly injures his ankle and knee and is medically disqualified from pursuing the instructor position. Next, Josh is transferred closer to San Diego to be a police officer at the Marine Corps Air Station Miramar.

"When I got injured as an infantry instructor, I was scared that something was off about me," Josh carefully voices. If I asked for help I would be seen as worthless, because that's the way the Marine Corps operates. You don't ever ask for help."

When Josh first returns from Iraq, his commanding officer does stop by the house and advises Nina to give Josh space and "just let him be who he is now," but no one knows who the new Josh is or is becoming.

In combat there's not going to be someone there
to hold your hand, so if you were raised in that type
of environment, that definitely will not help you."
—Marines.com

I probe a bit more about how Josh actually suffered his TBIs.

"From explosions and falling. I fell out of a helicopter. Then a suicide bomber blew himself up inside a building, and a wall came down on me," Josh answers matter-of-factly. "The building falling didn't do as much damage as you think it would. They dug me out and asked if I wanted to go to medical or stay with the team. I said, 'Stay with the team.' That was it. Nobody ever talked about it again."

You fall out of a helicopter. Along the way, you also break bones and are cut up. Then a building collapses on you and you just keep going. No wonder the Marines recruitment videos show do-or-die feats these military men and women must endure before they can even enter a wartime battle. These Marines are not Gomer Pyle with his aw-shucks cheer. These are the few, the proud, the ultra-gutsy.

"In the building explosion, I had some scrapes and cut up my head, but that was just a cut," Josh says, brushing off his injuries like he is a kid who only needs a Snoopy bandage. "They gave us coca leaves like crazy, basically unprocessed cocaine, so you could stay up and do your job and never have to fall asleep."

Did Josh and his teammates ever catch much sleep on their clandestine operations?

"No. We were on a schedule of 96/24," Josh explains. "So you're up for 96 hours then down for 24. Four days awake, 24 hours off, for three months. We were constantly on the move."

Intense sleep deprivation, a battered body, and always-on vigilance on top of being a long-range assassin for three months solid, did not do Josh any favors. Now six and half years after serving in Iraq, Josh is unraveling. More quickly than he wants to admit.

A fellow Marine who knows Josh from his first days at Camp Pendleton is now Josh's master gunnery sergeant. The E-9 officer pulls Josh aside saying Josh is different in his demeanor and warns him to keep himself in check. Two days later, when a fellow Marine accidentally fires a round during a weapons clearing, Josh grabs the gun away from the solider and slams him in the mouth.

"The master gunnery sergeant saw it and yanked me back, saying, 'You're going to medical first thing in the morning. You're going to get a post-deployment screening. You're not being charged. You did the right thing. You took the weapon away, but you don't punch the guy in the mouth,'" Josh explains of his superior's reprimand.

Josh adds that when the gun fired, he was so startled that it was just a natural reaction to neutralize what he saw as the enemy. "The enemy at that time," Josh notes, "was my own Marine."

In many ways, the enemy is Josh himself. Finally, Josh is not asking for help, but getting it. The next morning, a general surgeon hands Josh a stack of evaluation paperwork to fill out. Josh is torn about answering honestly. His mind floods with comments from a number of his senior officers telling him since Iraq that something is wrong with him. Now, he feels pinned down, taking fire, yet somehow sensing freedom. Josh recounts that life-changing exchange with the surgeon.

He feels pinned down, taking fire, yet somehow sensing freedom.

"It took me about two hours to answer all those questions," Josh begins with this portion of his post-war journey. "I gave the paperwork back and the doctor just glanced at the paperwork. His first question is, 'Do you have access to weapons?'"

"Yes, I do. I'm third in charge of my platoon," Josh explains to the surgeon. "I have access to hundreds of pistols and rifles and shotguns, and a little bit of C-4 every once in a while. Of course I do."

The doctor retorts, "Not anymore. Who's your senior enlisted?"

Josh gives his master gunnery sergeant's number to the surgeon who then methodically dials. Seconds later, the doctor minces no words to the officer on the phone. "Your sergeant failed," he booms. "He failed badly. He's not coming back to work."

For the next six months, Josh is placed on light duty medical evaluation. Every day for six hours, Josh meets with a psychologist to determine if Josh can continue in the Marines.

"I was doing a lot of research and realized that if I'm honest with these people, I'm going to be kicked out of the Marine Corps. I can't lose everything. I've got three kids, a fourth on the way," Josh explains of his half a year in medical evaluation. "After about the first three months, I started locking up and not telling them anything because I didn't want to be pushed out."

The repetitive daily questions include how Josh is feeling and if he is experiencing anger and getting enough sleep. No one contacts Nina to get her perspective on her out-of-sorts husband.

I turn to Nina directly and want to know how she was fairing through the medical and emotional examining of Josh.

Me: So how was your relationship at this time?
Nina: I'm just taking care of the kids.
Me: Josh, you'd come home and just disappear?
Josh: Eat, go to bed, wake up the and do it all over again.
Me: Did you have dreams?
Josh: Horrible dreams, constantly, crazy dreams.
Me: And Nina, that would wake you up too?
Nina: Hm-hm. I've blocked a lot of that out.
Me: Bad things happen when I go to sleep.

"Bad things happen when I go to sleep." I've heard intriguing comments by thousands of people all over this planet, but Josh's disclosure is purely profound. I imagine in his dreams he relives the horrors of warfare and aiming his rifle to take people's lives from three-fourths a mile away. But I don't have the heart to ask.

Nina: It was rough when Josh first started getting treatment because it opened up Pandora's Box.
Josh: There was also the things I've seen in Iraq, but your mind twists things in certain ways in your dream state.
Me: Like people coming at you rather than you coming at them? Like you're the one being attacked?

❧

Both Josh and Nina knowingly nod and then lovingly glance again at each other. When you've been to hell and back, sometimes it is better to just let the scorching ordeal cool down on its own. I sense it's not the time to stir the ashes, but talk about fresh hope ahead.

After the six-month evaluation period, the doctors feel Josh is stabilized and he returns to full, active duty. A couple of months later, while out on patrol training, Josh is in a combat fitness test and lifts a fellow Marine onto his shoulders and hustles. Josh feels a searing pain in his lower back as soon as he picks the soldier up, but presses on, carrying the guy two hundred yards. When Josh goes to let the Marine down, the pain rips into Josh's lower extremities.

"I just collapsed. I couldn't move at all," Josh acknowledges. "I felt nothing but sharp pain throughout both of my legs, down to my ankles, and my feet had gone numb almost instantly."

Military hospital specialists determine that Josh's back injuries in Iraq have finally reached their screaming point—Josh's degenerated disks are compressing on his spinal cord. He is ordered off active duty for good.

"At that point I went off the deep end. Everything came back. This was 2010. I fought every step of the way to try to stay in the Marines, but finally, I lost," Josh discloses, his face tensing at the realization. "I'm the guy that can get anything done. If my commanding officer told me to do something, come hell or high water, it's getting done. But now, my body had given out. I felt like a complete and total failure because I couldn't will myself over this."

Brave. Driven. Broken. Crashed. First Sergeant Deeds hits the end of the road. Or, is it the beginning of a new route?

For the next year and a half, Navy doctors who serve the Marines try a number of therapies to ease Josh's pain and mental state. A senior Navy officer, a seasoned psychiatrist with a top security clearance, meets with Josh consistently. This Naval psychiatrist personally knows the military strategists who developed the intelligence program that Josh's team implemented in Iraq.

"More than a decade later this psychiatrist hears from me, somebody that used their program in combat," Josh reflects. "It was very informative for him to see how badly guys that he respected messed up—how they messed up brains."

Every day for almost eighteen months, Josh drives from Miramar to Balboa to meet the Naval mental health professional to see if they can calm his "messed up brain." But no one else in the military could speak with him. Josh is cut off from his Marine unit and ordered not to talk to any of his fellow Marines. Even the MPs at the front gate of the Miramar base where the Deeds live, the MPs that Josh trained, will not say a word to him.

"They were given orders to act like they didn't know me. I'd ask a question and they wouldn't answer. I'd pull over to try to talk to them and they wouldn't answer," Josh recalls with a heaviness in his voice. "I asked for help and got the silent treatment because I wouldn't tell other Marines what I had done while I was deployed. It was really crappy. It was just horrendous."

After his long days of therapy with the Naval medical experts, Josh comes home to find although Nina loves him dearly and wants to understand his inner turmoil, she just can't really go there to the Iraqi terror. Nina tries to avoid having nightmares herself and wants to protect their in utero son and their other three children from both parents being psychologically strained.

"I tried to talk to Nina, but she didn't want to hear a lot of the stuff," Josh explains. "Looking back, I don't blame her. I wouldn't have wanted to hear all that either."

Josh's safe place to share anything was with the top Naval psychiatrist. Nina emphasizes that this doctor and those who developed the intelligence program had no idea of the dreadful effects it would have on U.S. soldiers.

"He didn't know the cost at the time," Josh adds. "Nobody knows at the time when they create something. The guys who developed the nuclear bomb didn't know how it was going to be used."

In all his physical and mental pain, and alienation from other Marines and his own family to a degree, I wonder how all this affected Josh spiritually. I'm not sure how Josh feels about God after his childhood experiences and now all this adulthood sacrifice and betrayal.

"I just became angry, super angry. How could God let this

happen to me? Why would God let this happen to me?" Josh reasons. "Why would God let everybody be cut out of my life?"

THUD! To Josh, even God dropped him in an isolated black hole. I ask Josh what kept him going at this point.

"I don't know what kept me going," Josh states, his eyes staring straight ahead as if searching for a lifeline. "Maybe the hope that someday it will be better."

❧

Somewhere in the mix of moving back from Japan, Josh, Nina, and the kids start attending a San Diego-area church. They respond to a mailed flyer they received from the church. But integrating into a church community proves hit or miss. Josh attends because it's important to Nina, and it's one of the few things they all do together as a family. Yet Josh does not warm up easily to the congregation's men who extend kindness and friendship.

"They didn't understand the military," Josh shares. "They didn't understand the struggle it was for me not to eat a bullet every single day."

Our conversation drifts to the sobering number of military suicides in America. Nina explains that the civilian world—even the church—doesn't understand that on average twenty-two military members kill themselves each day in the United States.

In Josh's fragile state, he walked a thin line in joining these national statistics himself.

In January 2012, Josh is declared 100 percent disabled from severe PTSD, severe multiple TBIs, and roughly twenty other diagnoses including degenerative disk disease, glaucoma, and hearing loss. His back, knees, ankles, elbows, and shoulders are more like the bones and joints of someone twice his age.

Methodically, the medical discharge person takes Josh and Nina through Josh's one hundred-page report. The damage is done. The military's conclusion is final: Josh at age thirty-six that August is discharged from military service and is told he can never work anywhere, ever again.

"I'm thirty-six years old and I can never get a job. Any job. Nothing," Josh repeats out loud. "The military is afraid that I'm going to go off the deep end on some civilian who will end up dead and I'll end up in jail."

The same U.S. Marine Corps that trained and placed Josh in intelligence gathering behind enemy lines now acknowledges that Josh is too ill to serve his country and too ill to work in any capacity now and in the future. The military provides full disability retirement to Josh for a lifetime and they pay for his family's medical expenses.

"I'm thirty-six years old and I can never get a job. Any job. Nothing."

The military also pays for the Deeds to move anywhere in the country, and they choose Colorado because of its economy, schools, and veteran medical care. The medical care that Josh continues to need for his unending migraines and deteriorating spine and joints.

Moving to a pro-military part of the country, but with few Marines around, Josh finds it even more challenging to fit in with men he can trust. The Deeds search for a church, but between the throngs of people and loud music that can trigger Josh's headaches, it proves wearisome to try to find people who can relate to them.

Some folks wonder why Josh, who looks normal on the outside, can't work. Others grow impatient with Josh and Nina canceling social plans because Josh is sloughing through another painful flare-up.

"Some guys I've met complain about pushing a button and watching a bomb go off. They have no clue. I want to say to them, 'I don't care that you killed five hundred people with a bomb. You're thirty thousand feet up. You have no clue what up close-and-personal combat looks like. No clue,' " Josh stresses, his husky voice going a notch deeper. "I have done the things that you dream about in your nightmares. You have nothing compared to me."

Josh is being raw and candid. He feels comfortable now in our interview just letting the words charge forward. Yet he softens his tone and admits it's taken him some time to consider the struggles of his fellow service members.

"I have come to realize that we all have different thresholds of pain. I can look back and say, 'Your PTSD is nothing compared to mine,' but that's not being realistic," Josh concedes. "Maybe his PTSD is worse than mine because he has a different threshold, a different maximum than I do. So I can't judge him for his pain, just as he can't judge me for my pain. Everybody has a different maximum."

Nina shares that Josh's pain maximum is incredibly high and it's what kept him afloat when the Marines only allow for mild over-the-counter anti-inflammatory medicines.

"While you're active duty, you are allowed no pain meds. You get Motrin and water. That's it," Josh firmly explains. "If you want anything else, you're out of the Marine Corps. You have a gunshot wound, a broken leg? Motrin and water."

But while Josh is going through the two and half years of medical evaluations, the military doctors begin loading him up on a mix of medications. Once he retires, they add even more.

In early 2015, the Veterans Affairs (VA) doctors give Josh an iPad to keep track of his arsenal of prescription drugs. "I was a zombie, taking two or three pills every two hours every day," Josh concedes.

Me: Nina, were you concerned?

Nina: I was not allowed to be. If I was trying to voice my concern about those things, then according to Josh, I was meddling and trying to prevent him from getting better. So I just threw myself into our kids.

Josh: So early 2015, I'd had enough. I went from taking all those medications a day to zero. I was done.

Me: Just overnight?

Josh: Overnight. Done. And our relationship really went downhill after that to the point that she up and left one day with the kids. Nina moved out, filed for divorce, and had me served with papers.

Nina: It was a legal separation to protect the kids and myself. In the mindset Josh was in, he's like, "F-ing fine. I'll divorce you then. Just change it to a divorce, not a separation."

Me: And you did that because basically you'd hit your max?

Nina: I had a fear for my life and fear for my children's lives at that point.

Me: Because of his anger and threatening behavior?

Nina: Oh, Josh was not himself. He had become an absolute monster, and normal helping with the children things flipped him too much. I was constantly trying to protect the kids, protect myself. I was living in a state of constantly having my purse ready to go, and hiding it so he couldn't take my car keys. I was living as if my husband, who I love and am completely devoted to, would turn on me at any moment.

And I knew that I was the only person that Josh had left. I know one of the biggest lies that Satan tells Josh is that he will be all alone and everybody will leave him. I was not about to let that be a part of our story. But at the same time, I wasn't going to allow Josh to destroy his family. That's not loving him well if I'm going to be a part of what he was doing. So I had to make that extremely difficult decision.

Nina finally lets down her own guard and lets her own dismay and angst gush out. How could she not? I wondered how she held up through all of Josh's trauma and onslaught of post-Iraq torment.

What is it *really* like to live with an unpredictable spouse, the man she no longer recognizes when he returns from the Middle East? After twelve years, enough. Was enough. Nina backs away to save her husband and her kids . . . and herself.

Nina and the four kids stay with friends for a couple weeks and plan to move to a homeless shelter, but other friends pay for them to stay in a hotel. Then Nina and the kids move back to the house.

"Josh absolutely hit rock bottom when he had to leave the house," Nina continues, "when Josh no longer had our family, our dog, our home."

I can sense the tension festering. Josh is building toward something in their story, but I'm not sure what. What could be tougher to hear than how he's already suffered, how the family has languished because he followed through on his commanding orders?

"Nina got the house, and I couldn't take my service dog with me. So I was living in my car without my wife, without my kids, without my service dog," Josh shares, breathing in deeply. "I decided to end it all. End the pain."

Nina gently whispers, "September 19, 2015."

❧

Josh pauses. His jaw clenches. His eyes squint at the memory of that day as if he's aiming his rifle at a hazy target a thousand yards away. He swallows his hesitancies and bulldozes through recounting the darkest days of his forty-some years.

Josh drives to southern Colorado mountains about sixty miles from home and parks his car by a trailhead. He takes a gallon of water and starts walking west into the trees and mountainside slopes. He trudges on for two days and two nights, not knowing if he is still in Colorado.

"I know how search crews work. Anything beyond thirty miles, they stop looking. So I figured I'd go out far enough, so there was no way my body would ever be found," Josh details. "Without a body, it's just a missing person. So my family would never know, and I didn't really want them to know. I just wanted to end the constant pain."

In his methodical fashion, Josh explains how wild animals are scared away by the scent of humans who have washing detergent and fabric softeners on their clothes. Josh strips down to his underwear, knowing his own urine and feces upon death will mask his human odor and the animals will then eat his carcass.

Sigh. Josh thinks of everything. Except for the unexpected out of his control.

Before daybreak on the third morning, September 21, Josh edges his way to the top of a ridgeline. The final minutes of his life are crunching to a halt.

"It was just me in my underwear with my pistol up on that mountain. I cleaned my pistol, broke it down, loaded it," Josh recounts. "I made sure that there's no possible way that once I pulled the trigger there would be a misfire."

Josh clears his throat and shifts in my dining room chair. "Then for whatever reason, I asked God, 'Give me a sign if this isn't what you want me to do.' And it was at that exact moment that the sun peeked up over the top of the mountain, right before I pulled the trigger," Josh discloses, again pausing to steady his emotions.

The final minutes of his life are crunching to a halt.

"I don't know if it was God talking to me in my own voice or if it was just me talking to myself in my head," Josh continues, "But I heard, 'Go back and give it one more shot. Ask your wife for forgiveness and give it one more shot.'"

Just seconds from ending his battle-worn life, Sgt. Joshua C. Deeds, USMC (Ret.), eases off the trigger of his pistol. One more shot. Not a shot at an enemy combatant. But a shot for life, for marriage, for family.

"God planned it in such a way that I would reach my end once I got to the top of that mountain, and he knew that I would ask for his help . . . one more time," Josh concludes.

Josh about-faces and heads down that mountain slope, back in the direction of his car. Over and over, disbelief that he heard that almost audible voice drifts through his mind. He remembers little else from his return trip. He runs out of water the first day and drinks from creeks.

Across rugged high-altitude terrain, Josh wends his way back toward his car and breaks through to the road about five miles from his vehicle early the third day. Josh reaches his car and tugs off an orange sticker that informs him the vehicle is scheduled for tow-away in about a half hour. Saved again in the nick of time, he drives to Operation TBI Freedom in Colorado Springs and they put him up in a hotel room at the Army's nearby Fort Carson.

"I started the long road of repairing my relationship with Nina," Josh says, looking directly at me now, ". . . you are the only person who has heard that story out loud outside of our family."

"It's reality," I simply respond to Josh's account of almost taking his life. I place my pen on my notepad. "I can totally see why you made that choice."

I have close friends affected by a loved one's suicide, and I decided years ago that none of us know fully what goes on in someone's mind and emotions before they are pushed to the final brink. When my incessant pain from my car accidents rammed me close to the brink myself, I developed a field-tested empathy for those who want out of their pain.

Josh battled years to stay on active duty and to get better. No longer living with Nina and the kids, Josh's world darkens. But God will not let Josh surrender his life. Even while Josh is trudging alone in the wilderness toward that mountaintop, Nina senses something is dreadfully wrong with her man.

"I didn't know where Josh was. But that first night when he left, I sent a text to one of our good friends and said, 'You need to pray for Josh right now. I don't know what is happening, but I feel like we are absolutely fighting the gates of hell right now for him.' "

When Josh returns and the two start talking again, Nina asks him what happened on September 19. With a measured calm, Josh recounts his backcountry trek toward his suicide attempt.

"That's when we realized our stories intertwined," Nina explains to me. "Josh and my stories are always intertwined no matter what we are going through and what we are fighting. We are one person." Nina turns to Josh with a look of knowing reassurance. "I felt like I was fighting for your life," she half-whispers. "That's God."

✖

By January 2016, Josh moves back home with Nina and the kids. Instead of taking nearly two dozen pills a day, Josh's original meds are reduced in half. Feeling less groggy and out of control, Josh digs deep to repair trust in his marriage, with his kids, and with himself.

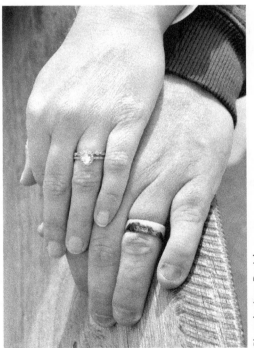

Photo by Jerry Daniel

"I'm down to four meds a day now four years later, and I will never go back to twenty-plus pills a day. I won't go back to ten a day," Josh emphasizes. "I don't know what kind of damage has been done to my liver, kidneys, or heart by taking all that medication every day, but that's no way to live. You might as well kill yourself."

Killing yourself is a sobering fact among military personnel, active-duty, retired, and reserves. In 2018, the Corps experienced a 25 percent increase in active-duty suicides from the previous year.[1]

How do I forgive myself for the things I've done? That's what I struggle with at this point.

All this comes too close to home for Josh. Of the five other soldiers in his unit behind enemy lines in Iraq, one never made it home. Within a few years, two others die of cancer. The remaining two kill themselves.

Josh is the sole survivor of their grim wartime mission.

The only living witness of what terrors they endured for the sake of America's freedom. And I wonder what kind of conversations Josh and God have had over the mayhem Josh helped dole out in Iraq.

Josh: I've done some pretty heinous things in combat that I would question. I've talked to God about this several times. I've never really been answered. He was watching me do it all. He never spoke to me while I was doing it. How do I forgive myself for the orders that I followed and for causing much more pain and destruction than an intended order? How do I forgive myself for the things I've done? That's what I struggle with at this point.

Me: Did anybody ever address that with you?

Nina: We're part of Samaritan's Purse Operation Heal Our Patriots, and that program is outstanding. A chaplain has worked with Josh quite a bit. Josh knows that it's up to him whether or not he forgives himself.

Josh: I know God has already forgiven me. I need to forgive myself.

As I once heard a speaker explain that forgiveness is both a point and a process, Josh continues in the process of putting down the gavel and not listening to self-accusatory messages about his wartime job.

We switch to the topic of Josh waiting on the VA to fix his knees and back and staying on Adderall to calm his brain and taking preventative and active migraine medicine, plus his sleep aid. The migraines invade about twice a week now and Josh has developed a coping routine.

"I drink a Monster, put on my sunglasses, take the migraine meds, and work through it," Josh explains. "I can go outside and work in the yard or take a drive and pick up the kids from school. I can work through it. Honestly, like Nina has told me many, many times, my pain tolerance is extremely high."

"That's what's so hard," Nina adds, her voice trailing off.

"I can work through my migraines now," Josh continues, "but during a migraine, I can't sit down and have an in-depth conversation without dropping twenty F-bombs in a sentence. No, it's not going to happen."

Josh notes that talking like a sailor, well, a Marine, does not reflect social graces with civilians and church folk. But with his TBIs, his verbal filter sometimes go awry, and he inappropriately blurts out a thought at the wrong time. Like barking at the slow-moving woman in front of him at the grocery store that she is a fat bi - - -.

Oops. Josh's unpredictable pain and surges of impatience make it challenging for the Deeds to commit to social functions, but they are cautiously building a small cadre of local friends. And through it all, Josh and Nina are putting down deeper roots in their faith.

"So our life hasn't been peachy keen, but for whatever reason, I've had this incessant need to lean into God," Josh brings up.

"I didn't want to acknowledge or show that I'm not in complete control of my own destiny. But I've had that need since I was a kid."

Nina acknowledges her take on Josh's persistent faith. "I think God's very patient with you."

Josh pauses at Nina's reflection and then shares how he almost ditched God back in his early days in West Virginia. Josh points out how his painful abuse was not wasted. "We came to the realization a few years ago that as horrible as my childhood was, it prepared me for what I experienced in combat," Josh states. "God was prepping me for the things I would have to do and see in Iraq."

We linger in silence for a few seconds. My mind trails to the stealth intensity Josh endured trying to stay alive in Iraq. I bring up the 2014 war movie *American Sniper* starring Bradley Cooper as Navy SEAL Chris Kyle. I wonder how close the film is to Josh's Iraqi reality.

"It's pretty realistic. He was a legend. I am nowhere near his caliber in what he did—ever," Josh says with fresh fervor. "I've got thirty-one under my belt. He had hundreds. There's no comparison to that. No way."

Seeing the movie with Nina in January 2015 did trigger some flashbacks for Josh; memories he doesn't want to unleash. I do not press him on those details, which are buried relics with little value to the living or the dead.

Instead, I wonder how Josh continues to bend and come back from so many obstacles that would crush so many of the rest of us.

Me: In physics there's a bending point, for example, with metal on a bridge. If you go past that bending point, the bridge will collapse.

Josh: But I'm not like that. I will bend, bend, bend, and bend again, and go way past that point. The bridge will snap and fall, and then I realize, "okay, that was too far." But then I pick myself up, rebuild that bridge, and it will be stronger next time.

Bend, bend, snap, rebuild, stronger the next time. In a sense, this describes Josh's marching orders from his earliest days. How has his post-war strife affected his own children's upbringing?

Josh: Looking back, we're one of the few families that have been upfront with our kids from the get-go.

Nina: Age-appropriately.

Josh: A lot of families hide it and hide it until something catastrophic happens, and then the kids don't understand what's going on, and their whole world is destroyed because they were never prepared for what could actually happen.

Nina: When Josh got out of the Marines, he was angry with me initially for letting the kids know the diagnoses and talking to them about his health. The kids were 9, 8, 5, and 2.

Me: What kind of conversations do you have with them?

Josh: We're pretty honest.

Nina: We've always been honest, but before it was, "Daddy has trauma. Daddy is hurt. His brain is hurt." Now they have a very in-depth knowledge of the injuries.

The aftermath of dealing with brain injuries in themselves limits Josh in his ability to hold down a civilian job. Or, as Josh clarifies, "I'm good at shooting people at long distances, and I was good at being a police officer, and no police department is going to take me. And, I don't know of any civilian jobs that will let me shoot people at long distances, so I'm kind of stuck in my options."

To counter all the unknowns of Josh's daily health conditions, he works hard at just being with the kids after school and during summer breaks.

"I watch TV with them and take them to movies. I hug them a lot. Praise them a lot," Josh shares. "I tell them I'm proud of them. And I explain to them different issues that come up that I have to deal with."

All four of the Deeds children have been in counseling to work through what Josh calls "secondary PTSD from my episodes that have rubbed off on them." As far as Josh's continued care through the VA, he sees a doctor every couple of months and is waiting for more successful therapy or surgery for his spinal and knee injuries.

"Most of my days, if I'm not with my kids or my wife, I spend fighting for medical care that I should have already gotten. It's a constant struggle, constant fight," Josh notes with a lilt of exasperation in his voice. "Or, I help other veterans that aren't as far along in their healing or medical journey as I am."

Josh has been involved with a few veterans groups since retirement, looking mainly to encourage combat veterans like him. He gets the pain. The loneliness. The fight to fight on.

This never-quit resiliency has remained a guiding distinctive of the U.S. Marine Corps long before it adopted *Semper Fidelis,* "Always Faithful," as its motto circa 1883. Nina fills me in how she sees *Semper Fi* demonstrated by God.

"God's faithfulness has seen us through all the hard things. He can deal with our anger. We can bring that to him. Part of our story is realizing the richness of our relationship with the Lord," Nina elaborates. "We could take a different route and be like I'm done with this whole Christianity thing, period. But for me, it's not about a religion, it's about my relationship with Christ."

Josh nods in agreement.

"To me, it is God's faithfulness and that's the only reason I am able to love Josh the way that I am called to," Nina adds. "I know I have plenty of reasons not to, just like he has plenty of reasons not to hang in there with me."

Josh takes a minute to reminisce about their dating life back in Memphis when he would read Scripture to his favorite gal. "It was just me reading verses to her and not going in depth. Now we have very in-depth conversations about the Bible together," Josh explains. "We've grown very far in being able to have deep philosophical and belief conversations about Scripture. Whereas before, I was just reading a book to her, just reading words."

Sharing that they discuss and apply God's Word to their wounds of war and beyond, Josh and Nina give each other a final adoring glance. How do they summarize their relationship and marriage now of twenty years?

"Deeply in love," Josh quickly replies. "Growing closer every day."

Nina smiles and shares, "We're 100 percent committed and wanting to love each other well in the way God's calling us to. We have each other's back. I know that even when Josh is in pain and having a difficult day, there is nothing that he wouldn't do for me."

Semper Fidelis, Josh and Nina. Here's to you remaining . . . Always Faithful.

I Wonder Is there anything that can't be forgiven?

Dig deeper. *Bend.*
Additional insights and reflections on page 244.

Five

Living in the Shadows

*"In faith there is enough light
for those who want to believe and
enough shadows to blind those who don't."*

—Blaise Pascal

CYNDI* LIVES IN THE SHADOWS. The shifting grayness that is not quite crystal clear, not quite cloudy.

I am not sure how to tell you about Cyndi. You see, Cyndi is homeless. Cyndi is a witch. A homeless witch. Our worlds are expansively apart and yet maybe not.

Maybe Cyndi and I are more alike than I would like to think.

If you're looking in the morning daylight, you may not find Cyndi. Cyndi prefers to skip the first hours after sunrise and cocoon in her makeshift home wedged in a corner of an auto body shop. Cyndi's ex-husband owns the repair-n-paint business and lets her hole up in a ten-by-fifteen-foot room with her son and his girlfriend.

In this tough-as-steel part of town, amenities include sharing a toilet and bathroom sink with all the employees and customers. Privacy is a foreign word when you're homeless.

Most days Cyndi has no place to be. No place to go. She's a part-time fry cook and concessions worker at area event centers. Some days she does clerical work for the street mission group next door. A bit more to the west, Uplift, a faith-based work opportunity center

---

*Names are changed in this chapter to respect privacy.

finds homeless folks day labor jobs. The work center also offers free coffee, showers, and a laundry room to those who need these basics.

Cyndi frequents Uplift regularly. Although she doesn't espouse the Bible beliefs of the staff, they are family to her. Cyndi feels at home among the laid-back crew who prefer tattoos, bandanas, and dark T-shirts to demure dress codes.

Cyndi is a sweatshirt- and baseball cap-wearing kind of gal. No black hat, cape, crooked nose, or warts. No green teeth, pointy finger-nails, or crackling shrill voice. No broom. One look at petite, and a bit rough-around-the-edges Cyndi and you don't think, *Oh, she's a witch, a maven of darkness.* Nope. Cyndi could be your neighbor down the street or the manager at your local convenience store.

Cyndi is outgoing and chatty until you cross her the wrong way. Then cover your ears because she will blister you with profanities. Cyndi thrives on learning and is an innovator. Cyndi's even consulted an herbalist in Europe about making a potion to stop her daughter from drinking.

"She won't take it because it will make her throw up violently or have diarrhea every time liquor touches her mouth," Cyndi firmly explains. "And it's good for seven years, and mine's better than the doctor's."

It is not recommended to cross a witch. I certainly hope I don't tick off Cyndi with my endless questions about her ambitions, her loves, her spirituality, her future. I decide to go with the easy-going interview approach. I invite Cyndi and our mutual Uplift friend, Karen, to a nearby Burger King.

Surely a girl without a stove, or a kitchen for that matter, would like a burger and fries. Finished off with a shake or sundae. Nah. Cyndi has some esophagus issues and opts for just a large black coffee.

Karen sits with us for a bit, making introductions, then slips out of the booth to let Cyndi and me crank up our candid conversation. Cyndi's quick-thinking mind and jovial interjections intrigue me.

We are soul sisters on wisdom and wit. But I doubt we'll connect on true matters of our soul. I gently remind myself to leave any judgmental conclusions back in the parking lot. For now, I want to hear everything I can about this new acquaintance sipping on a paper cup of Joe, just inches from my digital recorder.

"What do you call that flap? When you eat and swallow, the flap closes and the food stays there. But then. . ." Cyndi pauses, making an urping sound. I nod in knowing agreement.

"They call it heartburn for a really good reason. It burns like fire. I have to stop and let the muscles relax so the food can go down. That is PAINful," Cyndi says, grimacing. "I live on Tums. I take pure peppermint. Peppermint soothes the stomach. I've even given peppermint to the cat when he heaved up hairballs."

Forget the niceties. I appreciate Cyndi's candor. Esophagus woes. Allergies. Car accidents. Cyndi and I are gelling on common ground. The tell-me-about-you interview is shifting into overdrive.

You see, Cyndi lives in the shadows on shifting ground that is not quite concrete, not quite quicksand. It is tough at times to connect the bouncing dots in Cyndi's story, but there are anchoring facts in understanding her odyssey:

- Born December 11, 1958, in an American Army hospital in Frankfurt am Main, Germany.
- Father descends from five different Native American tribes; he served twenty-one years in the U.S. Army and thirty-five in civil service.
- Mother is of multiple European ancestry including German, Liechtensteiner, French, Swiss, Austrian, and Spanish.
- One brother, three years older.
- The family lived off base in Heidelberg, Germany, for thirteen years, while returning for short assignments in the States.

Cyndi's father was an officer in the U.S. Tank-Automotive and Armaments Command (TACOM) who helped design and oversee tactical weapons and combat vehicles. He was rarely home because of special assignments. Meanwhile, Cyndi's mother stayed active in officer's club activities and social galas.

"My mother has a royal European bloodline and is a royal courtier. I call her the grand duchess, and I kept my distance growing up," Cyndi shares with a hint of scoffing in her voice. "I was raised by the nanny, the governess. I'm Cinderella. I was a servant in my own house."

❦

The tension with her socialite mother escalated when Cyndi's father switched to Army retired reserve and began working in electronics for Ford in Flat Rock, Michigan. Their home life spun wildly when, just four days back in America, Cyndi stepped off the school bus and a drunk driver slammed into her.

The thirteen-year-old fractured both legs, cheekbones, nose, and several ribs. The impact hurled Cyndi thirty-eight feet in the air, ruptured her spleen and left her with a triple concussion. She endured four and half months in the hospital and a year in a wheelchair. Welcome to the good ol' USA.

As the tenacious teen recovered, she convinced her mother, who was working as an interior designer at JC Penney, to take up bowling and join a league to make friends. When it came to her mother's love of fine dining and fine manners, Cyndi grew bored and carved her own path toward womanhood.

"I wanted to be out in the woods, hunting. I did do the sewing machine thing, but at night I snuck over to my neighbors' dairy farm," Cyndi says, smirking at her youthful independence. "I got a job milking forty head at 4 o'clock in the morning. I got back home at daybreak. You think my mother was up at daybreak? Come on!"

Cyndi was close with her father, but he was called back into active duty for special operations in Vietnam. Then the war sucker-punched them all. Her dad was missing in action and presumed dead. Cyndi's mother folded in a nervous breakdown heap. Cyndi's brother kept his distance by camping out in a teepee on their five-acre property. No one really wanted to be around her mother, who regularly struggled with what Cyndi now knows was bipolar disorder.

"She was a moody woman. She'd come after you with a wooden spoon. It was like I didn't know if I was coming or going with this woman," Cyndi says staring into her coffee cup. "After I got to Michigan, there were no more governesses, and I got tired of all the crap."

Cyndi father was found alive and returned from war after eighteen months, but the battle lines at home intensified. At age fifteen, Cyndi took her parents to court and became an emancipated minor. "I became a ward of the state. I had enough of Cinderella," Cyndi explains. "The prince wasn't coming, okay? I had to get the hell out."

The exasperated teen loved her father dearly, but confronted him alone in the garage. Cyndi had it out with him next to the '65 Pontiac Grand Prix that she started driving to school and to another job at Sambos.

Cyndi lives in the shadows with a past that is murky mixed with misjudgment.

"I'm out of here. You've lost me. You never were a good parent. You can be a good husband, but you people have no idea what it means to be a good parent," the fed-up daughter tersely told her dad. "I've led a very lonely life. It's like all of us are within ourselves doing our own thing. Me? I'm lost. Someday I'm going to get married and make my own family. I can do that."

Cyndi takes a gulp of her cooling-down coffee and glances over at the guy jabbing his French fries in a wad of ketchup. We both take a few seconds' breather. I contemplate asking the questions I need to ask, but I am not sure how my probing will be received. Nothing seems to faze the sixty-plus Cyndi, who just disclosed her soap opera-sounding childhood. Little did I know that we were just warming up for a bucking bronco ride into her twenties and beyond.

Cyndi lives in the shadows with a past that is murky mixed with misjudgment. She's faced off with one bending point after another, which fortifies her unswerving spirit.

Photo by Beth Lueders

In 1977, at age eighteen, Cyndi married her high-school sweet-heart, Stan. She fondly recalls that they went steady for six months, were engaged for eight months and married for six years.

"As a teen, I would never go out with a guy unless he had a motor-cycle or a horse," Cyndi says with a slight husky chuckle. "Definitely not if he was wearing tennis shoes."

The woman has some specific standards for her men, but she soon confides, "God, I have piss-poor character when it comes to men. Bad taste, girl." Cyndi lets out a heavy sigh, then studies her coffee remnants before looking up again.

Now we're tracking in her years with Stan and his grandparents in the Tennessee Smoky Mountains, thirty miles from the nearest town. Stan's maternal grandparents raised Stan from fourteen days old when his mother was placed in an institution.

Grandma eagerly taught Cyndi the essentials of Southern living—quilting and canning and serving up Southern fried chicken and okra. But as much as Cyndi tried to please her husband and raise their son and daughter, born seventeen months apart, Stan proved to be, as she describes, Dr. Jekyll and Mr. Hyde.

"Stan was an aggressive dominant alpha husband, and we'd do hand-to-hand combat in the kitchen. And I would come back at him," Cyndi shares, pressing down on her lower lip in a half-grimace. "Those were the years of beatings and broken bones. He was a vengeful monster."

Things intensified when Stan, Cyndi, and kids, Nicholas and Vanna, moved to Florida for a fresh start. Stan was working construction, but met some cagey guys who lured him into taking cocaine and selling drugs to pay for his ruinous habit. One day, Cyndi came home from work to find their house cleared out and Stan driving off with the kids and another woman.

Cyndi pieced together their trail and followed after them in several states, pleading for her kids at numerous police stations. Cyndi could never quite catch up to them, and eventually, without her knowledge, Nicholas and Vanna landed in foster care. Cyndi later learned that Stan stole about $150,000 in cocaine and was found dead of a cocaine overdose.

After her multi-state search for Nicholas and Vanna, Cyndi circled back to Florida, waitressing and modeling underwear. In 1982, she married Stephen and they had daughter, Nikki. Stephen turned out to be verbally and physically abusive too. He detested kids and was unwilling to work. After three years they divorced, and Cyndi and Nikki moved to southern Colorado, where her parents had moved.

Next, Cyndi met husband number 3: Nick. Nick wooed Cyndi with his jet-black locks and Latino good looks. They married in 1988 and had two children, Merry in 1993 and Sam in 1995.

As Cyndi's fortunes would fall, Nick started sleeping with his brother's wife. Nick had some 'splainin' to do, but didn't fare well with his excuses. When baby Sam was only four days old, Cyndi left and got her own apartment, giving Nick one year to clean up his act. One night she invited Nick, his brother, and wife over for dinner and dessert. The witch instincts in Cyndi hissed as she let her life-energy field explode.

"I cursed Nick with 'you will die old and alone sitting on a sack of money,'" Cyndi recalls, her face contorting at the memory. "'As long as you deny your witchcraft, your body will deteriorate because the gods will have no mercy on hypocrites.'"

Now I know that Nick has some connection to the occult too. Cyndi has some 'splainin' to do about that, but first Cyndi takes me through her moving back to Florida with their two kids and Nikki. Nick and Cyndi divorced in 1997 and she gained sole custody of the kids. As a single mom, Cyndi dug deep and participated in a self-sufficiency project that helped her complete computer school and learn to budget and manage a home.

She describes those years in Florida with a degree of accomplishment yet regret. "My kids grew very damaged, very street smart, very hood and 'gang-y' because Mommy worked and they skipped school and ran the streets," Cyndi explains. "I had no adult supervision for them. My kids did pretty much what they wanted. I worked ten at night until six in the morning. What could I do? I slept or had another part-time job, or I was putting myself through another technical school."

In March 2008, Cyndi moved with the kids to Texas for new beginnings and became a Texas state correctional officer at a maximum-security facility. Pulling down a substantial salary, Cyndi finally felt she'd landed in cotton. But then her teens got in trouble smoking weed and Cyndi was called into court because of their truancy issues.

The judge advised Cyndi that she would need to make a choice: her children or her career. Cyndi resigned from her prison job, and life soured even more. Her car's fuel sensor failed and she canceled her auto insurance. The Department of Motor Vehicles would not allow her to keep the car in her driveway without insurance coverage, so the DMV suspended her driver's license.

No job. No car. No driver's license. Then Cyndi's landlord left town after illegally renting a house to her and others. Cyndi and the kids were facing life on the street. Daughter Merry was still communicating with Nick, and he offered to pay for a U-Haul truck and move them all back to Colorado.

"Nick was saying, 'I love you, baby. I'll buy you a car. I'll take care of a home for you,'" Cyndi says, reliving his promising words. "I loved Nick and he's the father of my kids. He's a whore, but I'm a realist."

Cyndi saw no other way out of her predicament, and in the winter of 2015 arrived with Merry and Sam back in the Rockies. At age seventeen, Sam would finally meet the father he never knew.

"When I came back here, I had hoped that Nick had changed, but he was worse than he ever was," Cyndi laments, her eyes narrowing as if in pain. "Nick pulled me out of that U-Haul truck and kissed me and held me and said, 'I love you so much. Damn, you look good.' My heart just melted because I have loved him more than anyone else. But Nick is a little manipulator and I know it."

Reportedly, Nick was living with a woman for six years and ended up marrying her because of his immigration problems. This news only added to Cyndi's woes of being jobless and homeless.

"I stayed here in Colorado because I'm destitute. I have a lot of work credentials and experience and I'm overqualified for most everything," Cyndi explains. "But you have to understand, if you don't have a proper birth certificate, proper driver's license, and proper vehicle, you will not go far in this country, let alone this state."

So Nick lets Merry stay at his house, while Cyndi, Sam, and his girlfriend set up a makeshift shelter in the back room of Nick's auto shop for free. Now we return to the revelation that Nick has witchcraft in his personal lineage too. And I need to interject here with my early impressions of witches from the *Wizard of Oz*.

Let me tell you those little monkey things were almost scarier to me than even that green-freakish Wicked Witch of the West.

None of these creepy Oz characters are in the same upscale pagan league as nose-twitching Samantha on *Bewitched* who married handsome mortal Darrin Stephens. Cyndi has married a mortal or two. Well, actually three, although at least one of them, Nick, was a witch.

Cyndi describes her dad as a shaman, so I have to look up the difference between a shaman and a witch. Google notes 10.9 million results for "shaman vs. witch." Apparently, I am not the only one curious about these mysterious persons in the underworld. In perusing a few websites, I discovered shamans are individuals who access the world of good and evil spirits and healing powers of Mother Earth, especially by entering an altered consciousness state. Shamans practice divination and ancient healing traditions within Nature to bring health and balance to their community.

In *witch* research, you find the very word bathed in centuries of negative connotations. Can you say, Salem Witch Trials? Witches today are individuals who practice magical spells or rituals and work folk magic to alter the energies of the world around them. Witches tend to call Mother Earth into their environment instead of "crossing the hedge" to enter the natural realm.

Witches practice traditions connected to pagan roots, and those witches who follow the Wiccan beliefs follow a god and goddess. More benevolent witches also believe in karma or the awareness, as Cyndi explains, "Whatever you do will come back on you."

Still, with all the polished definitions out there about followers of witchcraft, I want to know what Cyndi believes and practices as an Earth worshiper. The second time we meet, we find some chairs in the foyer of the Uplift office just east of Cyndi's makeshift auto body shop home. I jump in with an open-ended question.

"What do you call your religion?" I ask Cyndi, genuinely intrigued by her faith and how that helps or hinders her in making a comeback from her years of hard knocks. I'll let her tell you directly.

I'm Wiccan and Celtic. I am a solitary witch, a hedge witch, which is the witch of the forest. I live on the edge of the forest in the middle of nowhere. A hedge witch is always a healer. In ancient days, hedge witches lived at the edge of the forest some distance from the village. If a village needed a midwife or herbologist, hedge witches were called upon; they were healers.

Hedge witches lived away from the village because they were different. They loved you but they were afraid of you. They respected you but didn't want to hang out with you. That's basically the life of a hedge witch, and it's really no different for me today. I see witches or witch wannabes and they know a few words to spark your interest and let you know that they're Wiccan. Then when you start asking them questions, interrogating them basically, you see they know little about being a witch. I just turn my back and walk away.

I curiously share with Cyndi my other experience of interviewing a Wiccan, a high priestess who leads a coven of about a dozen other witches. I spent several hours dialoguing with this woman in a library study room and over a Chinese meal, but she seemed like she was holding back details of her faith practice.

Cyndi and are in a natural pacing with my questions and her candor. I ask and she tells. Would she consider going in with a coven?

"People have wanted to be in a coven with me, but no, I'm not going to make a coven because here's my words to other supposed witches," Cyndi replies with a sternness in her voice. 'I don't like you and I don't trust you. And all you want to do is absorb my knowledge and my experiences and my recipes and my information and get into my book of magic.'"

A book of magic? Cyndi, do tell more.

"Every witch has got a Book of Shadows. Once you're in a coven, everybody is allowed to get in your book," Cyndi explains. "So why should I let other witches with thin books look at mine, which is thick with forty years of my religion? I will pass my book down to my daughter Merry if she straightens up."

Cyndi is revved up, hardly coming up for air now.

Cyndi drifts into her heritage of witches among her five children and eight grandchildren. She describes Merry as borderline sorceress and believes her daughter is a "pure blood with great potential." Much of the genetics of passing down supernatural powers is more than I can absorb during our conversation, so I politely nod and move on to statements that witches and Wiccan folks sacrifice animals.

"We don't sacrifice anything! That's Hollywood TV crap," Cyndi quickly shoots back. "Our religion is based on Mother Earth. Basically you're humanitarians, you're environmentalists, you're tree huggers, you're for clean water, clean air, and clean soil."

Cyndi is revved up, hardly coming up for air now. "What a rotten religion I'm in, huh? Do you think I'm dancing naked around the fire in the middle of the night?" she asks. "So what? Yeah, we do that, but we cleanse the Earth."

Wait. Hold it. I thought Cyndi is a solo witch. She meets with other witches? Cyndi explains that her kids are her tight witch family.

They find Garden of the Gods on the west edge of Colorado Springs as truly sacred. Those towering red sandstone formations make Garden of the Gods one of the country's top tourist destinations. Cyndi claims the nearby town of Manitou Springs is sacred too and home to hordes of witches and witch wannabes who live in the historic, adventure-rich community.

Although Cyndi doesn't want to join up with other area witches, she shares her view on witches being tolerant. "We don't judge people. We don't condemn them. We pretty much have an open heart and an open mind," Cyndi notes. "If you're gay, it's okay. If you have orange hair, it's okay. If you like to have multiple sexual partners, it's okay. As long as you ain't hurtin' nobody."

We delve a bit deeper into the kinder, gentler side of witchcraft beliefs.

"If you take drugs, that's not okay because you're polluting your body and your body is the temple. You can't do that," Cyndi clarifies with a scolding tone to her words. "You have to respect and maintain your body. You are what you eat. That is a strict rule."

❧

Being homeless and living on a scarce budget messes with Cyndi's desire to cook more nutritious foods that better maintain her body's temple. There is one more obvious vice that shows witches are not perfect. Cyndi asks if we can step outside so she can light up. She doesn't need my judgment on her cigs. She takes a long puff and ensures the smoke curls away from my face into the steady breeze.

"I like Marlboro Red 100s, but I can't afford them, so I smoke Pyramids. I'm determined to quit. I'm over sixty. It's not good for me," Cyndi gets out before taking another drag and exhale, "I am really anxious and stressed out, but I am not depressed. I refuse to be depressed at my situation."

Cyndi smokes and reflects on her "situation" of being a three-time married solo witch stuck in the middle of city concrete and glass. Her plan to keep on bending and coming back tumbles from deep in her thoughts.

"I will absorb positive energy and I will take one day at a time. I will ask for opportunities and ask my spirit helper for strength and guidance," Cyndi shares. "I will ask the Lady of Fire to light my way to make sure I stay on the straight and narrow and make sure that I don't deviate from the path. Umm . . . I have deviated over the years."

Yes, well, Cyndi has ventured along some off-course trails in her six decades. I ask Cyndi how her personal beliefs help her bend and adapt when life gets messy.

"I have studied the different Christian religions, but there's a difference between studying and having faith. I don't have any faith," Cyndi voices, her head turning upward. "I've read the Bible, gone to religious schools. I've investigated. I believe every religion on the planet is pretty close. It's just the difference between faith and simply studying for information and research."

"But you have faith in the Wiccan and Celtic way," I pose as we begin a slow walk.

"Yes, I do," Cyndi calmly replies. "I have a tremendous amount of faith in Nature because I can see it, feel it, touch it, talk to it."

"So in a sense, the gods are . . . ," I get out before Cyndi quickly interjects with a history of the gods of nature.

"Cernunnos is the god of fertility. He is the god of the hunt and the animals—and the god of everything that is green upon this planet," Cyndi states, her arms making a sweeping circle. "That is my god. I chose him because he's ancient. Hecate is my goddess because she is the goddess of magic and the queen of all witches."

With my digital recorder still rolling and picking up Cyndi's recitation of her nature worship deities, she lists her moon goddess and sun god before giving a shout out to Gaia, the Earth goddess.

"And that's it for me. I've got the earth, animals, the moon, and the sun, and the magic. That's all I need," Cyndi summarizes. "That serves my purpose. And, of course, I've got the ladies of the elements of the planet, which is the pinnacle."

I decide not to ask for an explanation. There's only so much earth religion terminology I can process in a day. We meander toward Nick's auto body shop, and I wonder if Cyndi will invite me to see her temporary shanty amid the banged-up cars and stifling paint fumes.

In the alley behind the shop, two guys appear strung out, pressed against a cement wall, their upper bodies hunched forward as if they are posed to hurl any second. I can't tell if they are sober and depressed or stoned and mellow. Sometimes there's a nearly invisible line between the two.

Cyndi calls out to them and they both give a groan and a nod of greeting. They are in the Set Free program where Cyndi assists with clerical work. It is tough to transition out of years of substance abuse, but these two men are trying.

Cyndi and I return to her recollections of deviating from the path and she regrets giving her financially struggling kids money when she should have saved the $5,000 for a car.

"Yes, I smoke, and that's a bad thing," Cyndi says, flicking her Pyramid to the parking lot asphalt, smashing and twisting the butt to death. "I'm going to continue onward and upward and pull myself up by my bootstraps. I believe the gods will present opportunities for me, and I will be justly rewarded for being good. Whatever you do will come back on you threefold, whether it be good or bad. Karma's a bitch. And the Fates are cruel. So be good and do what you're supposed to do."

Photo by Beth Lueders

Cyndi chatters on about her starting to smoke at age fifteen and then quitting a number of times over the years. When she planned a pregnancy, she'd stop smoking for a year to detox her body. Later, she didn't start back up with cigarettes until each of the kids were walking, talking, and potty-trained. Then she'd slip out to a tiny patio garden and meet up with a cozy chair, a lamp, and her ashtray while she read classics by Louisa May Alcott, Mark Twain, and Robert Louis Stevenson.

The busy mom soaked in her alone time in her woman-made oasis. But those days are history, a history Cyndi partly adores and partly feels misgivings about. We circle around to the front door of Nick's shop, and Cyndi budges the door open, motioning for me to follow her.

🌿

An ample man sanding down a car's back fender raises his head slightly in greeting us. "Poppy!" Cyndi cries out over the swirling sander and through the acrid aroma of fresh paint and solvent. I simply smile and nod as we weave our way around scattered car parts to get to Cyndi's room down a dank hallway.

I'm honored that Cyndi trusts me enough to enter her quaint corner of the world. Duct tape is Cyndi's interior design lifeline. Strips of the gray hold-most-anything-together adhesive dot Cyndi's belongings. Most important to her, the tape keeps the aquarium for Fred, her son's four-foot ball python, from splintering more.

I've never been a snake fan, especially after accidentally hitting a side-winding black one with a riding lawn mower in high school. Thwack. Yuk. Sorry, Mr. Snake. Just writing this sentence gives me a bit of the creeps remembering my summer in the Congo when a ten-foot boa constrictor strangled a goat just yards away from the mud hut I was staying in. No doors on the hut. No motion detector alarm system. No love from me for snakes of any kind.

When Cyndi picks up Fred and he hisses and curls around her

shoulders and neck, I have to look away. Mercy. I have a bachelor's in agriculture, and I dissected a number of weird critters in school labs, but a much-alive snake swirling and twisting just feet from me gives me the willies. The things we writers endure to get the best story. Mercy.

Sure, ball pythons are non-venous snakes, but they'll bite and constrict to kill. No, thank you. While Cyndi baby-talks with Fred, I glance around the room. How do you describe the mishmash from your kitchen, bedroom, living room, family room, and garage all crammed in a space the size of a sports utility vehicle?

Cyndi and Sam and his girlfriend keep a stash of Toasted O's cereal, ramen noodles, and Velveeta near a coffee maker and hotplate to the right. Their living quarters beat straight-on-the-street living, but this crib is no posh penthouse.

Clothes and jackets are jumbled in lopsided piles on the stark floor. Jumbo plastic jars that once held convenience snacks now serve as a mishmash of cupboards. At the back of the room, a cream quilt with green and burgundy leaves hangs to separate Cyndi's third of their bedroom mattresses.

It's hard for me not to think about downtown urbanites sipping wine and blathering on about their latest business dealings just twenty blocks away. The contrast is sobering. In American urban centers, hundreds of invisible people like Cyndi wander around with oversized backpacks or with a wobbly shopping cart lugging their sole possessions. Homelessness is not camouflaged in niceties.

No customers and not even Nick are allowed to enter Cyndi's room. A darkish blanket covers the doorway. "Things are going well for me, and I'm surrounded by positive energy. I've got four crystals on the floor in each corner, and I've got an incantation on this door blanket. So no negativity can enter in here," Cyndi explains as she uncurls Fred from her neck.

"Nick can't come in my room without my permission, because if he moves the blanket and steps in, he'll start getting sick," Cyndi says, placing Fred back in his aquarium. "I've really put some power on that, because he's a witch and he's strong. But he left the religion and turned into a Christian, so his body is deteriorating because he was born a witch. His mother's a witch. So that's why Nick is so sick and in and out of the hospital."

It is not recommended to cross a witch, but Cyndi divulges more of Nick's health problems. "You are what you eat. He's 310 pounds. He's way overweight. Your wife don't cook? Eat fast food. It's none of my business," Cyndi adds before we slip around the doorway blanket and head back into the shop's paint-fumed air.

Cyndi and I weave our way outside to the back of the building. The brisk breeze dancing in my nostrils is a welcome respite. We pause at the shambled mess of a back door to Nick's business.

"That's my bedroom right there," Cyndi points out. "Somebody tried to break in, but me and my son beat them with pipes. They busted the door completely down and came in with big metal pipes. My son and me fought them off. It's all on camera. I have a board and a brace across that door, but I've got to get a lock."

Cyndi shrugs as if saying such is life in this crime-heavy section of the city. We slowly saunter on the sidewalk between Nick's shop and Set Free, ignoring the va-room of vehicles swishing past us.

"My girlfriend Alvea lives here," Cyndi says, directing me to a spot above a small Mexican restaurant. "She's my best friend next to Karen. I've got Alvea and Karen. That's enough. When I make friends with somebody, that's it, they're my friend. Everybody else counts as an acquaintance."

I sense our hours together are winding down, yet I still have some unanswered questions. Cyndi perks up talking about an opportunity next week to join a free culinary arts baking program through a local nonprofit.

"Things are going good for me, finally," Cyndi shares with an uptick in her voice before I circle back to her mother who is now in her late eighties and living about fifteen miles away. "My dad's buried here. My mom and dad were married sixty-nine years. Every Friday she has her hair done, and she goes to the Governors Club.

She's a member of all that high-society crap. I'm happy for her. Whatever floats her boat. I'd rather be in the country riding a horse."

Cyndi is still the independent little girl now living in a petite woman's body. Our conversation drifts around to how Cyndi views the difference between her spirituality and Christianity.

"As far as the Wiccan way, I could pretty much get away with a lot of stuff that Christians can't," Cyndi divulges. "My gods are much more lenient, where Jehovah is very, very strict. I think it's impossible to be a true Christian because his rules are so strict."

Cyndi's proclamation piques my curiosity. "Like what?" I shoot back.

"Fornicators and adulterers will be judged alike. Homosexuals are an abomination to the Lord. Witches are an abomination to the Lord. That pretty much covers a lot of things that witches don't have to worry about," Cyndi quickly rattles off. "We're promiscuous, and that's okay with our gods. As long as we don't hurt anybody."

There's no time to address Cyndi's list of a do-what-you-want lifestyle vs. a life devoted to God's protective standards. The woman of faith in me ruffles at the generalized opinions, while the journalist in me squelches a quick-fire comeback. I totter on that line between knowing truth and sharing truth. I choose to delve deeper into understanding Cyndi's bond with her earth-honoring gods.

"What do you do to call upon your gods or practice with them?" I genuinely wonder. "Are you able to talk with your gods?"

"I usually go into the forest, a desolate place—Garden of the Gods is best if you sit out and meditate," Cyndi offers.

"But you don't get to do that very often," I knowingly respond, "because you're here in the middle of the city."

"Right, I'm not practicing at all. I'm neglecting my religion horribly. If you go all the way around the fence and you go to this wooded area, you can commune a little bit with the gods, but it's hard because it's not peaceful," Cyndi explains with a long sigh. "You look around how Mother Nature is suffering. There are days I feel all wrinkled and old and deteriorated.

"I can stand on earth barefooted when the moon is full, back there somewhere behind the building but not on the concrete. I do that just to rejuvenate myself and make myself a little healthy. But not long ago, I planted a flower and it died."

It pains Cyndi to be a long-time witch and earth worshipper and be so hemmed in how she connects with nature and her deities.

"I'm exposed to the homeless, the drug addicts, the tweakers. It's violent and aggressive and a lot of criminal activity. I can't believe this horrid place, how it's affecting my body and how I'm deteriorating," Cyndi bemoans. "And, of course, you cannot practice your religion in a negative environment or everything will backfire on you."

"How would you practice if you could?" I ask, watching Cyndi look out at the cars and trucks zipping by.

"You'd have to be surrounded by positive energy. There's nothing positive in this part of town," she affirms. "I would have to go to Garden of the Gods and do a cleansing ritual and cleanse my body."

I hear Cyndi's anguished frustration. "So you haven't been able to do any of that since moving here?" I ask.

"I'm stagnated, which is absolutely horrid. It's horrid on my body and it's horrid on me. I've done a few healing spells on Nick, but other than that, no. I wanted to do a potion on my daughter to keep her from drinking, but the rules say you can't go against someone's will," Cyndi elaborates. "You cannot touch anyone's free will. It's forbidden. You cannot control people through love spells and all that. That's black magic. My religion has thirteen creeds, and I abide by those creeds."

We're now back in front of the Uplift center and Cyndi launches into an addendum about her religion's respect for the environment. Cyndi's commentary sounds like an antithesis to the hang-loose gods she just described.

"You can't throw trash on the ground. You have to recycle. You can't pollute the environment. If driving a car which has a catalytic converter, don't over-drive, because it is not good for the environment," Cyndi advises. "So basically you can drive back and forth to work, to the grocery store to pay bills, and that's it. You don't joyride. You walk; you ride a bike; you do everything in your power to help the earth."

I'm pretty convinced that God, the Creator of the universe, does not object to earthlings looking out for the planet. I glance at my notes and look for a redirect to how Cyndi, through it all, has kept bending instead of breaking.

"It's better to be a tree than a mountain," Cyndi says, moving toward the tiny oak tree planted in a square of sidewalk in front of us. "The tree bends with the wind where the mountain gets eroded."

"So are you a tree?" I ask, looking quizzically in Cyndi's eyes.

"Definitely. I'm an oak tree," Cyndi replies, reaching out to hold a dainty tree branch. Look at the trees here. They are tough. The weather is just bipolar. Mother Nature has had a very hard time in Colorado for twenty to thirty years."

Cyndi nestles the end of the thin tree branch in her palm. "So what's going to happen this winter?" I inquire. "Is it going to be a cold winter?"

"Yeah, it's going to be a really bad winter, and it's important that we do have a lot of snow so in the spring it will melt and feed the Colorado River. You look at the buds on the branch in your hand and you can see what stage the tree is at. Is it sick? Is it healthy?" Cyndi explains like a perceptive botany professor. "The trees will talk to you by showing you the signs of the development of the branches. See right here? She had buds, and she lost all her leaves, and now she's saying that winter is soon upon us."

I lean in to appreciate what Cyndi has garnered from being a student and congregant of nature.

"Almost every one of her buds has got three tips. That means we're still going to have sunny weather," Cyndi confidently explains. "Look at the shape of how full she is. She's recovered. She's a monster. She's tough. And like me, you have to be."

Cyndi is describing bending for nature and humans. She gets how we are created to make comebacks through any season.

Maybe Cyndi and I are more alike than I would like to think.

I Wonder Where does faith in Creation or the Creator intersect?

Author's note: Cyndi's story takes an unexpected turn. I share it in Chapter 10.

Dig deeper. *Bend.*
Additional insights and reflections on page 247.

Six

Second Chances

*"America is the land of the second chance—
and when the gates of the prison open, the
path ahead should lead to a better life."*
—George W. Bush

"THESE DECISIONS ARE NOT MADE LIGHTLY.... It's our belief that young offenders who have grown into exemplary individuals, and who have clearly learned from their mistakes, should be considered for a second chance."[1] So pens Colorado governor John Hickenlooper in releasing another list of pardons and commuted sentences before leaving office.

Rhidale Dotson is on the shortlist and promised by several higher ups that he will be one of the fortunate chosen ones to have his sentence reduced for early release. On December 14, 2018, Gov. Hickenlooper grants pardons for forty-six individuals and commutes another six inmates with sentences of life without parole.

"These decisions are not made lightly."

I zip to the online site of the letters to the fifty-two inmates now delighted with an early Christmas present. "This Executive Order granting a pardon to. . . . " I scroll down past the A through C letters, complete with the shiny gold seal and the governor's loopy blue-ink signature. Armenta. . . Ashton . . . Baucke . . . Bergener . . . Carroll . . . Churgin . . . Doyle. Finally to the Ds. Wait. D-o-y . . .Rhidale's last name is Dotson. *T* comes before *y*.

No-o-o-o-o-o-o-o-o-o. Maybe there's some mistake. Maybe the governor's office got the letters out of alphabetical order. I nervously scan the other inmates' names starting with D.

No-o-o-o-o-o-o-o-o-o. No Dotson. No Rhidale Dotson. No pardon. No clemency. No early release. No hiding that I am grieved. Sad. Disappointed. But my angst on behalf of Rhidale woefully pales to his personal pain. How does *he* feel right now?

The news from the governor's office jolts me. But how is Rhidale coping with this uppercut to his head and a cross blow to his heart? To add to the misfortune, two of Rhidale's inmate buddies did get pardons and will be out within a couple of years. But Rhidale? Will the forty-one-year-old live out the rest of his days in the out-of-the-way prison?

Or, will the new governor review Rhidale's request for clemency and press his gold seal on a letter written just to Rhidale. Rhidale Dotson. No mistake with the D-o-t-s-o-n. *T* before *y* next time.

"These decisions are not made lightly."

Rhidale Dotson, #86988. I know his crimes. I know his voice. I know his aspirations. I know him fairly well, but we have never met. Not until November 2, 2018.

❧

Awkward. Distrustful. Tense. How else can I describe walking into a prison visitation room filled with criminal offenders staring me down? I am, after all, invading their turf. It's early Friday afternoon, and I'm trying to appear nonchalant among twenty-some male inmates perched on plastic chairs crammed around tiny cafeteria-style tables.

The prisoners in their blue-green uniforms, plus their visitors, all eye me wandering around trying to find my assigned table. I am forced to hover a moment at empty tables mixed among the already seated prisoners. Number 8. Nope. Number 11. Nope. The tables are randomly numbered. *Why didn't the guard just point me toward the right table?* My ego crawls with a tinge of embarrassment.

Fair-skinned, doe-eyed me wants to crawl inside myself and disappear. Or, at least walk back out behind the locked behemoth steel door. Out of here. Done. Past the tough-guy guards. Past the frisk-you-down security team at the guard gate to drive back the ninety miles to civilization. Past the stretch of dried-up tumbleweeds and parched melon fields surrounding this state prison for men—up to 1,007 of them, many with maximum sentences that will ball and chain them for the rest of their lives.

It's a land that knows how to hedge against tough times. Back in the early 1900s, immigrants who were trying to scratch out a living via coal mines and farming faced death if they didn't comply with the Mountain Mafia, Southern Colorado's crime bosses. Think names like Spinuzzi and Carlino. Think gambling rackets and liquor boot-legging. Think "dooz what I sayz" and cement shoes in the nearby Arkansas River.

Travel forward a century and there's whispers of mafia godfathers still barking out demands in nearby Pueblo, once called Little Chicago. Maybe the Colorado Department of Corrections constructing the Arkansas Valley Correctional Facility (AVCF) in 1987 sent a message to every local *capo crimini,* the Don, that a new boss rules the state's southeast.

No matter who you are, no one rules the weather here. Angry winds shear off roofs from already battered sheds. The blazing sun splits gaping crevices in waterless fields. Yet the area's dry air, hot days, and cold nights produce some the world's sweetest melons—cantaloupes, honeydews, and watermelons—many with the coveted "Rocky Ford" name.

Like countless AVCF prison inmates, some regional melons don't get a second chance. These bad melons become dinner for cattle and other livestock. Not every melon makes it to market, not every felon makes it back outside. I want Rhidale to be one of them.

"I have a prepaid call from . . . [Rhidale], an inmate at a Colorado Correctional Facility. . . To accept this call, press 5 now."

Whenever I answer my office phone and hear the warbled-voiced, computerized message of a woman saying, "I have a prepaid call," I wait through her twenty-second instructions and hear Rhidale say his name and then finally his baritone "Hello?"

A friend who taught a class, *The 7 Habits of Highly Effective People,* in the state prison system learned that I was working on this book. She suggested I interview Rhidale, one of her top students. Rhidale and I started our phone conversations in summer 2015.

❧

I certainly do not know what it's like to be Rhidale growing up in the thick of gangs. Crips vs. Bloods. North Side Mafia vs. Sureños. The closest thing we had to a gang in rural Nebraska were competing sports teams and 4-H clubs. Antlers vs. Hornets. Herefords vs. Angus. It's hard to call cattle and horse judging at the county fair exactly a smackdown of rivalries.

We prided ourselves in winning gold-embroidered ribbons, not in bragging about killing police officers. No body cameras around, just Kodak 110 Instamatic cameras that gave a different meaning to point and shoot.

Although Rhidale grew up in the state next door, it seems like our upbringings were worlds apart. Yet we've both outsmarted adversity a time or two with a bend-and-come-back-stronger mindset.

Born in spring 1977, Rhidale was raised the middle of three boys on the east side of Denver, Colorado. When his parents divorced and his mother remarried, the nine-year-old found three stepsiblings grafted into the family. When Rhidale's father remarried, his two stepsons quickly bonded with Rhidale and his two Dotson brothers.

"From the time Rhidale came forth, he was independent. I noticed how quickly he comprehended most anything from early on, whether it was an instrument musically, or whether it was academically," explains Rhidale's mother, Priscilla Sutton-Shakir, on our initial conference phone call with Rhidale. Priscilla wants to share a bit about why she's always believed in her son. "He didn't even have to study for a test. Rhidale just has a brilliant mind."

A perceptive mind that allowed him to get 100 percent on tests without studying. An astute mind that earned him a perpetual spot on honor roll and into accelerated classes and bypassing seventh grade. And a determined mind that declared he was going to build the first flying car. Along with his sharp intellect, Rhidale followed in his mama's steady faith.

After all his years of high performance, Rhidale put on the brakes.

"To hear him talk or pray—this kid could pray like he was a mini me." That's quite a compliment for a semi-retired businesswoman who is a licensed minister. "I knew he was going to be great on this earth because I prayed over all of my sons. I remember saying, 'Lord, cause Rhidale to make his mark in the planet for good, the good of all humanity.' These things I prayed for him in the womb. I took him to church. That was his upbringing," Priscilla adds before exiting my conference call with Rhidale.

From that first phone call until the present, I occasionally add money to Rhidale's JPay account, and he dials out from a wall phone in his prison pod. The prerecorded message advises me that all calls will be monitored, but neither Rhidale nor I let that hinder our Q & A sessions. When you get into a lively conversation, you lose track that some prison employee may be listening in.

So what happened to this bright boy with the heart tender toward God? In eighth grade at age thirteen, Rhidale faced his first C in a science class, and his parents and stepdad were profoundly disappointed. After all his years of high performance, Rhidale put on the brakes.

"My brothers didn't get in trouble for their report cards. Nothing happened to them for their lower grades. All this hoopla went on about me, and I was like, *What am I working so hard for? This doesn't make any sense,*" Rhidale recalls. "My older brother, Ron, was Mr. Popularity in high school. He got anything that he wanted. He had all the females.

"He was my idol, my hero. And my younger brother, Ray, he skipped class and did all these other things and didn't get into trouble. So that was my defining moment. I said to myself, *I'm tired of this! I'm gonna do whatever I want to do. Man, I want to be free!*"

But Mr. Independent paid a horrendous price for his freedom, and he's still paying for what he thought would unshackle him from his parent's expectations. "My ambition was, 'I'm not gonna let my mom's standard and my dad's standard define me,' " Rhidale shares during our first conversation. "I'm gonna find out what's cool for me."

Cool among his peers meant carving out his own niche and street cred. His older brother was part of one of Denver's Crips gangs styled after the notorious Los Angeles-style violent street gangs to infiltrate Denver's northeast side in the mid-1980s. One of their intracity Crips rivals, the Crenshaw Mafia Bloods, were an offshoot of the late '70s primarily African-American street gang also originating in the southwest 'hoods of L.A.

Surrounded by these anger-fueled young men pulling in the money, the girls, and the prestige, Rhidale hungered for their do-as-you-please lifestyle.

In poignant irony, while the Dotson boys were chummy with gang members, their mom and stepfather were leading the anti-gang program Open Door Youth Gang Alternatives that they established to mediate and intervene with gangs in Denver, statewide, and eventually nationwide. With their parents investing extra hours outside the home, Rhidale and his brothers drifted outside the home too, keeping their street life from their parents.

While the big boys of the Crips and Bloods were declaring their domain along Colorado Boulevard, Rhidale from about age ten ran into encounters with the little brothers, cousins, and nephews of Crips who were trying to make a name for themselves to someday join the gang themselves.

"I spent a lot of time fighting. I got suspended. My biggest thing back then was that I really hated bullies," Rhidale explains. "And a lot of these guys that thought they were tough, they would jump on other people that I knew, friends of mine. I was the one that was able to handle myself. So I was feeling like a champion for people, a little hero. I wasn't ever afraid to fight. Actually, I got a lot of my confidence from fighting because I'd win."

The winning at fights with other schoolboys seared a name for Rhidale that would later prove invaluable behind bars. Emerging into his teen years with his knack for quick learning, Rhidale began to test the waters on staying out of the gangs while planning to set up his own posse.

Around age thirteen, he stole his brother Ron's Impala car, and barely peeking over the steering wheel, Rhidale cruised all over Denver.

"I was just bold and ambitious and didn't care," Rhidale recollects of his restless teen years. "From that point on, I started getting a larger reputation, a criminal reputation. I ended up finding out I had more aptitude to do more of the rebellious things. I was fearless. Where other individuals would be reluctant to fight somebody or go steal from a store or go do whatever, I was like, 'Hey, I'll do it.'"

Rhidale modeled that fearless attitude to his younger brother, Ray. Together, the Dotson boys schemed as partners in crime. They began sneaking into people's homes— sometimes in the middle of night and sometimes in daylight when people were at work—to steal game systems, guns, and other items of value that could be easily pawned. In time, Rhidale and Ray upped their heists to include stealing cars and selling them to chop shops.

"The first time we actually got arrested was at the Aurora Mall when we stole some watches from a JC Penney," Rhidale remembers. "We thought we were clear, and as were walking out the store, all of a sudden this man picks me up and slams me on the ground. I ended up peeing all over myself. I was so scared. It was terrible."

While the police spared the boys from going to jail, the law officers could not spare the Dotson sons from the heated exasperation of their parents. The tension at home seethed as Rhidale connived being a better criminal who would not get caught.

He sold a few drugs now and then, but opted for a more sophisticated scheme of robbing money from the guys who made drug sales. "I was always pretty successful with the females," Rhidale says with a chuckle, "so I even had a little team of females that would set up the guys carrying the drug money. Yeah, it was crazy."

Feeling too restricted by his mothers' rules, Rhidale at age fifteen turned to living on the street, sleeping outside or in a dive motel. Sometimes he'd return home but eventually get kicked out. "My mom always does everything in the pursuit of excellence, so the standards were ridiculously high with her. I was doing my best to stretch out and wanted to live life on my own terms," Rhidale asserts. "Mom would beg me to come back home because she didn't want me out there knowing that I was headed the wrong way."

The wrong way pointed to trouble at school too. During Rhidale's junior year, he was offered a full academic scholarship to a number of Colorado colleges. But just two weeks after the scholarship news, Rhidale was in the classroom and worrying whether his pager was catching phone numbers for money-making business opportunities outside of school.

Teachers and family were pulling for Rhidale, but he explains, "Basically the streets were calling me. I reasoned, 'I'm getting to the point where I could pay for my own college if I wanted to. So forget this!'"

Rhidale backed out of his agreement to focus on his academics and take advantage of the scholarship. The next year as a senior, he was expelled for bringing a weapon on school premises and transferred to a second-chance alternative school.

Ditching his textbook education, Rhidale pursued running his own crew. Partying. Smoking weed. Stealing. Selling. None of these subjects made it on the tests his peers were taking in school. "My crew was getting connected with people that were much older than us. This was a whole other type of lifestyle. It was fast," Rhidale recalls, but he stops to emphasize his next point. The warble-voiced woman interrupts and tells us we have sixty seconds left on our twenty-minute call. Rhidale agrees to call me right back.

"I have a prepaid call from ... [Rhidale], an inmate at a Colorado Correctional Facility... To accept this call, press 5 now."

"I was never, ever a gang member," Rhidale continues. "In fact, I had a disdain for them. I had a disdain for most gang members because I felt that they were followers, and I figured myself to be a leader. It didn't make any sense for me to follow anybody when most of them were less capable."

Sound conceited? Perhaps. Or just describe Rhidale as a realist. His mind for business and getting ahead was more fine-tuned than many of the gang members he encountered. But at seventeen, Rhidale and a friend were arrested for an attempted car jacking. Rhidale faced ninety-six years for a number of initial trumped-up charges, but took a plea deal. Sentenced as an adult, he pled guilty to conspiracy to commit aggravated robbery and served three years in the Youthful Offender System.

In school, Rhidale was well-liked and gregarious, so out on parole in 1998 at age twenty, he carried his persuasive status to his new ambitions of building a studio and launching a record label. "I love music, and as a hobby I was producing and creating music for other people," Rhidale says, his upbeat voice showing his passion for tunes. "I eventually decided I could make a business out of music and that would help me achieve my dreams. So I built a whole studio piece by piece."

With all his business investors and artists lined up, Rhidale started recording, but encountered a lack of business sense and focus with some of the investors. He soon parted ways with these financiers, their money, and their purchased music equipment, but this put him in a monetary bind to meet his recording deadlines.

"I was gonna, as they say, pull a couple of 'licks,' meaning pull a couple of robberies to get money quickly," Rhidale explains. "That would take care of my cash issues right there, and then we could finish recording and make our launch date."

In March 1999, Rhidale and his crew pulled a lick by responding to an ad selling a keyboard and case. At the seller's home, Rhidale's buddies escaped with the goods and left him alone with the homeowner.

"I never intended to hurt anyone and had a BB gun instead of a real gun. When my friends ran out, I didn't know how to get out of there safely. So I struck the guy a few times on top of his head and ran," Rhidale admits of the fumbled robbery.

Almost two months later, Rhidale ran across a newspaper selling a Roland MC-303 Groovebox that was particularly appealing to the eager musical entrepreneur. On May 17, Rhidale and a buddy met up with the musician selling the equipment.

But the second robbery turned south quickly when Rhidale, his friend, and the seller got into an ugly tussle.

When you feel your life is falling apart—or, you simply have nothing left— this is you bending.

Rhidale and his cohort's gun went off in the brawl, but no one saw blood. Breathless from fighting, the twenty-two-year-old Groovebox owner succumbed to what appeared to be an asthma attack. Rhidale and his crime partner grabbed any music equipment they tested that might show their fingerprints, and fled.

Rhidale considered calling 9-1-1 to report the seller's breathing struggle, but realized that would alert the police. Instead, the man's father came home and found his son dead in the basement with a bullet wound in his back.

Rhidale's robbery buddy tried to pawn some of the stolen equipment. This led to Rhidale's arrest and connection to both robberies. In the first music equipment theft, the seller was a retired police officer. Stealing from and smacking a retired law enforcement officer does not win you brownie points. A grand jury indictment charged Rhidale with several crimes, including the second robbery resulting in felony murder (legal responsibility for a death to those present and participating in events leading up to the murder).

Rhidale endured a jury trial in which his mother and fiancée were pressed to testify against him. On September 25, 2001, the jury found Rhidale guilty. On November 2, 2001, the judge's gavel SMACKED. Rhidale was sentenced to life without parole.

"I have a prepaid call from . . . [Rhidale], an inmate at a Colorado Correctional Facility. . . To accept this call, press 5 now."

What was it like to hear the judge decree "life without parole"? Those three words are a javelin to the heart. What does Rhidale remember about that soul-searing moment? In the introduction of this book, I defined a bending point like this: "A bending point takes you to the edge where doubt can drag you into discouragement, or despair leaves you for dead. When you feel your life is falling apart—or, you simply have nothing left—this is you bending."

What was it really like for Rhidale tottering on The Edge? He takes me back to early 1999, prior to his felony murder arrest. Back to his Denver apartment with his fiancée in the room. Back to the moment he believes he heard directly from God.

"I literally heard God say, 'This is it.' And I had this vision of what both outcomes would have been if I had continued doing what I was doing. I was going to end up hurting lots of people," Rhidale says of that turning-point experience. "I also knew that God was giving me one more chance. I sensed God saying, 'You know me. You know I love you. You know I have better things in store for you.'"

In the following moments, Rhidale made a vow that he has never turned aside from, not even in his darkest hours behind bars. Not even in those pitch-black agonizing brawls with himself and the enemy of his soul.

✿

Rhidale recounts his transparent pledge that day as if he were twenty-one again. "Lord, I'm going to serve you. As hard as I was going for myself and everybody else and these streets," he vowed. "I'm going to serve you a hundred times better than that, a hundred times stronger than that."

Back on his apartment floor that night in spring '99, Rhidale dropped his six-foot-one-inch frame to the carpet, pressing his face into the thick fibers. The entire universe seemed to pause as he remained prone before his Maker. "I gave it all up," he says, slowly releasing his breath at the memory.

When Rhidale retells this part of his life, he shares how he had no idea that a trial and prison sentence were next on the docket. "God has a serious way of actually making you the person he means you to be," Rhidale explains. "When he refines the gold, he doesn't wait around!"

Rhidale first shuffled off the correctional facility bus at Arkansas Valley on August 2000 to start serving his forty-five years for the aggravated robbery case. Good-bye family. Good-bye fiancée. Good-bye freedom. Hello a thousand unknowns.

I would hope Rhidale's introduction to the state penitentiary was an upgrade from various prison books and movies. *The Green Mile. Dead Man Walking. Shawshank Redemption.* Vicious felons preying on the newbies, the fresh blood. Malicious inmates molesting other inmates. There are things I want to ask Rhidale, and things I don't even want to know.

Rhidale reassures me that he earned his "strong reputation" behind bars as a juvenile. Because Rhidale had just turned eighteen, he was charged as an adult and moved to an adult pod.

"With other grown men, hardened criminals, the worst of the worst," Rhidale says, describing his fellow savage-minded inmates. "With the type of time that I was looking at, I had to fight the most vicious. I had to fight for my survival during that time. Luckily, I was very good at fighting, so I got a reputation for being able to hold my own; not only hold my own but dominate in that arena. I can fight."

Photo Courtesy of Arkansas Valley Correctional Facility

Rhidale careens our conversation to his early years on the inside. "I trained myself to be automatically dangerous," he continues. "I worked out all the time. I did things to stay physically fit, fast, and explosive. I made myself a weapon."

Wow. A human weapon. There's fighting and then there's killing. I've seen some of the destructive weapons prisoners devise. I've toured the Museum of Colorado Prisons, as have more than two hundred thousand other people from all fifty states and more than fifty foreign countries.

What do I remember most about the displays and exhibits covering more than 140 years? The crudely made shanks—knives cobbled together out of silverware, bolts, toothbrushes, pencils, and sharpened wood—and bound together with tape, string, toilet paper, matchsticks, and a plethora of other bonding materials. There's even a YouTube video on how to make a shank or shiv out of Jolly Rancher candies. Yes, creativity is not lacking for some prisoners.

Small-town me has never committed a crime that I know of, and yet, I have. We all have. We all mess up and say and do things that are not our stellar best. Gossip. Envy. Pride. My rap sheet is lengthy, just not something the U.S. criminal justice system cares about.

We all create our own prison. Or the choices of others heave us behind bars not of our choosing. For some of us the jail walls are etched with haunting memories. For others, our emotional confinement is bitterness and anger. Or, the dungeon of despair. Countless individuals pace in an addiction lockup and others in a holding cell of greed.

But even as I type this sentence, I feel incarcerated by my own body. Chronic pain is my captor. A villain I call the Silent Tormentor. Not exactly Capone and Gotti, but just as heartless.

In 1985, a car roaring through a red light slammed into my compact Mustang idling still at a rush-hour intersection. The driver hit my vehicle almost head-on and rammed my twenty-eight thousand pounds of silver steel backward. I'll never forget that terrible jolting back and forth between the assailing driver's car and the car behind me—a bumper car collision on steroids.

We all create our own prison. Or the choices of others heave us behind bars not of our choosing.

Whiplash, herniated discs, and strained back muscles harnessed me to physical therapy for months. Two years later, another reckless driver smashed into the back of my friend's car. As a front-seat passenger, again my neck yo-yoed in ways it is not designed to move.

My low back did not escape injury either. More grueling months of physical therapy. More orthopedic surgeon appointments. More squeezing, screaming nerve pain down both legs. At times I reasoned that death was the only way to cope.

I eventually pieced my life back together and weaned myself off the pain medications and therapy. Fast-forward a couple decades to 2013 and another aggressive driver zoomed through a side-street stop sign—in the dark with no working headlights—and boomed his hefty 1980s model Mercury into the driver side of my crossover SUV. My neck snapped violently to the right, and the force ripped my seatbelt from its base. Another round of an ER trip, physical therapy, and years of rebuilding my beat-up body.

I have not experienced a pain-free day in thirty-three years. That's 12,775 days with chronic back and neck pain, and by the time you read this it may be closer to thirteen thousand, but hey, who's counting?

Several times when Rhidale called me for our phone interviews, I could not move my head more than a few inches. My lifer confinement is a temperamental back and neck that call the shots most days on whether I face an invasive headache or a vice grip of knotted muscles. I never quite know when I'll be locked down in my own private cell of misery.

Yet as much as my health betrays me and keeps me in chains at times, I am not incarcerated in a faraway prison for potentially the rest of my life. On rough days, I wrestle with feeling isolated from a normal life. I know Rhidale can relate to this. Maybe you can too.

"I have a prepaid call from ... [Rhidale], an inmate at a Colorado Correctional Facility... To accept this call, press 5 now."

How has Rhidale kept bending instead of breaking over these past two decades? I ask him about his most grueling days behind bars. Immediately, he reminisces to when his father died in May 2009. After Rhidale learned of his father's cancer months earlier, the two increased their communication.

"We made sure we laid everything out on the table. He'd always been one of my strongest champions," Rhidale says with a tenderness in his voice. "When I got the news that my father had passed, I had a couple of tears, but I had to wipe my face and act like nothing had happened."

I probe a bit. "Because to show weakness, the guys would be calling you a big baby or something?"

"Nobody's crazy enough to do that!" Rhidale shoots back, half chuckling. "At the time, I was still weighing two hundred-something. No one would be audacious enough to mess with me. It's just that in prison, you don't show many signs of weakness. That's just part of the culture. And what's crying going to do? Nobody's going to help; I'm not going to get a hug from anybody."

I think of the scene in *Shawshank Redemption* on Andy's first day in prison. The old-timers bet on who of the new inmates will break and cry first. The overweight newbie sobs the first night and his outburst leads to the chief guard savagely beating the distraught inmate to death. Rhidale is right. In prison, you learn to hold your emotions in check.

On the day of his dad's funeral, Rhidale was in court and returning in shackles on the prison bus. "I wanted to talk to my family, but of course, I didn't get to talk to anybody that day," Rhidale recalls, his voice pausing to catch up with his disappointment. "Usually when you get back from a writ, your phone doesn't work for a while for security reasons. So when I finally got to the facility, I was in a bad headspace.

"The good thing about coming back to this facility was my friend Cedric was here. Our families grew up in the same church together. He's the closest thing I have to family in here. So at least there was somebody who knew me, and knew what I was going through. But I was still in a bad headspace."

A bad headspace in prison rarely leads to good. As soon as Rhidale returned to AVCF, he was given a cellie, a cellmate. But the guy tried to steal from Rhidale. Dumb move.

"He went through all my stuff—that's an absolute no-no. I had to get into a fight with the guy," Rhidale says, his voice tensing from just the memory. "He asked to be put on the opposite side of the yard from me, so he'd be safer. He, being a gang member, that's not a good look on him. This guy was a Crip. Cedric was a Blood. There's an automatic enmity there."

A few days later, the big homie of the short-term cellie sent him on a mission to get back at Rhidale. "This guy ends up coming back to my side of the yard with his homeboys and tried to sneak up on me," Rhidale points out. "So it ended up being this huge, huge gang fight. A lot of people got hurt. By the end of the night, there were about thirty of us in plastic cuffs and we ended up going to the Hole."

The Hole. Every prison has solitary confinement to help adjust an inmate's attitude. This holding area gets its name "hole" because it's typically located under a prison's first floor. One ex-prisoner describes the Hole as "desolateness and the feeling of utter aloneness . . . as if my soul had deserted me."[2] That's intense.

Even though video captured that Rhidale was the not the instigator of the fight, he still faced twenty-eight days in the Hole. A bed and cement slab that serves as a desk with a swinging stool underneath were Rhidale's only cellmates in the constricted space.

"Mentally it's tough. You have all this time just by yourself to think. You have to deal with yourself," Rhidale details.

> *"Mentally its tough... you have to deal with yourself."*

"You're in there with yourself twenty-four hours a day, except maybe you get out briefly once a day to take a shower or walk up and down the tier a bit."

In the Hole and still freshly grieving over his father, Rhidale struck up many a tête-à-tête with God. "When I go to God with questions, it's never, 'Okay, I'm going to give up on you.' It's more, 'Okay, help me understand what this is. Why take away my Dad now? Why should I have to deal with these major conflicts right now?'" Rhidale shares. "I had to realize I needed the time to make me stronger and someday better able to lead people. Now I can relate to people who have gone through these situations or worse."

Aggression and violence seethe in prisons. A grudge can turn south quickly, until, as Rhidale describes, "violence escalates like wildfire." In his early years of incarceration, Rhidale recalls a number of write-ups and times in the Hole, and one incident of knocking out a belligerent inmate during a basketball game.

Rhidale hit bottom with the ladies too. Ava, his fiancée before he entered AVCF, called almost daily at first, then once a week, and the letters dwindled too. She could never visit because of being on probation for her own run-in with the law. Their relationship ended in 2003.

Two years later a romance budded with Christina, a friend of Rhidale's brother Ray. Christina visited weekly and she and Rhidale talked on the phone daily. "It was a beautiful thing for a long time," Rhidale says. But after about four years and helping Rhidale through the loss of his dad, Christina moved on too.

Thud. The emotional darkness trampled Rhidale's heart. Why care anymore? I let Rhidale take a moment before asking about how he keeps bending and not breaking when he is saddled with a no-end-in-sight life sentence.

✺

Rhidale always sounds so positive and at peace. What changed in the man who considered himself a human weapon?

"When you have a forty-five-year sentence like I did originally, it sounds like a dark and dismal situation, but you can still see daylight. Daylight is what we call it. You can still see hope. You know that eventually all you have to do is do the time and eventually you'll be able to be free again one day," Rhidale explains.

"With a life sentence it feels like you can't breathe. Most anybody you talk to that's got a life sentence, that's the way it feels, like you've got a heavy weight on you and it's constantly constricting you. It's like having a boa constrictor, or a python, around your neck constantly squeezing."

Ugh. Ugh. "Wow. That makes total sense," I reply, looking for the right words to reply to his sobering description.

"If what you focus on all the time is, *I have a life sentence. They want me to die in here*, there's no hope. That mentality can pull you into this really, really, really dark place," Rhidale shares. "You feel helpless and so low that you can almost drown in your depression. It feels like you'll go so deep you'll never be able to recover from it."

During a pensive stretch in the Hole in 2009, Rhidale slid ever closer to going under in his oppressive thoughts. Yet he determined to wrestle it out with God. "I asked God, 'Is this hope that I have real?' My hope is to someday be free, to have a family, to experience life beyond prison, after prison, Rhidale says.

"And clearly, as clearly as somebody in the room with me, I heard a resounding 'YES' resonate in my spirit. I'm a skeptic, I'm a realist. So I'm asking, 'Did I really hear a yes? Is that really what I heard or am I just grasping for straws?' So I open my Bible and start reviewing God's promises. And I read Jeremiah 29:11, 'I know my plans for you.'"

Rhidale also chronicles the Genesis 50 story of Joseph thrown in prison and completely forgotten by those he helped. Rhidale's heart is lightened when he reviews how God had a rag-to-riches plan for Joseph to be freed by Pharaoh and appointed second in command of the entire nation of Egypt. And, ultimately, Joseph's leadership saved the lives of untold people, including his own.

"God had a plan for Joseph in that turmoil. I also went back to the ultimate model, who is Jesus, who did everything perfectly without sin, and he had to go through things that none of us can even fathom as far as experiencing pain, especially while doing it in perfect love," Rhidale clarifies. "Remembering what Jesus did gave me the motivation to pull myself up and start getting back on the path of doing something better."

❧

"I have a prepaid call from … [Rhidale], an inmate at a Colorado Correctional Facility… To accept this call, press 5 now."

After that cellie-caused riot in 2009, Cedric, as a higher up in the Crenshaw Mafia Bloods, and known as Baby Brazy, was shipped to a super-lockdown facility in northeastern Colorado. But while there, a number of Crips tried to kill Baby Brazy by attempting to throw him off a tier. Within a year, Rhidale's longtime buddy was back at AVCF.

"When Cedric came back to this facility, it was a beautiful thing. We finally decided it was time for us to make the most of it," Rhidale explains. "Our whole mission became, 'If it ain't about home, it ain't about nothing.'"

Home. Getting back home with family and friends. Both men decided to man up for authentic change in their lives and laser-focus on their goal to get out of prison.

"I came to the decision in 2010 that I had to stop making excuses," Rhidale explains. I had to ask myself, *Am I really doing everything possible to get home? Am I really doing all that I can to be the most that I can, to be all that I am capable of being?* I couldn't lie to myself. I knew I wasn't doing everything possible. I was just giving lip service to what I wanted."

In early fall 2010, Cedric handed Rhidale a piece of paper with a rough proposal to help gang members do something better with their lives. Cue the angelic choir and watch the light bulbs flash on. Cedric was onto something that could transform the entire U.S. penal system.

Cedric approached the prison leadership with the idea to create a stellar program to encourage inmate gang members to commit to personal transformation from the inside out. With his own background of being a gang member, Cedric turned to Rhidale to develop the organizational systems and skills side of what became the Gang Awareness Program (GAP).

Receiving the proper approvals to pursue developing the program curriculum, Rhidale and Cedric, in spite of not being gang brothers, launched into intense research. Starting with no framework or guidelines, Rhidale began to ask fundamental questions like: If a man wants to change, how does he really do that? How do you change a man who's been a certain type of person for a very long time?

Rhidale started reading dozens of books on psychology and cognitive behavioral models. He perused literature from Alcoholics

Photo Courtesy of Arkansas Valley Correctional Facility

Anonymous and Narcotics Anonymous about addicts turning their life around. He frequented the prison library and ran across the eye-opening book, *Changing Criminal Thinking*, and its work on developing a therapeutic community model.

He researched in between working up to thirty hours a week answering phones for the prison's call center and taking college courses. Rhidale discovered additional motivation for GAP as he participated in a *7 Habits of Highly Effective People* class led by a team of business professional volunteers from the outside.

"I started taking notes on everything. I've got thousands of pages of handwritten notes," Rhidale says, stressing that once he becomes passionate about something he can work sixteen to twenty hours a day on a project. "It was a priority to show that I could handle my work responsibilities, and all my other responsibilities, and continue to grow even in a place where business as usual is mainly about wasting time and violence. I worked twice as much as the average person in here because most people in here mainly play cards and work out."

In the process of examining the workings of personal change, Rhidale begin to fine-tune his own perspective and actions. He found himself staying out of fights, and if he did get in a tussle with someone, he felt guilt and remorse and would apologize to the other inmate.

"I begin to realize that I have to answer for my actions. I have to answer to God. I had to learn how to forgive," Rhidale explains. "I had to learn how to allow myself to be forgiven for my actions too."

Rhidale dug deep to examine what he believed to be true about himself. Was he a coldhearted criminal or a child of God with the potential to live in the free world and contribute value to people? On June 12, 2011, during a lockdown alone in his cell, Rhidale decided no more compromises, no more excuses. He landed on the following epiphany:

> I'm 100 percent responsible for everything that does, or does not, happen to me. I have the power to make things different, get things right, produce the results that I desire. Events + Responses = Outcome. The only things that I have control over are the things that I do. That means, no matter what happens, my reactions will affect the outcome. Everything I say, think, and do, needs to become intentional and aligned with my purpose, my values, and my goals. I will be successful. No excuses. I make this commitment today, Sunday, the 12th of June, 2011.

From this personal responsibility commitment flowed the finalizing of the GAP curriculum that Rhidale and Cedric presented to the AVCF and eventual state prison authorities. "We met with practically every warden and deputy warden in the state, and we blew their socks off," Rhidale exclaims with a happy chuckle. "That's how we got our opportunity to start the program."

The premise of GAP is to change the pattern of imprisoned gang members from being takers in a game of competition to being builders in a reality of creation. Takers vs. builders. Competition vs. creation. Game on.

"When you come from an environment of a gang, which is all about competition, and then you come into prison, which is even more about competition, the biggest takers win. In the game of competition, the perception is that there is not enough of anything and so you compete for the resources, you compete for status—and often viciously," Rhidale explains. "But it's really just a crazy game that you're playing."

The Gang Awareness Program is designed to help people stop playing the game of competition and start transforming their identity into a builder of the future they desire. GAP encourages becoming a builder through an investment in relationship and individual transformation. Although not a Christian-based program, Rhidale and Cedric intertwined biblical principles in the curriculum such as doing good, caring, contributing, loving, and forgiving.

"We focus on creating a clear and definite picture of what truly matters most to a person and then inspire action to do something toward that every day," Rhidale emphasizes. "We try to get people to realize it's not okay to become part of the status quo in here of becoming irrelevant and slowly dying. We strongly encourage investing in yourself."

Back in 2012, GAP initiated with a small group of inmates who received the training. By 2014, a core group of eleven grew to fifty-eight individuals living in a blended pod environment of several rival gangs and ethnicities working out their personal changes of attitude and actions.

"We wanted to create an environment where it was safe for

individuals to go through transformation and emerge as this different person without having to lose complete contact with everyone else in the facility or in their life," Rhidale explains. "We don't believe in isolating somebody to then become this completely different person. What that can do is cause serious enmity. People need to see you being a part of this program so everything we do is backed with our complete transparency."

Under continual retooling, GAP has been shelved, restarted, and renamed over the years, but the underlying tenets are still stirring a lasting makeover within prisoners' hearts. The gradual personal changes are happening despite the gang culture of conforming to what others dictate. As one of the chief GAP leaders and a founding member of a nondenominational church and its worship team leader within AVCF, Rhidale often finds himself lifting other guys out of their crisis moments.

Not exactly a priest on duty in a confessional booth, Rhidale does find his fellow prisoners come to him for counsel and help.

Like a 2:00 a.m. visit to his cell and an inmate confessing, "I'm contemplating suicide" or "I'm thinking of killing this guy." Not exactly a priest on duty in a confessional booth, Rhidale does find his fellow prisoners come to him for counsel and help.

Other prisoners were jumping one newer guy at the facility because he was gambling and talking trash about other offenders. He approached Rhidale and asked Rhidale as a "good dude" to help protect him from others who wanted to rough him up for owing them $15. Instead, Rhidale bought the guy $15 of merchandise from the prison canteen so he could pay off his debt and told the grateful inmate he was back at square one.

Summing up his philosophy with his fellow prisoner, Rhidale explains, "Rather than me saying, 'All right, you owe me,' I was saying, 'Okay, just do better.'"

To just do better himself, means Rhidale chooses to be a servant-leader among his peers and pushes against the status quo of self-pity in being confined behind bars—potentially for the rest of his life.

"I'm showing people it doesn't matter what your situation is. You don't have to be defined by your situation. You can create your own circumstances," Rhidale shares. "I'm trying to leave a legacy of love, caring, and kindness as much as possible. I'm not Gandhi. I'm not a saint or anything, but I'm making good choices, and I'm staying occupied with things that actually matter and that make a difference."

Part of making good choices for Rhidale includes his writing apology letters to all of his crime victims, victims' families, and his own family members who were impacted by his wanton decisions as a young man. In Colorado, the Department of Corrections holds apology letters to victims and victim families in an Apology Letter Bank and leaves it up to those individuals to initiate if they want to read an offender's letter. Rhidale has no idea if those directly affected by his criminal activity have read his letters, or ever will, but he is moving forward.

"I can't do anything about the past. Those mistakes have been made. Some of them weren't mistakes. Some of them were deliberate choices that have consequences and those things are going to have results no matter what. But what I can do something about is the reputation, Rhidale maintains.

"When I draw my identity from my past, I have to drag all that stuff with me. When I draw my identity from my future and who God has called me to be, there's a huge difference. I find a way to anchor myself to what God has done for me. Or, I anchor myself in the future, which is always brighter than my past."

This changed mindset and solid faith is what Rhidale credits for his experiencing peace and staying motivated to inspire others. "Even if it doesn't inspire the masses, it inspires enough people that are actually changing their lives and becoming better," Rhidale says, his voice resonating excitement. "A majority of the guys that took that first GAP course that we offered in 2012 are doing awesome things."

Justin is attending Ohio State University via correspondence courses and developing his own behavioral curriculum for systemic prison change. Al organized a relay for cancer walk at the prison to honor his mother who passed away from cancer. Alex is a GAP leader who is enrolled in college and wants to build a nonprofit GAP organization on the outside when he is paroled.

"I have a prepaid call from … [Rhidale], an inmate at a Colorado Correctional Facility… To accept this call, press 5 now."

The facility is considering video chat visits via tablets for prisoners and their family and friends on the outside. Rhidale hopes this happens soon because his family doesn't have the finances to make the long trip to see him. Sometimes when he talks with his brothers on their occasional phone calls, Rhidale is reminded of the gang member lifestyle he witnessed day in and day out in the '90s.

By the late 2000s, the Colorado Bureau of Investigation estimated that Denver's original Rollin' 30s Gangster Crips—sixty-eight males and one female–had beefed up to 8,800 members in nearly eighty gangs. By that time, the founding Crips members themselves had racked up a rap sheet of plead guilty or found guilty of more than 150 crimes including: drugs, theft, assault, burglary, robbery, forgery, sexual assault, attempted murder, and murder or manslaughter.

Rhidale is grateful he never committed to a gang, and after half of his life in prison, he better understands why the image-cool posse of gangs attracted Cedric and other inmate friends.

Without a gang pledge, Rhidale has earned respect, and as he calls it, a "strategic presence in this place." I sense his calm, approachable nature from our first phone call in 2015, and I sense his protective friendship when we sit in the prison visitation room three years later. On that November afternoon talking about his business consulting and coaching plans once he is released, I can fully see Rhidale meeting his on-the-outside goals.

Before I get up from the lunchroom-style table to drive back north ninety miles, Rhidale asks if we can pray together. He holds out his hands and I rest mine in his grip. Here, boldly before his fellow inmates, guards, and God himself, we commit Rhidale's opportunity for a commuted sentence into the Lord's timing.

Two months and one week later on January 8, 2019, I nervously wait for our scheduled noon call to hear if Rhidale made the cut on the governor's final commutation list.

At 12:03 p.m., I haven't heard from Rhidale. There is no text possible from Rhidale to say he's running late. No email to reschedule our phone call. I must wait for the operator message, then press 5 and hear his voice. "Hello?"

My computer dings and it's a friend sending a text. 12:04:08. Rhidale is almost always right on the minute for our scheduled calls. Then again, sometimes the prison facility is on lockdown and he can't call. The Longest Mile, the Longest Wait. I don't like the suspense of this wait.

Gov. Hickenlooper was out of office at 11:59:59 p.m. the previous evening. If Rhidale did not make the final list this time, maybe the new governor will step in on Rhidale's behalf. I can't imagine going through all the letters and appeals and waiting. Waiting. Waiting. Ugh. I'm feeling a bit nauseous just thinking of the process prisoners go through in their quest for life again on the outside.

"*These decisions are not made lightly.*" 12:11:40 p.m. No call. I check to make sure my phone is not off the hook and is still working. I'm super quick because I don't want Rhidale to call and get a busy signal. Do I have the right date? I check my iCal. "Rhidale NOON."

This can't be good unless he is making call after call to his family and friends. 12:13:11. I start transcribing an interview for an article. I unsubscribe from a spam email and finalize an invoice. 12:21:03. Maybe he was thinking 1:00 p.m. and said noon by mistake? Maybe I should head upstairs to grab lunch?

I stand up from my desk and turn . . . then sit back down. How can I eat when Rhidale's situation is so devastating? Eating seems like celebrating, and I don't feel real celebratory. The phone silence feels like defeat. The end of Rhidale's current hopes.

After nibbling on leftover grilled chicken, I'm back in my office. 12:44:52. What do I say if he calls with bad news? It's not like he flunked a test or missed the field goal in the last seconds to lose the game. I'll be beyond bummed if he has to serve several more years indefinitely. Surely, the prison officials are not messing with him. He will get clemency at some point . . . right?

The day drags out painfully. No call from Rhidale. I search online for the governor's list of soon-to-be-released prisoners. Did the governor review Rhidale's request for clemency and press his gold seal on a letter written just to Rhidale? Rhidale Dotson. No mistake with the D-o-t-s-o-n. *T* before *y*.

Rhidale calls a week later and confirms that the governor did not grant a commuted sentence. Rhidale is disappointed but not defeated. His voice is scratchy and weak from making dozens of phone calls to his family and friends. I am honored to have made his call list.

Rhidale Dotson, #86988. I know his crimes. I know his voice. I know his aspirations.

"The greatest test of courage on Earth is to bear defeat without losing heart," states Robert Green Ingersoll."[3]

Rhidale bears the defeat of not seeing his sentence shortened—this time. He chooses to not lose heart. He chooses to bend and not break. He continues to view each new day as one day closer to freedom on the outside. One day closer to a second chance.

"These decisions are not made lightly."

I Wonder How do we still find hope when we feel imprisoned by the long way ahead?

Dig deeper. *Bend.*
Additional insights and reflections on page 249.

Seven

Remaking of Life

*"Grief is in two parts. The first is loss.
The second is the remaking of life."*
—Anne Roiphe

WE LIKE TO TELL OURSELVES that it will always be someone else's community. Someone else's children. Until one day it is not.

For Wayne and Gwen Wrich, that one day dawns itself again. And again.

How does one family lose so much and still hold steady? Could I ever endure similar angst and remain steadfast? I truly never want to know.

It's easier to observe people's pain and grief from a distance—a little farther away where you can hide your own tears. The Saturday I sat with Wayne and Gwen in their vintage-style farmhouse, Gwen cried pretty much nonstop through our hours of sharing. Wayne broke into stifled sobs here and there. All three of us passed the tissue box around.

What could I say? I could barely form a question or two. Words wobble and tumble when it comes to consoling this Midwest farm couple who press through harsh winters and hailed-out crops and still get up every day, often before the sun opens its eyes. I know of few others who can speak of unthinkable loss with such empathy and wisdom.

Life has dared Wayne and Gwen to break and break and break

again, but they continue to stand firm in their bending and refuse to quit. What is their secret for righting themselves repeatedly?

To reconnect with these friends I first met in my college days, our mutual friend, Angie, and I take a late March drive three and half hours northeast of Omaha into the unending openness. We pass acre after acre of slumped cornstalks and shorn soybean stubble, remnants of the fall harvest. Here in pastoral Iowa, piercing winds bluster wildly, unrestrained by urban concrete and congestion.

A cordial easiness rules the Heartland, but I felt on edge. Why? I couldn't shake loose from a badgering question: *How will I ask them . . . how will I ask them about the barn?*

On our drive that eases into evening, Angie and I chat cozily about our lives, and she shares a bit about Gwen and Wayne and their adult special needs daughter, Wendy, who lives with them. About ten miles from the Wrich farm, a skunk saunters onto the highway. THUNK. I am aghast but grateful that the odiferous mammal died instantly. The rental car reeks as we rumble up the farm's rocked driveway. Wayne and Gwen quickly help us unload the car so we don't linger long in Skunksville.

After Angie and I settle in, Wendy patters to the sofa and nestles close to me. She rocks toward me and then sways backward, leaning in and pulling away in her own willowy cadence. My mother's wedding ring set is a shiny invitation for Wendy to take my hand in hers. The slender brunette turns the silver rings below my bottom knuckle. Slowly, methodically. Around and around. She is contented and curious watching the petite diamonds shimmer in the lamplight.

Although Wendy cannot speak words, she still speaks. I hear her. And smile.

The night slips to sleep, and all of us soon join in the restful slumber. I awaken Saturday to the delightful scent of coffee and bacon beckoning me upstairs. Gwen and Angie are gabbing in the kitchen. Wayne is out tackling morning chores and hosing off the rental car's eau de skunk cologne. I marvel at the remodeled kitchen's crisp, white wainscoting and modernized appliances.

Martha Stewart has nothing on Gwen's sense of décor.

Now that it's light outside, I glance out the broad window above the kitchen sink, commenting to Gwen about the two rows of dainty Craftsman panes along the window's top edge. But then my interior design banter crashes to the floor of my thoughts.

Is this where she stands every day and looks out? I'm not sure my emotions could handle that view.

About fifty yards just across the front lawn, the expansive, gable-roofed barn towers, its triangular top rising to a distinct peak. Neatly coated in white paint and accented with green window shutters, the broad building emanates strength yet frailty. The sloping roof fits like a cozy jacket, sheltering the aging structure from the elements.

As 10:00 approaches, we crack open a more reflective conversation. Wayne, Gwen, Angie, and I pull up chairs to the oak table in the open dining area. Wendy is resting in her room. I open my notebook, turn on my voice recorder, and start with "Tell me about your early days of marriage."

Wed in January 1981, the Omaha-area natives start their marriage living on an acreage outside of Omaha. Wayne works as a combine technician at John Deere and Gwen at Children's Hospital. A neonatal nurse, Gwen goes into early labor for their first child in February 1985.

Shortening her twelve-hour shift, Gwen leaves work at 3 p.m. to relax at home that night with Wayne, watching the TV premiere of *Rocky* on the new channel 42. After the movie, the expectant parents drive to the hospital where son Keith is born at 3 a.m.

Outside of post-delivery severe hives for the new mom, parenthood proves smooth. Two years later, an opportunity presents to farm with Gwen's oldest brother and his wife and move to rented land in central Iowa.

Three months into Gwen's second pregnancy, a blood test shows a suspected abnormality for spina bifida, Down's syndrome, or another probable birth defect. Working with newborns with compromised health, Gwen understands the ramifications. A follow-up amniocentesis a month later, delivers better news.

"I remember getting the phone call about the results and hearing that the chromosomes were perfectly normal," Gwen recalls. "That was euphoria. Everything else seemed okay."

But okay only lasts so long. Wendy arrives December 27, 1987, and weighs in at four pounds, twelve ounces. Wayne and Gwen bring their bundle of joy home after learning their newborn has a tiny hole between her heart chambers that will need monitoring as she grows.

"We started our journey of she's got heart issues, and we're moving to a farm in the wilds of Iowa," Gwen explains. "We moved when Wendy was five weeks old. That was scary because I was leaving the best health care I knew, and I felt like I was going to Mayberry."

As the Nebraska natives settle in the state next door, Wayne and Gwen are not ready to settle into the latest diagnosis of developmental problems for their baby girl. Maintaining strong ties to the Omaha children's hospital where she worked for eight years, Gwen seeks a workup on Wendy at six months.

When the Omaha pediatric neurologist matter-of-factly states, "She'll never have an IQ more than 35," Gwen instantly bristles, but Wendy interrupts with a smile and giggle. The doctor then tempers his words with, "But of course it's just a number. We don't know what that means. We don't know the determination she will have or her personality. We don't know what kind of care you're going to invest in her."

At home, the care investment for Wendy includes an occupational therapist and developmental teacher. Wendy's chromosomes are normal, but something is not quite right at a deeper level genetically. As with many developmentally affected individuals, there is no medical label for her condition and no specific disease support group to join. Later diagnosed with "failure to thrive," Wendy weighs only twenty-one pounds by age four.

Wayne and Gwen are just beginning to discover how heart-wrenching times forge an openness with people who live a section or two away across pastures and creeks or along rutted roads that come spring need smoothing by the county grader.

Midwestern folks just calmly pitch in when life goes south. I remember growing up and watching many a local farm family buoyed by the strong arms and hearty food of others. A dairyman breaks his pelvis—neighbors show up to milk the cows morning and night. These unflappable helpers mow, rake, and bale the hay. And stack every hefty alfalfa square in the shed.

Midwestern folks just calmly pitch in when life goes south.

Farmers and ranchers who live off the land know how to circle the wagons when tough times set up squatter's rights. Wayne and Gwen are only ankle deep in hardship at this point, even after their first year of farming squared off with one of the driest years in Iowa history.

In the winter of 1989, the Wrichs learn about a 1950s house on 150 acres, north near Aplington, Iowa. Their oldest child, Keith, will start school in the fall. Wendy is beginning to take steps at age two and a half. In the middle of the excitement of the move, Gwen learns she's pregnant. Not expecting to be expectant, the couple focuses on packing things up. Gwen takes a part-time on-call nursing job in nearby Marshalltown and goes in for the baby's first three neonatal ultrasounds.

The family celebrates Christmas and two days later on Wendy's third birthday, December 27, 1990, the doctor's office calls. The baby is breach . . . but there is more.

"I remember the doctor saying, 'I hope I'm wrong, but I think there's something wrong here,'" Wayne says, his voice fading.

The next day, the obstetrician conducts the ultrasound himself and breaks the grave news.

"He told us Laura's feet are missing and there is one hand. She has an arm to the elbow on the left and a full limb on the right," Gwen explains. "She has knees, but she has something called arthrogryposis, where the joints don't bend."

Shock. Anguish. Heartache. The doctor advises an early delivery by C-section. A few days later at church, the hurting, numb family stands before the congregation to receive an outpouring of prayer.

"We didn't know what we were facing, but we imagined that our baby would be okay," Gwen shares, the tears flowing faster. "She would be missing some parts, but otherwise healthy. That's what we were clinging to. The people I worked with were so supportive. I took off work to prepare for another child that would need a lot of care in just three and a half weeks."

While waiting for a C-section the morning of January 25, Gwen starts into labor. Quickly, the surgical obstetrics team works to deliver the five-pound, two-ounce Laura. Because Laura's knees won't bend, somehow during the C-section her collarbone breaks.

Few words are uttered by anyone in the room those first moments after delivery. Laura is holding steady but does not cry—a malformed bone has fused her gums together beneath typical-looking lips. Before the newborn's swift helicopter ride to the University of Iowa Hospital in Iowa City, the nurses pull Gwen upright in her bed to see her swaddled baby girl. "She looks like my mom!" Gwen immediately exclaims at the sight of her thick, dark-haired girl.

A tracheotomy is performed within a few hours to assist Laura in breathing easier. An ear, nose and throat (ENT) doctor newly recruited from Philadelphia Children's hospital and specializing in maxillofacial reconstructive surgery becomes interested in Laura's needs.

The next weeks blur as the Wrichs juggle the needs of all three of their children. Wayne stays at home with Keith and Wendy. Gwen remains two hours away at the University of Iowa Hospitals and

Clinics on a floor dedicated to babies with tracheostomy needs. Gwen's new routine is three days on hospital watch with one day back home. They maintain this pace over the next two months.

During surgery, the ENT specialist finds Laura has a cleft palate and he frees the bony gum attachment. Soon the newborn is sucking on her pacifier. In the whirl of Gwen's exhausting schedule between hospital and home, neighbors and community folks stop over with mounds of food, and neighbor Myrlin plows snow from the lane.

Wayne remembers their friend Sandy's commitment to deliver a meal. "I was just a mess," he describes, "and we didn't have the snow all cleared, but Sandy backed her car up the lane to bring food to us."

After the operation to divide a tiny bone in Laura's mouth, she can cry and smile. Geneticists and a slew of specialists and medical students at the teaching hospital pore over Laura's case. At one point, Gwen, the vigilant mother and neonatal nurse, insists that her three-month-old receive less of the sedative phenobarbital for seizures and a high fever.

"Laura needs to fight, and I need to see her eyes," Gwen tensely directs Laura's on-duty nurse. "I need to see her coping." In a tussle with the prescribing intern a few minutes later, Gwen shoots back, "I need to see my baby smile."

Later that afternoon, Laura is rushed to surgery for a twisted bowel. The newborn finally heads home to the farm on March 25, grinning here and there with a coo to let everyone know she's a fighter.

With two special needs daughters, the Wrich family values people taking an initiative to reach out. Kind-hearted neighbors, Myrlin and Burdell, "were always there for us," Wayne points out.

"They were people who lived their faith, they were the hands and feet of Jesus to us," Gwen adds, directing her eyes toward Wayne. "Our faith remained intact, and I learned from others about what you can do for people in times of great crisis."

Gwen can still envision the moment Myrlin first met Laura. "Myrlin was one of the first to come over to our house. Some people would be scared, but he came in and sweetly said to Laura, 'Aren't you the pretty little thing?'"

Laura Lois, the brunette little angel missing part of her wings, reaches four months and sixteen days. She's learned to smile and giggle. On her good days, her eyes give that extra spark—but her lungs are just not healthy enough and veins too tiny to battle through another round.

Photo by BrynMaRae Photography

At the hospital on June 10, Wayne, Gwen, and six-year-old brother Keith all hug and kiss Laura, letting her go peacefully. Keith is unafraid because he knows his baby sister is with angels now. He gently holds and kisses Laura with the simple love of a child.

I pause to let both Wayne and Gwen catch up to their tears. My own eyes mist up thinking about other dear friends who lost an infant daughter. Baby Emma was also diagnosed in utero with a chromosomal defect and doctors warned of a shortened life. On the day of her birth, dark-haired Emma took one breath outside the womb and passed away. Emma was strikingly beautiful, her delicate internal systems were just unable to keep up. One breath on Earth instantly ushered her to meet the breath of heaven.

I will never fully understand why such tiny innocents are taken away far too soon. I've questioned God a number of times on miscarriages and early deaths. I just don't get it. Why not take heartless mass murderers instead? I lean in to discern how Wayne and Gwen weathered their loss and still feel God's unshakable love.

Gwen describes the awkward balance in their grieving for Laura. They wanted to be approached by others, but sometimes they did not. Wayne remembers an off-the-cuff remark at the post office.

"Aren't you the guy who lost his daughter?" The words body slammed Wayne's heart.

"The man just said it so bluntly. I felt like bawling. I shook my head and walked out. I couldn't believe it. After that comment, I felt somewhat paranoid. I didn't want to go anywhere," Wayne shares, his forehead tensing. "It's like you smash your finger or cut it off. You've got that wound. It heals up, but it still can be cut open real easy. It hurts. The wound is always there."

We take a brief stretch break, knowing the rest of the story is looming around the corner. I feel like I've already evoked enough tears from my gracious hosts. Somehow in the heartache, this even-keeled couple exudes hope that life may bend you, but you eventually stand stronger. I wonder: *How can they really model this strength when they've lost so much?*

The tissue box in front of us serves as a comforting lifeline as we dare to make it through another tough conversation. I glance at my notepad and ask, "How do you keep going when you hit your almost-breaking point?"

With a knowing look, Gwen holds her eyes on Wayne and offers, "We each have our own style of coping. What did the grief do, get in your face?"

"Yeah," Wayne slowly answers.

"We each have our own style," Gwen repeats. "By the same token, Wayne will be the rock and I'll be the mush. Then I'll be the . . . ." Her words halt. "I dunno. I just remember when we were driving and I knew. We had found Lee and . . . ."

The tempo of our conversation tilts upward. Wayne and Gwen talk eagerly about their youngest, born in February 1993. Gwen regains her pep describing curious and brave Lee, who at age three stripped down to just his boots at the blazing hot county fair. Ever a free spirit, Lee is the family's laid-back, silly comedian, yet intellectually bright. In junior high football, Lee is more interested in the social camaraderie than catching the ball or tackling an opponent.

Somehow in the heartache, this even-keeled couple exudes hope that life may bend you, but you eventually stand stronger.

An accomplished violinist, Lee was recruited as a fourth grader to join his school's fifth-grade production of *Fiddler on the Roof*. After the music teacher heard Lee play the fiddler's opening cadenza melody, she asked Lee to play the iconic piece throughout the performance whenever Tevye pondered yet another daughter's wish to marry.

Gwen still chuckles at the memory of Lee sword-fighting other students with his bow backstage and at a moment's notice hopping back on stage to share his musical prowess.

Lee is the same think-outside-the box lad who made a wolverine puppet in second grade with his mom sewing red eyes on a brown sock. But the creative thinker took this wolverine design to new heights. Or new scents. After asking to borrow some of Mom's perfume to spray on his handheld wolverine, Lee, on his own, also layered the cloth creature with aftershave, foaming bathroom cleaner, and Lysol.

During his class presentation with wolverine facts, Lee opened a zip bag to reveal the reeking critter, complete with "scent gland" to ward off its prey. At Lee's next parent-teacher conference, his teacher uproariously recounted the second grader's smelly demonstration.

And as a loveable cuddler, Lee still settled in on Mom's lap at age twelve. I smile just thinking about this tow-headed seventh grader with his eager curiosity and zest for life. I thought of Lee as I packed my bags to travel back to the Midwest.

Yet in planning my trip, hesitancy ping-ponged in my thoughts. How could I ask permission to go into the barn without seeming indifferent to Wayne and Gwen's private pain? What if they just didn't want to relive their anguish?

Gwen naturally transitions our dining room conversation to that Sunday afternoon, December 11, 2005. Gwen awakes from a nap and plays some computer solitaire. Wayne and Lee wrestle on the couch and then Lee heads out to do his chores. The almost-winter sun grows dim when Gwen asks Wayne, "Where's Lee?" Finding it odd that Lee is taking longer than usual to clean the rabbit and chicken pens, both Wayne and Gwen go outside and call for their son.

"We don't know where he is and we start to get that sinking feeling," Gwen remembers. "We're running around, and there's a little bit of a wind, so you couldn't quite hear yourself."

Wayne continues, "I went into the barn."

"And I'm running around, looking," Gwen adds, drawing her fingers tight around a fresh tissue.

"I start up the barn ladder and see Lee and yell," Wayne blurts out before all of us tear up.

We take a breather. Gwen shows me Lee's violin in a shadow box atop a shelf in the sunroom. She answers my question before I can find the words.

"Would you like the see the barn?" Gwen offers, motioning outside to the towering barn.

❧

I step into the chilly wind that flattens my hair as if I'm bracing against a car wash dryer. *Am I really doing this?* I've come this far, but I bristle against my tears. *What will I find after all these years?*

I reach the barn's east side door and creak open the latch, swatting through a sticky blanket of cobwebs. Swiping through the fine mesh, I'm startled by a white blur on the floor. A flat-faced animal skull lies caked with scattered straw. Those oversized eye sockets stare back, almost taunting me to take another step. The elongated snout, the heavy jaws. Was this a possum? A relative to what Lee was shooting at that Sunday?

Lee taking in wispy breaths. He was saying good-bye. And I wonder if he knew it.

The husky scent of moldy hay and pungent chicken manure awakens my memories of growing up in rural Nebraska. Something deeply visceral compels me past the skeletal remains. I glance up quickly and to my right. I eye the weathered wooden ladder, resting with three of its rounded rungs above the edge of the loft floor. Few had come near the ladder since the harried steps of the first responders.

I didn't come this far to back out now, I reason, shuffling toward the ladder. My mind drifts to the scene of Gwen cradling her son in the dank hayloft. The sun sneaking beneath the sprawling flatland and Lee taking in wispy breaths. He was saying good-bye. And I wonder if he knew it.

I will my feet to ease up a couple ladder rungs until my eyes are even with the hayloft floor. My nostrils prickle at the whiff of aging reed canary grass and cornstalk bales, no longer fit to feed any animal. I hesitate to go farther. I just can't cross the invisible fence that separates me from what I sense is holy ground. Wayne's and Gwen's weighty words from our interview rewind in my mind.

"I go up the ladder and Lee is laying there, still breathing," Gwen gets out, her eyes reddened from her tears. "Lee has his hat on, but he has a bullet wound in his head. By him is the old gun that we had in the shop."

"It was my dad's," Wayne softly says, fixing his eyes on the wood grain of Gwen's chair next to him. "Dad brought the rifle back from the war in France."

Lee took a hunting safety class and hunted a couple seasons with his brother and dad. Possums and raccoons were a problem on the farm, getting into the shed and chicken pens. Maybe Lee cornered one of the persistent rascals in the hayloft.

Our conversation drifts back to that grim late afternoon.

"He is still breathing and I'm talking to him. I yell at Wayne to call 911 and tell him to stay down from the loft because the paramedics need to know where to go," Gwen recalls of those first moments in finding their twelve-year-old. Lee is unresponsive and his breathing slows. "It's almost like he was waiting for me."

Lee wants to respond but his brain is shutting down. "It's okay. Mommy's here. It's going to be okay. You're strong, you can fight, or if you're just getting too tired, it's okay," Gwen reassures her struggling boy. "We love you so much. I want you to fight and keep listening to me. Keep breathing."

Lee's breathing stops and Gwen starts CPR. "I tell Lee it's okay to go be with Jesus," Gwen softly says. "In some ways, I did feel peace."

The four of us pause a moment to collect ourselves and pass the tissue box again.

"It seemed like forever for the ambulance to arrive. I remember being with Lee on the couch that afternoon. We liked to wrestle and play. Lee bumped my glasses off and I got upset because I thought he broke my glasses," Wayne says, his voice fading. "Lee suggested,

'Maybe I should do my chores,' and I said, 'Yeah, that would be best.' That was the last thing I said to Lee before he went outside." Wayne's eyes mist at remembering this final conversation with his fun-loving son.

The response team takes over CPR and hurriedly transfers Lee from the loft. The ambulance speeds away from the farm as best it can on the slick December roads, followed by a state patrol car. Wayne and Gwen are right behind in their red Silverado pickup for the agonizing nineteen-mile drive to the hospital.

The deafening silence echoes even louder in their hearts. Stunned and speechless, the couple well-acquainted with grief stare at the whirling red lights leading them east on the paved country road to highway 57.

"I think we're going to lose Lee," Gwen somehow musters. "I don't think the Lee we know will be with us if he can survive." The clinical reality pierces Wayne's strength shield. He emotionally buckles and white-knuckles the steering wheel to counter the assailing pain.

"We have got to get through this," Gwen consoles Wayne, squeezing his shoulder. "You are my rock. We are going to be okay."

About a half hour later at the hospital, the hurting parents are led with their pastors into the same private family room where they had gathered fourteen years earlier with Laura. As Wayne and Gwen steady themselves to see Lee, the doctor eases into the room.

Lee is gone.

"We all broke down. When we did go in to see Lee, I remember throwing up in a trash can," Gwen half-whispers. "He looked beautiful, but I was so overwhelmed with it all."

Approaching his now-gone son, Wayne grabs a washcloth and bites down on it with his quivering lips. No one prepares you to stand at the side of your lifeless child. Especially not a second time.

❧

I listen to and arrange words for a profession, but at this juncture I just have no words. When Lee passed I was living a thousand miles away and did not hear the news right away. Now a stretch of years later, it is an honor for me to learn of the courageous life of this young boy and see firsthand how his parents have continued to bend instead of break.

Wayne and Gwen share the over-stretched pieces of their life that have mended since they lost both Laura and Lee. The coroner and local authorities visit, and based on the setting and medical evidence, believe Lee slipped and fell off hay bales in the barn, firing off his grandfather's old gun. Wayne and Gwen still grimace wondering how long Lee lay there wounded.

In recalling the death of the gregarious, adventurous Lee, heartening moments do lighten our interview. When two coworkers from Gwen's school learned of Lee's passing, they instantly responded. "I'll never forget that Retha and Phyllis called each other and immediately jumped into the car," shares Gwen. "They came here and just sat with me."

Retha and Phyllis simply offer their presence to Gwen and Wayne through the night and into the next day. Charity, a respite nurse for Wendy, shows up in the middle of the night to help with Wendy when the sun comes up. Few words are needed. That Monday morning, Marlys, another woman in the rural community, arrives at the Wrich farm.

"Marlys came without even knowing us really. That was another inspiration. Marlys could relate because her son was also killed in a shooting accident," Gwen explains. She came in and gave me a hug and said, 'I just want to tell you that you will be happy again. I just want you to know that. We love you and we'll pray for you.' I'd never met Marlys before in my life. I think she assumed I knew who she was, but I didn't at the time. She wanted to share some comfort and strength that she had received from her own loss."

The teachers at Lee's middle school make themselves available to Lee's classmates who need to process and talk. About a half dozen of Lee's buddies visit the farmhouse and share with Wayne and Gwen how Lee influenced their lives.

Quiet Cesar speaks up about his struggle in understanding football plays and how Lee in their huddles before a play would explain to Cesar which direction he needed to run. Evan shared how Lee would make them all laugh in the huddle.

Wayne recounts the men in the Aplington area who reach out upon hearing the news of Lee's death. "There were all these little acts of kindness. A guy who was a feed salesman hadn't been here in a while, but he showed up with a ham. He'd lost his son who climbed up a ladder and got electrocuted," Wayne remembers. "Another dad couldn't even come in the house. He was just bawling. He brought us food. You remember all those little things."

The little things like the knowing tears or that bear hug like the one Wayne shared later with another grieving farmer at his own son's funeral. "At the memorial service, I didn't say hardly anything to him" Wayne shares, "but we just threw our arms around each other and squeezed."

In their times of unthinkable sorrow, Wayne and Gwen discover friends without words are often the most extravagant of healers. Dutch Catholic priest, professor, and writer Henri Nouwen describes these unsung heroes of loss. "The friend who can be silent with us in a moment of despair or confusion," Nouwen writes, "who can stay with us in an hour of grief and bereavement, who can tolerate not knowing…not healing, not curing…that is a friend who cares."[1]

Caring friends, family, and local folks who tolerate the not knowing, not healing, and not curing help the Wrichs bend through the shock, the pain, and the longing for what might have been.

❧

"You will be happy again," Marlys promises. But how do you get there? I wonder.

How does anyone find any semblance of a lighter heart when you've tragically lost those closest to you? How do you really rise up from the deepest caverns of loss? How do you function well every day looking up from your kitchen sink to see the overpowering right-there barn where your child died?

Photo by BrynMaRae Photography

It feels almost insensitive to ask about the barn. The curious reporter in me wants to know, the friend in me wants to bypass appeasing my inquisitive nature to avoid brushing against tender scars of the heart.

"I've only been in the barn once...since Lee died," Gwen says, interrupting the internal barrage in my head. "Do I need to go in the barn? No, not really. Do I want to go in the barn? No, not really. It was hard right after Lee died."

For months, Wayne dutifully tended to the chickens, rabbits, and 4-H projects in the barn. His eyes squint tight as if he's back in the barn doling out feed rations to the bunnies and hens.

"I remember one of the hard times I had when I walked in the barn and there was Lee's blood," Wayne stammers out before a long pause. "I just couldn't do anything else that day. We had his rabbits. We had to give them away because I'd just bawl every time I'd go into the barn to feed them."

"We don't get it. I don't think this side of heaven we are meant to get it."

While Wayne faced being in the barn itself, Gwen faced her work as a school nurse and seeing children—many of them Lee's classmates. Some days she cocooned in her office and left early. Two months after Lee's death on his birthday, February 11, Wayne and Gwen ordered fudge bars for dessert that day for the entire middle school. Every February 11, a gift of fudge bars topped the lunchroom menu until Lee's class graduated from middle school and then high school in 2011.

The date of the 11th holds other significance for Wayne and Gwen too.

Seven months after losing Lee, Wayne and Gwen choose Sunday, June 11, 2006, as the day to get more closure on their grief. They invite their pastor and two couples from their small group Bible study to meet in the barn—Pastor Harrison and friends Jim and Jane and Brent and Marsha.

"I did not want to treat the barn as a horror spot. And it was,"

Gwen firmly gives voice in standing up to her angst. "We all crawled up into the hayloft and sat down where Lee died. We talked and prayed and even laughed. That helped me when things got hard in my mind. Your mind wants to think about the worst part. I wanted to replace those images with loving images."

After that gathering in the barn, Gwen could counter the tough thoughts cycling in her head. "I'd think about the seven of us sitting around talking and praying in a very holy time," Gwen explains, instinctively letting out a sigh. "I could then relax and sleep, just like a hand is on your head and God is saying, 'It's okay, child.'"

Saying "it's okay" is not just bluster for this mid-America family. Wendy's limitations, Laura's short life, and Lee's shooting accident would crumble many a parent's resolve and their hope for comfort.

How could this happen to good people? I challenge my own thoughts on what is fair and not fair in life. They still worship God in their deep anguish? Why?

"The encouraging thing is our pastor that night in the hayloft didn't say, 'Here's the answer,' " Gwen puts forth, her tears no longer draining her face of color. "I don't need answers, because we don't know the answers. We don't get it. I don't think this side of heaven we are meant to get it."

Gwen gestures to a plaque on the counter that reads, "Having faith in God includes faith in His timing." She explains, "I don't get our losses, and I'm not going to get this as long as I breathe. But I'll trust that God will continue to get us through it. He will bring us around it."

Through. Around. Over. The direction of moving forward for the Wrichs remains part mystery and surprise. Part defying the harrowing blows, part recognizing that there is more to life than its finishing point.

"All sorts of people have things like this happen to them. How do they handle it?" poses Wayne. "Without faith, there's nothing else to hold on to. I don't see how people handle life without Christ. I just don't see—there's nothing else there to really grasp."

Even at Lee's visitation service, the distraught Wayne and Gwen were reminded of the source of their sturdy lifeline. Son Keith, a junior in college, pulled his parents aside and confided with straight-forward candor. "There's two ways we can go with this," Keith shared. "We've got to choose which way we're going to go."

Together the family chooses a firm grip of faith and a renewed sense of how precious life really is for every person. For the Wrichs, the loss of Laura and Lee reveals a tenacity of spirit and tenderness to the pain of others.

"The grief becomes part of who you are. Blessings come in the form of somebody remembering," Gwen says calmly. "As tough as it is, the worst fear is forgetting."

(left to right) **Wayne, Gwen, Keith, and Lee**
Photo taken about one month before Lee passed away

Photo Courtesy of the Wrich Family

Recollections of Lee's spunk and his sensitive soul come easy. The day Lee stepped up in fifth grade for a friend is one fond story that would make any parent proud. Brilliant yet encumbered by anxiety and frustration one day at school, Lee's classmate disagreed with a teacher's instruction, shut down, and would not leave his desk.

The teacher, guidance counselor, and principal all try to coax the boy from his seat to no avail. They brainstorm and call in Lee who talks with and reassures his buddy. A few moments later, Lee put his arm around his friend as they head out of the classroom to apologize to the teacher and simply move on to music class.

That was Lee William Wrich. Live the moment. Tackle the challenge. Choose joy. It's what his family continues to learn through his passing.

A basket of nearly two hundred memorial cards remains visible in Wayne and Gwen's home office. "Do I pull them out and read them? No. They're there," Gwen says. "They are kind of a reminder of God's promise of faithfulness through people." And there's the scrapbook of handwritten notes on bright colored paper from Lee's friends. Evan wrote in pencil, "I will never forget his determination and will to do things."

For Wayne and Gwen, never forgetting carries over to being there for others. Living in rural America, people know relatives, friends, fellow churchgoers, and local farmers who've lost loved ones to tragedy too. The farmer found dead on his tractor after his gun slipped while shooting at ground squirrels. The bank teller who sobbed when Wayne, empathizing with her grief, offered his heartfelt condolences. The teller stumbled for words. "Thank you for remembering."

In the spring before they graduate from seventh grade, Lee's classmates plant a red maple tree alongside the middle school football field with his name on a rock beside the tree. As seniors, his classmates vote Lee's maple tree and rock as their class' favorite local spot.

A framed photograph of the class of 2010 gathered around Lee's tree hangs in the Wrich sunroom. "I look at it all the time and think about those thoughtful classmates," Gwen shares. "I pray for their lives and dreams, and pray for wonderful futures for each and every one of them."

Wayne and Gwen note that it can feel easier to not say anything to those who are hurting, but easy can rob people of comfort. We talk a moment about the countryside cemetery just south of Wellsburg where Laura and Lee are buried, a grassy oasis bordered by pine trees amid flatland fields of corn.

One can't miss the engraved violin and cross on Lee's gravestone or the image of a little lamb that graces the top right of Laura's memorial stone. The Bible reference 2 Corinthians 12:9–10 (New International Version) is etched on the bottom edge of Laura's stone. Gwen explains the significance of the Scripture that says "My grace is sufficient for you, for my power is made perfect in weakness . . . ."

"These verses talk about imperfections and weakness. When you're at your weakest moment, there is the challenge to be your strongest," Gwen shares. "We don't show God how strong we can be, we find out how weak we are without him."

The paradoxes of the Bible have long intrigued me. Strength when we are weak. Rich when we are poor. Steadying peace when utter turmoil invades. Wayne and Gwen assure that these traits come directly from God's hand. I envision Michelangelo's fresco painting on the Sistine Chapel's ceiling—the Creator stretching to touch the fingertip of Adam.

We reach a silent pause. No one reaches for a tissue. We rest our conversation. Our thoughts settle. I've heard people talk about sensing the nearness of God. We have crossed to that moment ourselves.

❦

About eight months after Lee died, another tragic death rocks the local community. Treye, a freshman at the University of Northern Iowa, is stabbed and killed trying to break up a fight off campus. At the time, Treye's mother, Lisa, lived three blocks from the Ackley school where Gwen works. Gwen wants to encourage Lisa somehow.

"I didn't know Lisa. I don't think I even knew her by sight, but I knew of her," Gwen says. "I knew that Treye was the son of somebody in the community. And Lisa was a grieving woman. I know. I've been there."

So one afternoon after Treye's murder, Gwen calls Lisa and asks if she'd be up for a pizza. Lisa is surprised by Gwen's kindness and accepts the offer of a food delivery. Gwen buys a large beef and mushroom from Pizza Ranch and drives to Lisa's house.

Stepping inside, Gwen shares a few simple words. "I don't know that I'm able to share any amazing words with you, but I just wanted to bring you pizza."

"I'm not doing very well," Lisa musters, her eyes glistening with tears.

"Hon', you are doing amazing. And do you know why?" Gwen reassures. "Because you answered the phone and you let me bring you a pizza. And you answered the door. And you're vertical."

"But, I haven't dressed and . . . ."

"That's not required," Gwen instantly responds. "If I were home, I would be in my pj's. I just want you to know that you're doing good. There's no timeline on your grief."

In a bit of foreshadowing of their own grief, the Wrich family visited the Victorian House in Waterloo, Iowa, the summer before Lee's death. One of the museum's exhibits featured a vintage home set up for a family experiencing the loss of a child. Smallpox, cholera, and other diseases at that time proved heartless on little ones in particular.

One room in the 1880s home displayed a closed casket of a child, thought to be about Lee's age. In another room, a number of mourning clothes lay neatly on a family bed. One outfit was for the two-month period of grief, another for six months, another for eighteen months.

"There was respect or acceptance that you don't get over grief next month or you don't get over grief in four seasons. Stages of mourning were recognized for a long period of time," Gwen says, turning to me. "People were allowed to subtly wear something that communicated, 'I have experienced a loss.' People were allowed to wear their grief. Remembering is an honor."

Even for those of us who never personally met Lee or Laura, remembering them is an honor. I can see Lee wowed by the swank vintage house turned museum. Surely the almost-teen wisecracked about the froufrou finery, the textured wallpaper, the oh-so-delicate china, and the grand floral-carpeted staircase. How could Lee resist gliding down that handsomely curved banister?

I slip into my own reflection. We like to tell ourselves that it will always be someone else's community. Someone else's children. Until one day it is not.

I stare intently for a moment. At nothing. My eyes linger out the window. In front of the barn, relentless winds bend the lanky tan grasses and dried wildflowers to the west. A lone strip of stockpiled snow is too stubborn to let spring arise.

I ask Gwen and Wayne where they are at now with their grief. Wayne gently arches his eyebrows and gives a pensive reply. "It's never done."

The remaking of life comes with no finish line.

I Wonder When pain and loss invade repeatedly, what helps us most?

Dig deeper. Bend.
Additional insights and reflections on page 252.

Eight

Tattered Memories

*"We, the children who survived, bravely endured
being hidden in difficult conditions . . . . We coped
with the continual terror of being found out, and
discovered within ourselves, the tremendous
self-discipline required to disguise our identity
in an environment where evil abounded;
behavior that amounted to heroism."*

—Dr. Shalom Kaplan-Eilati,
Lithuanian Child Holocaust Survivor

TATTERED PIECES OF HOLOCAUST HISTORY drift across Ilana
Zandell's memory. Ilana isn't entirely sure about her earliest years.
Other recollections of growing up in Lithuania stubbornly burrow
deep, as if crossing their arms and refusing to talk.

Ilana remembers nothing before the attic in the Kovno ghetto.
The attic where Ilana and four members of her family—father,
mother, brother, and grandmother—crammed into the cubbyhole
in the ceiling.

Much of what Ilana knows about her early years is stitched in her
memory via conversations with older relatives. These are the brave-
hearted men and women who modeled to Ilana how to keep bending
day by day with unwavering determination. No matter what.

In August 1939, when Ilana is just six months old, Adolf Hitler
brokers the German-Soviet Nonaggression Pact, promising no

military clashes between the two countries for at least ten years. A year later, the Soviet Union annexes the Baltic Republics of Lithuania, Latvia, and Estonia.[1]

On June 22, 1941, Hitler and his militia renege on their commitment to the Soviets and invade the Soviet Union. Hitler again shows his true colors.[2]

In Lithuania, many citizens at first welcome the German invasion as a way to be free of Soviet rule. But as the German armed forces escalate their mayhem, confusion swirls around whom to trust. Many anti-Semitic Lithuanians turn in their Jewish countrymen to the Nazi authorities. Pro-German Lithuanian mobs also kill hundreds of Jews, unfairly blaming them for the Soviet repression.[3]

For roughly five hundred years, Kovno thrived as a cultural and religious center for Lithuania's Jews and became the country's provisional capital in 1920. But two decades later, in July 1941, the local Jews are herded into one of the oldest suburbs of Kovno, the Jewish village of Slobodka. An estimated remaining twenty-nine thousand Jews are sealed off in the Kovno ghetto from the rest of the world.[4]

The fenced-in corral of cramped primitive houses permits less than ten square feet of living space for each person—roughly the size of a one-car garage for Ilana's family. In other ghetto homes, four or five families wedge into one shack. Trigger-happy guards. Rationed food. No running water or sewer system. A crush of diseases pillages the Jewish captives.

By that fall, the Nazis inflict selections, a killing of the most undesirable Jews who are too old or infirm. In addition, the German mobile killing squad, the *Einsatzgruppe*, and their Lithuanian auxiliaries, murder without respect to gender, age, or ability. In rural Lithuania, the Nazis force countless Jewish farmers to carry their own shovels to dig their own graves.[5]

Ilana's family ducks again and again in the crosshairs of the Nazis, but manage to slip under the enemy's most ruthless radar.

On October 29 at the Ninth Fort just outside Kovno, the German

SS, the *Schutzstaffel*, and Lithuanian police, shoot nearly 9,200 Jews. The bodies, half of them children, are shoved in a collective sand-pit grave. This single abhorrent operation is the largest mass murder of Lithuanian Jews.[6]

For the next year and half, the Kovno ghetto is relativity quiet with the Jewish captives forbidden from having more children and instead enduring slave labor in local German-run factories and workshops.

In the autumn of 1943, the Germans convert the Kovno ghetto into a concentration camp.[7] In spring 1944, the merciless German regime orders a *Kinder Aktion*, a roundup and deportation of the local children from the Kovno ghetto. Hitler's snarling protégées snatch approximately two thousand five hundred Jewish youth to entrap them as laborers back in Germany or toss them aside as soon-to-be corpses.[8]

Fortunately, Ilana remembers none of the heart-wrenching commotion outside her family's living quarters. When the *Kinder Aktion* roundup assails, she huddles with her family in the attic.

Scared. Still. Silent. Each breath they inhale dares to be their last.

"My first memories of anything in Lithuania was going up to the attic. I remember my mother sitting in back of me and holding me," Ilana shares. "I also remember my mother holding a tin. I don't remember if there was anything in it. Then I remember coming back down again through the ceiling opening and stepping on a table underneath us."

Seventy years after the horrors of the Holocaust end in 1944, I learn about Ilana through a Denver-based Shoah project. *Shoah* is the Hebrew word for Holocaust. A friend and I drive the sixty miles to meet with Ilana in her comfortable home on the southeast edge of the Mile High City.

Ilana is warmly congenial but finds it hard to articulate what happened to her after the *Kinder Aktion*. Ilana's memories are wispy and faint, but we sit down in her living room to see what recollections she can grasp onto.

"I don't have any memory prior to the ghetto. The space where we lived was more of a hut than a one-room house, and it was kind of pushed in. I remember a table in front of a window with two chairs," Ilana carefully describes. "My grandmother, my mother's mother, would sit on one end of the table, and I would sit at the other end in a chair with my big rag doll."

Ilana smiles at recalling her oversized doll. "I couldn't decide who was going to go first on the chair, the doll or me," Ilana continues. "If I got on the chair, I couldn't reach down to get her; and if she was on the chair, there was no room for me. This was a constant dilemma for me. I remember that distinctly."

Ilana squints her eyes to somehow squeeze more memories to the surface. "I can see my grandmother sticking bread crust in a brown liquid and eating it. My mother tongue is Russian, and I remember hearing my grandmother speak something in Russian," Ilana shares. "That is my most distinct memory of the ghetto. My grandmother slept on a cot that folded up. I remember that, and of course, going up to the attic."

Ilana pauses and presses in her lower lip. I know it is frustrating at times to will pre-school memories to mind. Ilana was only five years old when the 1944 *Kinder Aktion* tore apart ghetto families.

"I have very few memories of my mother, but I remember my mother cleaning the ceiling with a broom," Ilana continues. "I even remember a blouse that she wore in the ghetto. It was the same blouse she wore when they had gone skiing one year."

Memories of Ilana's father, Solly Zeve, and his work with the family's tobacco factory and traveling the world on business are absent for Ilana. "I don't remember my father at all, and I don't remember my brother, Henry," Ilana explains with disappointment in her voice. "My father and brother were with me, but I don't remember them physically."

Beyond these brief flashbacks to the ghetto, Ilana's memory is blended with later stories from relatives who explained how she survived extermination at the hands of the Germans. What Ilana does remember next reveals how life in 1944 rapidly deteriorated for the Jews in her city, turning grim and grisly.

❧

Ilana's young widowed aunt, Lea, is a dentist and one of her patients is the superintendent of the area orphanages. Lea confers with her patient and they devise a plan to save Ilana, Henry, and their cousin Ellen. A friend of Ilana's father is a Jewish guard at the ghetto's gate, and he risks his own life for the Zeve family too.

"Next thing I know, my brother, my cousin, and myself are being taken out of the ghetto. I was carried out by a woman, and my brother walked next to her," Ilana recounts. "There was a man there too, but they were not a couple. I know Ellen left also, but I don't remember Ellen at all."

Ilana looks down for a few seconds. Her mind strains to match an image with her next words. "That was the last time I saw my mother," Ilana gets out before her tears escape their internal dam. "That's probably the hardest thing for all of us child survivors. Every single one of us.

I swallow hard hearing Ilana's anguished words. It never gets easy hearing how Holocaust children were separated from their parents and familiar loved ones. Such a malady of the heart sounds worse than whatever the Nazis inflicted on people's flesh.

Such a malady of the heart sounds worse than whatever the Nazis inflicted on people's flesh.

"My brother and I wind up at a house outside the ghetto," Ilana continues, dabbing her eyes with a tissue. "I remember being on a bed and crying for my mother. The people who helped us out of the ghetto were Lithuanians but not Jews."

Ilana's next recollection is of being in a Catholic orphanage without any of her family. "Henry is someplace else. I don't know where. We are separated," Ilana voices, the pain of it all showing on her somber face.

Ilana explains that Henry is almost five years older, so the trauma of the Shoah is more dramatic for him. She later learned that upon escape from the ghetto, Henry ended up at a few locations including a farm where he worked and learned to fit in. While Henry remained undercover, he started practicing the Catholic faith for a time to hide his Jewish heritage.

Ilana had her own conformity issues of being one of the only black-haired girls and a Jew in the "Aryan" orphanage run by a handful of nuns. At her first Mass and not knowing the way of Catholicism, little Ilana initially sits down instead of kneels during prayers. One of the sisters kicks her in the tush to correct her.

"Because we were still under Nazi rule, I had to act like everybody else or I could be removed from the orphanage and the nuns would be punished," Ilana explains. "There were dozens of Lithuanian kids there, and I had to fit in. I spoke Lithuanian, but I had no clue what I was doing."

Ilana remembers another unfamiliar experience during a Mass. "They put something on my tongue, which I learned later is the wafer. That was probably the best thing I ate at the time. I don't remember food in the ghetto, but I do remember the food in the orphanage was awful," Ilana shares before her face folds in a frown. "We had to eat a brown gruel-type thing."

Ilana's memories of the orphanage are muted and distant, but she does her best to bridge together the muffled remnants.

"One time one of the nuns took me away, and we were hiding in the church or the nunnery because the nuns heard that the Germans were close by," Ilana clearly recalls. "I found out later—if nobody came to pick us kids up—we would need to become Catholic. I remember that distinctly."

Ilana leans back in her thickly cushioned wicker chair and nudges her mind into a silent repose. It is hard to imagine being that young and facing complete separation from all of her family. In a bolt of fast-forward reality, Ilana is whisked from her mother's arms to a stranger's arms to a sea of orphaned kids under the tutelage of tight-lipped nuns.

Ilana is an alien in alien surroundings. Alien people. Alien bed. Alien food. Alien religion. Nothing is the same. So did she turn her emotions off and tuck them within? I was curious to know.

"We had no feelings. We felt nothing," Ilana says of her mental state and that of other Holocaust orphans like her. "I can't explain it. I was five. As a child, you live the life that is created for you. You don't pick and choose, and you don't know anything different. This was my life at such a young age. All this was happening to me, but I didn't process anything."

Photo by Dorease Rioux

193

How could she? The constant living with scarcity and living scared shut Ilana down from being a carefree preschooler, from being a little sister, and a beloved daughter.

While Ilana is shuffling through the culture shock in the orphanage, her parents and adult relatives are in for the fight of their life.

The Germans fiercely plough through Eastern Europe unfolding a depraved plot to destroy all the region's Jews. In Poland, bordering Lithuania, some forty thousand Polish children are kidnapped during *Heuaktion* (Hay Action), or essentially the harvesting of victims, and exiled to Germany as slave laborers.

After the war, Ilana learns from her father, Aunt Lea, and other relatives about loved ones who stood courageous against the Nazi henchmen. When Ilana's paternal grandmother, a robustly healthy naturalist, is about to be sent to Germany's Stutthof concentration camp, a Nazi soldier demands of her, "Can you work?" The elder Mrs. Zeve immediately snaps back, "Not for you!" The outraged henchman instantly shoots and kills her.

Ilana's maternal grandmother who lives with them in the ghetto faces a similar tragedy. After Ilana and Henry escape the ghetto, Grandma Babun is seized and forced into the hordes at the Ninth Fort who are murdered by gunshot and heaved onto a pile of bodies in one heaping moat-like trench. Post-war figures calculate that roughly eighty thousand citizens of Lithuania, Austria, France, and other Nazi-occupied countries were exterminated at the fort about four miles outside of Kovno.[9]

I wonder if the remaining Jews in the ghetto heard the handguns and machine guns blasting from the killing fort. Again and again.

"Once you were taken to the Ninth Fort, you could not be of any help to the German government. You were too old or too young," Ilana explains of Grandma Babun annihilation. "They got rid of people pretty quick."

And what about Ilana's parents?

On July 8, 1944, when the Germans execute their final liquidation of the Kovno ghetto, they burn the ramshackle homes and barbed wire enclosure to the ground. Ilana's father and several other ghetto Jews had been digging secret underground hiding places around the ghetto. But the Nazis unleash dogs and throw smoke grenades to force the hiding Jews above ground and into the open. About two thousand ghetto Jews die of asphyxiation or burning. Only about three thousand of Kovno's prewar population of roughly forty thousand Jews remain[10]—imagine only seven and a half percent of your community surviving—Ilana's parents and Aunt Lea are still among the living.

Only Solly, Sonja, and Lea know which orphanage and farmers are hiding Ilana, Henry, and Ellen. As things turn fatefully bleak, Lea vows to Ilana's parents, "I am going to save the children."

As the last of the ghetto Jews are herded together to be deported on trains, Lea devises a bold move. Being a blondish-redhead with blue eyes, she convincingly looks Aryan. In line for the trains, Lea steps out of the masses and keeps walking. She walks straight out of Kovno and into a local forest where she meets up with farmers who are patients of hers.

"People hide her, and she lives like that for a year, not knowing anything about what happens with my parents," Ilana elaborates before continuing her story about the Nazi trains. Ilana's eyes well up even more just thinking about sharing the details her father and others passed on to her when she was old enough to take it in.

Solly is transferred to Germany's Dachau concentration camp and Sonja to Stutthof, Poland, the first World War II concentration camp set up outside Germany's borders.[11] Two of Ilana's paternal aunts, Reva and Zena, and Zena's daughter Fanny, are also captive at Stutthof. Reva is a physician and is assigned to work in the Stutthof infirmary.

"The only way my young cousin Fanny stays alive is Reva hid Fanny between the dead bodies. Fanny has to lay there between the dead bodies when the Nazis are coming to inspect the infirmary,"

Ilana shares. "Because of that experience, Fanny later had some emotional problems."

Solly braves the brutality of Dachau, Germany's first concentration camp, established in 1933 by new-in-power chancellor Adolf Hitler. Hitler originally plans the Dachau facility to imprison just political opponents of the Nazi regime, but his list of infidel inmates soon expands to include Jehovah's Witnesses, homosexuals, gypsies, and eventually Jews.

Later, Dachau is the first German camp to conduct medical experiments on humans. When I read online about Dachau's human guinea pigs, immediately I think about Walter and William from chapter one.

The Plywacki boys volunteer to transfer to Dachau in mid-January 1945. They are at this squalid concentration camp at the same time as Solly. Do Solly and the boys ever meet? Walter is treated in Dachau's medical unit and then smuggled out by two male Polish nurses.

Dr. Reva worked in the Stutthof infirmary. I wonder if she collaborated with others, like the nurses at Dachau, to help Jewish children escape. If Dr. Reva was hiding her niece Fanny among Stutthof's dead, then it is quite plausible that she helped other child prisoners survive the mayhem.

I wish I knew. I wish Ilana knew. The key players in these conceivable clandestine rescues are now all deceased. Awhile back Walter and I lost email contact, and I feared he had passed away. My heart twists at the thought. My mind falls sluggish.

Gratefully, Walter and I recently reconnect via Facebook. I long wonder if Walter will turn aside from his staunch atheist stance before his final breaths. I so want to hand deliver a copy of *Bend* to him and see his kind face again.

The grief I feel about losing contact with Walter seems so minuscule to the personal losses of Ilana. None greater than the death of her mother at Stuffhof. Sonja died of typhoid at the camp—perhaps inside the infirmary in Reva's arms.

Sonja comes so close to defying the Nazi's cruelty and walking out of Dachau on April 29, 1945, when the U.S. army liberates the death camp and some thirty thousand emaciated survivors.[12] Sonja misses her release by one month.

While tens of thousands of Jews suffer inside the concentration camps teeming with disease and death, thousands of Jewish children like Ilana remain hidden from the horrific carnage. But their plight chafes with its own confines of inhumanity. Their secluded existence in the shadows hinges on one inquisitive neighbor, one careless remark, one loud noise, one misjudgment. In a flash, fiendish Nazis can descend and tragically rip the hidden figures from their underground isolation.

A few months after Germany surrenders to the Allied powers on May 8, 1945,[13] Ilana encounters a sobering impasse in the Catholic orphanage. Aunt Lea is now back in Kovno working as a dentist for the Russian government, who steps in after the Nazis' defeat. Lea has moved into an apartment and works on her pledge to keep Ilana, Henry, and Ellen safe. Lea retraces her steps with the Lithuanians who are protecting her nieces and nephew.

Hitler is defeated, but his poison continues to desecrate.

Ilana is the last one to be rescued. Lea visits the orphanage and the nuns lead Lea to a circle of young girls. Would Lea recognize the now six-and-half year-old Ilana? War forces children to mature awkwardly. Abandonment robs children of their carefree trust.

"My aunt had to pick me out of the circle, which she did. Did I recognize her?" Ilana wonders aloud. "I don't remember. I want to say yes, but I have to be honest; I don't remember."

What Ilana does remember is walking and walking all the way back to Aunt Lea's apartment that day. They stop at farmhouses along the way, but many of the Lithuania farm folk still seethe with anti-Semitism. Hitler is defeated, but his poison continues to desecrate.

Reunited with Henry, now ten, and Ellen, now eleven, Ilana must have giggled and pranced in joyful relief, but again, those memories elude Ilana. What matters most is the tight bond she feels with Lea.

"We were very close," Ilana says with a widening smile. "My aunt was widowed young and didn't have any children, so we were her children, her family."

In her government work, Lea becomes friends with a Russian general who helps her with the next phase of the family's post-war recovery. The general assists Lea with obtaining false identity papers to sneak out of Lithuania with the kids through a secretive underground resistance group.

"We were taken out at night in long trucks. I was terribly car sick, and I remember my aunt sitting in back of me with a towel," Ilana shares about their harrowing escape before the Soviet Union's Iron Curtain descended to ensconce Lithuania from the West. "We went from one displaced persons camp to another, to another, to another until we wound up in a camp in East Berlin."

Once the Allied soldiers liberate hundreds of thousands of Holocaust Jews, many have no place to go. Their original homes, jobs, family, friends, and entire communities no longer exist. Countless numbers of Jews in concentration camps stay in the camps' languid conditions months after liberation.

During the three-year German occupation of Lithuania, the Third Reich exacts the unspeakable genocide of a quarter million men, women, and children—ninety percent of Lithuania's Jews. The Baltic country's Jewish communities are almost entirely exterminated, creating one of the highest Holocaust victim rates throughout Europe.[14]

Of Ilana's eighty family members in Kovno before the Nazi invasion, only twelve survive by the war's end. Decades after the German-led carnage, Henry gives a talk to a group of Buffalo, New York-area high school students. "It's amazing what you can do to survive," he assures his young audience. "I had that drive. God took care of me. I'm the lucky one."[15]

Ilana feels lucky too, especially for the care of dear Lea. Ilana also knows how painful the loss of family is to Henry. Before they leave

Kovno for Berlin, Henry tries desperately to search for their mother.

"When Henry saw trains coming into Kovno, he would chase the trains to see if our mother would get off of one," Ilana shares, her eyes heavily misting. "All this was traumatic for him."

Being the youngest of the family's three child survivors, Ilana deals with more inward trauma. She is too little to chase trains, but still aches for her mother. Gratefully, Aunt Lea becomes a loving surrogate.

Ilana recounts their struggle in a displaced persons camp in Warsaw, Poland. Henry and Ellen contract measles and Ilana comes down with the mumps. "And my aunt took care of us. Somehow she got brown sugar, and she made us caramel candy," Ilana explains with an uplift in her voice. "She was an amazing woman."

While Lea is adjusting to being a new foster mom of three, she learns through a Jewish organization that Solly made it out of Dachau and is alive in Munich. "My father was liberated, and he spoke English, so he worked for the American government as an interpreter," Ilana explains. "My father was befriended by an American general, and my father was obsessed with getting us back. Somehow he gets word that we were in East Berlin."

While Lea and the kids are waiting in the overcrowded Berlin displaced persons camp, Solly rushes to meet them there. "My brother jumps up and recognizes my father immediately, saying over and over, 'Papa! Papa!'" Ilana recalls before growing a bit solemn. "I knew what Papa meant, but I didn't recognize my father. I had no recollection of him at all. I asked, 'Are you my father?'"

Ilana does not remember her father in the Kovno ghetto, and she does not recognize him a year and a half later. At this point in our conversation, Ilana repositions herself in her chair and glances out her living room's full-length windows to the mountains brimming Denver.

❧

"My father was never a whole man again. People learn to live with what happened in the Holocaust; unfortunately, my father never quite made it," Ilana says with a slight grimace. "He was just an angry, angry man most of his life. I did not have a good relationship with him."

Solly's post-war connection with the American general proves helpful in transferring the now family of five from bombed-out Berlin. The general provided a car and driver to move them from the displaced persons camp through Checkpoint Charlie and on to Munich. In Munich, they live in a house owned by Nazis whom the United States government directs to clear out to provide housing for Holocaust survivors.

Ever a businessman, Solly starts refurbishing old American military vehicles and sells them back to the Americans. Lea sets up a dental office. The three kids attend a Jewish school with other Eastern European children who have also been in the displaced persons camps.

"I called the Munich house we lived in the 'leftover house,' because whoever survived the war and came from Lithuania stayed with us until they emigrated to Israel, the United States, or wherever," Ilana explains.

The family settles in the house for three years before moving to an apartment. Ilana remembers her girlhood years after the war with a mix of emotions. After Lea picks up Ilana from the orphanage, Lea makes Ilana a stuffed cloth doll with a porcelain head, dressed in a charming outfit.

"Somehow, I dropped the doll and there was a big hole in her head, and I was crushed," Ilana offers. "My aunt made her a little cap, but the doll was never the same for me again. Every time I'd pick it up, I'd take the cap off and look at her hole, put the cap back on, and then I didn't want anything to do with her."

Ilana recalls how later in Munich her disinterest in dolls continues. "I had all kinds of dolls and dollhouses. I had dishes made out of porcelain. I never ever played with them. I used to stick them in a drawer. If I was invited to a birthday party, I would take a doll out and give it away," Ilana expresses with a straightforward tone. "I don't remember an attachment to anything in particular. It just wasn't important. I lost my mother. Kids talk about their favorite doll and favorite this and that. No. Not me. At our house in Germany, I was a tomboy. I climbed trees. I'd go into the forest. I needed my sense of freedom."

With all her loss at such a young age, Ilana's detached response to her broken doll and later doll collection is no surprise. One of my psychologist friends, Dr. Julie Cox, explains that the injury to Ilana's special doll symbolizes what happened to her mother. Ilana's maternal relationship was beautiful, good, and safe, and then her mother disappeared and died.

There is no fixing of Sonja's death. No fixing what happened as a hidden child during the Holocaust.

"Ilana's repeated insistence on taking off the cap once she knows the doll is broken," Dr. Julie explains, "indicates her young but pained awareness that irreparable damage had been done and there is no fixing it."

There is no fixing of Sonja's death. No fixing what happened as a hidden child during the Holocaust. No fixing of escaping Ilana's homeland to live in a foreign country. And soon no fixing of Aunt Lea starting a new life by emigrating to Israel in 1948. With each of these punches to her soul, Ilana covers herself with another layer of "I'm fine."

Sure, there are tender letters back and forth with Aunt Lea and the occasional phone calls, but all the women Ilana was closest to are now gone. Grandmother, mother, aunt. Even the nuns who risked their lives to protect her. And deep within Ilana's heart, an insatiable desire churns. She longs to know more about her own mother and her mother's family but will not be able to articulate that until adulthood.

In 1949, Solly and Ilana, Henry, and Ellen all move to the United States, where Solly's two uncles emigrated around 1920 to the Bronx,

New York City. The two elder Zeve men sponsor the visas for Solly and the kids. Of course, fifth-grader Ilana wants to fit in with everybody else. She picks up on speaking English quickly and works at not having an accent.

Before the relocation to America, Solly meets and falls in love with Bella, a young Jewish woman who stayed alive in the Holocaust by staying on the run outside of Munich. Bella moves to New York a year before Solly and the kids. As soon as the family settles in the Bronx, Solly and Bella marry. Solly returns to his roots in the tobacco industry and works for top cigarette companies as a tobacco blender, the one who develops tobacco products' taste.

"Bella was another very strong woman. She kept saying to me, 'Nothing happened to you. You were not in the camps. Nothing happened to you. You're fine,'" Ilana recalls. "And I had convinced myself that I was fine, and I wanted to fit in. My name is Ilana, which is very foreign, and a friend of mine started calling me Lainie and then Elaine. So for years I was Elaine. I hid behind that because 'I was fine.'"

But was Ilana *really* fine or just bending as if she were? At this point in our conversation, Ilana glides through her early years in the USA and picks up her story with the family moving to Buffalo her sophomore year in high school. Ilana meets Chuck Zandell who is a student at the University of Buffalo, and they marry in June 1959 in Chuck's home state of New Jersey.

As Chuck completes graduate school in petroleum geology at the University of Kansas, Ilana finishes beauty school and supports them. Their first son, Marc, was born in 1961, while Chuck applies to oil companies. It isn't until Sinclair Oil hires Chuck that he learns he was being turned down for jobs with other companies because he listed "Jewish" on his applications.

"Chuck could have written anything on his applications," Ilana explains, "But he said, 'No, this is who I am.'" Ever proud of her man, Ilana and the family move to Midland, Texas, for Chuck's new job. Son Jay is born in 1964, then daughters Sheryl in 1965, and Lesa in 1969. They reside in Texas for seven years and also spend nine months in Roswell, New Mexico.

Busy with the children, Ilana wants to raise them in Jewish traditions, but finds it challenging to discover a Jewish community in west Texas. She tells the experience of living in "so redneck" Midland and the city celebrating Brotherhood Day, inviting all the local clergy to visit other churches. When no clergy visit the small Jewish community center, Ilana and her friend turn their anger into organizing a Jewish smorgasbord during the next year's Brotherhood Day.

"We decided if we couldn't get through to people's heads, we were going to get it through to them with their stomachs," Ilana says with a grin. "We sold fifteen hundred tickets and cooked stuffed cabbage, challahs, and cheesecakes. People went crazy for it. And that was how we got them to come into our Jewish community, and it became an ongoing event for years and years."

Not one to back down from opposition, Ilana remains dedicated to her Jewish heritage, even if she is not much for organized religion. And she keeps pursuing classes when Chuck's job lands them in Madrid, Spain. Outside his oil company work, Chuck teaches classes via an extension of the University of Maryland. Ilana starts working on her psychology major via the same Maryland university system.

After the family moves to Denver in 1969, Ilana completes her degree via Metropolitan State College of Denver. Later, when the kids are older, Ilana wants to get her law degree, but decides the timing is just not right. But not one to sit around and waste time, Ilana launches a local wholesale fine jewelry business and it thrives for thirty years.

No matter how much Ilana digs into living and learning, her past is still simmering on the back burner. A past that includes when each of Ilana's children turned age five, she said to herself, *Oh, my God. I was taken away when I was their age. There was nobody to love on me.*

As much as Ilana tries to keep this painful reality stuffed away, she eventually meets with a psychiatrist. "I sat there telling him that I was well. You really do live in denial for a long time," Ilana shares with a roll of her eyes. "And I told the psychiatrist that I have all my skeletons in the closet. Well, my skeletons started to fall out of my closet when I turned fifty. I started to face my skeletons, and they came out bad."

With her kids all grown, Ilana finally has time to look back on her own upbringing. Comments by the psychiatrist nudge her into noticing how much she hates loud noises and cannot stand being in the dark. "I became more self-aware and finally had to face reality," Ilana says, delving back to her emotional awakening. "It was like a sleeping lion that suddenly came alive."

To further her healing and to gain some personal closure, Ilana at age fifty-four travels to the Baltic countries with Chuck in 1993. They visit Kovno, then the Stutthof concentration camp near modern-day Gdansk, Poland, where Sonja died. Ilana wants a death certificate for her mother and spends hours with research assistants at the camp looking through files.

"They pulled out the original folders of the Germans. The files were immaculately kept," Ilana recounts of seeing the decades-old German documents. They knew exactly the names of prisoners and where people came from and how old they were.

"My mother was on the last transport out of Kovno, and then they burned the ghetto down, so the camp never got any of the books. They had no information whatsoever on the last transport. I found nothing on my mother. I was crushed. I was just crushed. We got out of Poland the next day. I couldn't stand it any longer."

Before leaving Stutthof, Ilana asks Chuck to say Kaddish for her mother, a Jewish prayer of blessing for the dead. From Poland, Ilana and Chuck travel to Germany and tour the Dachau death camp where Solly was imprisoned. Right after the war liberation when the family was living in Munich, Solly insisted the kids tour the Dachau camp.

"I saw the straw where he slept, and I saw Dachau the way it was," Ilana says, her voice pausing for a moment. "And when I went back to Dachau on the 1993 trip, I was appalled at what I saw. It was all cleaned up. I could hardly go through the camp."

Disappointed and disillusioned by seeing the Holocaust camps as an adult, Ilana later visits the Holocaust Museum in Washington, D.C., and combs their research microfiche records to find her mother's name. Again, Ilana finds nothing. No Sonja Zeve, or Ziew, as the Germans spelled it. No Sonja with a maiden name of Babun. Even if history records do not prove Sonja existence, Ilana grips the few memories of her dear mother even tighter.

In 1991, a group of Holocaust child survivors across America first meet in New York City. Ilana is not emotionally ready to attend, but cousin Ellen does and tells Ilana about Eric, a child survivor from Denver who attended. Ilana takes two weeks to muster courage to call Eric. Soon Ilana joins Eric and one other male child survivor to start Denver's child survivor group. Their gathering regularly meets and features a facilitator to lead attendees through memories of their days under Nazi oppression.

"That was the beginning for healing for me. It took me ten years until I was able to talk about my experiences. Finally, I didn't have to put my skeletons back," Ilana elaborates. "I never spoke about them before, because I convinced myself that nothing happened to me. There were no emotional scars. There was nothing. I was fine."

This time Ilana's "fine" mask cracks much like the head on her childhood doll. This time there is a way to fix the pain with emotional honesty and the hard work of letting out the grief.

"Some in our child survivor group had been on the run, some with parents, some were in basements—however they found a way to survive. Going into hiding affected everybody differently. We just talked and talked. I felt safe to talk and felt understood without having to explain," Ilana expresses with a steady sigh.

"We all came from different parts of Eastern Europe, but there was one thing we did have in common: we all lost a mother, and that was the worst thing that all of us experienced and still felt."

Ilana thinks back to her days in Midland, Texas, when she attended a foreign film festival and watched a film about the Warsaw ghetto. "I sat there and would not allow myself to cry," she reflects. "Everybody around me was sobbing. Can you imagine that? And I never thought about the sadness until later as an adult."

The shock, the numbness, the denial all blends within Ilana's subconscious until finally five decades or more later she can catch up with what she calls the "absolute inhumanity" of what the Nazis did to her people and to her family.

When the multiple Oscar-winning movie *Schindler's List* debuts in 1993, Ilana does not want to see it at first, but then feels she wants to watch it for "everybody who didn't make it."

> *Schindler's List fractured the world's naivety about the brave Europeans who took a life-risking stand for the hunted and haunted Jews.*

"It was probably one of the hardest things I've ever seen. It took everything for me not to just scream," Ilana explains. "You know what I remember about the whole movie? The red coat. You didn't see the little girl being killed. All you see is the red coat. That was unbelievable."

In my mind, *Schindler's List* fractured the world's naivety about the brave Europeans who took a life-risking stand for the hunted and haunted Jews of Germany, Poland, Lithuania, and beyond. Some have characterized Oskar Schindler as a hero, perhaps sent from God himself, to save Jews amid Hitler's pandemic evil. I wonder how Ilana views a higher power in her own rescue, so I simply ask, "How do you feel about God?"

Ilana shifts forward in her chair and looks at me directly with her dark, winsome eyes. "I don't believe in God. I was raised Jewish, and I'm very Jewish culturally. I love my culture. I love my history and my Jewish books and cantorial music. It's rich and it's painful," Ilana summarizes. "Religion is a totally different thing. I don't believe in orthodoxy. I shun that completely. My husband was raised orthodox. I was raised as a rebel. Our kids do refer to themselves as Jews and have been bat and bar mitzvah'd. We observe all the holidays and go to temple on high holy days."

Daughters Sheryl and Lesa attend Temple Emanuel with their

parents, but sons Marc and Jay stay clear of the organized ceremonies except for a young family member's mitzvah.

"I'm not atheist, but in some sense I am. Do I think there is a supreme being? Not really. I think we make our own lives. I love Judaism, but in my own way. And you'll find that with a lot of Jews," Ilana further explains. "We are what we are, but we are also cultural Jews. There is something in us that is a culture—our food, our music. It's Eastern European. We have taken something from all over and made it us."

"Have you ever thought that God was watching over you," I ask, "and protected when you were living in that orphanage?"

"No. I don't have that feeling about God. It's always my mother watching over me. God and I have a funny relationship," Ilana adds with a hearty chuckle.

"When you say funny," I respond, "do you mean that God feels somewhat distant?"

Ilana answers clearly and thoughtfully. "I don't believe in prayer. I don't believe in all that stuff. I can't say I have a strong belief in God. I really don't."

We shift away from faith reflections and hover a bit on Ilana's relationship with her other relatives who made it through the utter Nazi vileness. Brother Henry has spun in years of anger, still shuffling along the edge of the Holocaust's harsh reality and at times shutting himself off from his baby sister.

Ilana has remained connected with cousins Ellen and Fanny. Returning from Europe in 1993, Ilana met up with her oldest cousin, Zvi, after a family wedding in Boston. The two could not stop talking. Zvi at age thirteen also survived the Dachau concentration camp.

"We talked and we talked, almost through the night. And whenever I got together with Zvi, we were two old war buddies," Ilana fondly recalls of Zvi who has since passed away. "My husband would say, 'What do you have to talk about?' And I'd say, 'I don't know. It's just talk. It's comforting.'"

Comfort was often missing in all those distressed years during and after the Shoah. Yet Ilana has consistently woven comfort and beauty into her own life. One look around the former hair stylist's home and you see her exquisite eye for art and refinement. We stand and walk toward Ilana's walls of captivating art.

Ilana's South African display features an abstract painting of multi-colored faces on contrasting black. On a nearby pedestal that reaches Ilana's waist, an ebony sandstone sculpture portrays a mother embracing a child. At my friend's coaxing, Ilana poses by this mother-child holding a striking black and white photo of her mother. Wavy dark hair, piercing dark eyes. A dainty double-strand necklace. A fashionable hat offset to the right. Sonja and Ilana share similar looks and style.

Ilana shows us another vintage photo from a collection passed

Photo by Dorease Rioux

208

down to her by an uncle who emigrated to Israel before the Holocaust. In this picture, Ilana's parents sit arm and arm. Solly is decked out in formal attire accented with a white shirt and white bowtie. Sonja wears a slender-fit white dress with ruffled cap sleeves. Perhaps the most captivating aspect of this young couple's photo is Solly's broad grin. No one would have suspected that a few years later their marriage would end at the hands of a heinous dictator.

Ilana also treasures numerous photos of dear Aunt Lea who set up a dental practice in Tel Aviv. Ilana traveled once to Israel to visit with Lea, and Lea visited Ilana and her family in America. The two women's mother-daughter-like bond held firm across the miles.

Ilana cherishes all remembrances of her Lithuanian relatives and finds solace in a number of Jewish art pieces she picked up in Israel: a watercolor of Jerusalem's wailing wall and a Tel Aviv artist's pen-and-ink interpretation of everyday life. Ilana herself is a decades-long member of the Denver Art Museum and frequents special exhibits. She loves opera and the symphony and the musical performances at Temple Emanuel.

Ilana wears a number of her all-time favorite pieces from her jewelry business days. A passion for plants and flowers add to her golf and skiing as well-rounded hobbies. Ilana and Chuck were active in Denver's Argentina tango community for years, but a health complication for Chuck in 2019 keeps them for now from the quick-paced improvisational dancing.

Before we invite our conversation to rest, Ilana details a memorable surprise when she returned to Kovno as an adult. Ilana was overjoyed to find a building still stands with "Chaim Zeve, 1910" carved in the stone design. Chaim Zeve was Ilana's paternal grandfather, the astute businessman who founded the successful tobacco factory and employed generations of family members and friends.

Chaim is a common male Jewish name and in Hebrew means "life." The first two letters, *chet* (ח) and *yud* (י) mean *chai* or "alive." When Jews say "cheers" or offer a blessing they will often exclaim *L'chayim*!, which literally means "to life!"

To life and coming alive when life says break truly is the heart-beat of this energetic mother of four and grandmother of six. Ilana consistently models that life is precious and there is no time for squandering it away.

"I'm going to live a healthy life in whatever is health for me. I feel very together now. I have gone the gamut. I used to live outside my skin, now I live in my own skin," Ilana shares as she eases back down in her chair. "I have learned to live with the Holocaust side by side. Like a friend of mine said, 'It doesn't own you anymore.'"

I nod and offer a knowing smile to Ilana's words as I ask my new friend how we come back from intense adversity.

"I don't know if anybody consciously really thinks about how they come back. They just do it. You always find people who go through so much worse. You always do," Ilana shares, her dark eyes steadied on mine. "You find internal strength. You live side by side with it for the rest of your life. It's never out of my mind. It's never away from me, but I let it be there."

And on the days when the little girl in the ghetto and in the crowded attic poke around in Ilana's thoughts, she takes them to the orphanage where the nuns handed her a white paper cone filled with pieces of raspberry candy and assured her that the sweet treat was a gift from her mother.

"Whether my mother sent the candy or not, I don't know. I think it was Lea who had all the connections with the orphanage. But as a young woman, I started buying raspberry-filled candies each December around Hanukah. Then throughout the coming year, every once and awhile, I eat a piece. But mostly, I keep some in a drawer as a reminder."

A reminder hidden in a drawer, much like Ilana's hiding in that orphanage, that no matter how bitterly excruciating life can get, there are still sweet moments that delight.

I Wonder What experiences from our childhood still hold us back today?

Dig deeper. *Bend.*
Additional insights and reflections on page 254.

Nine

Courageous Freedom

*"All the great things are simple, and
many can be expressed in a single word:
freedom, justice, honor, duty, mercy, hope."*

—Winston Churchill

THE BRUSSELS AIRLINES PILOT'S VOICE crackles over the intercom, "We'll be landing in Monrovia in a few minutes." Hawa Metzger unexpectedly starts to shake in her seat. Her body shivers and tenses. Her heart gallops. Perspiration builds on her forehead. A full-fledged panic attack controls Hawa's body, mind, and emotions.

Returning to her homeland of Liberia for her sister's wedding after nineteen years away, Hawa did not expect this reaction to her February 2016 trip to her country's capital city.

"My body started shaking because my mind was telling me, *Oh no, you might get stuck here,*" Hawa later tells me. "Even though there was no longer a war, it was terrifying for me to actually be back."

You would never guess that behind this vivacious woman's upbeat countenance lies years of sheer apprehension. Hawa is truly a resilient example of bending and pressing onward through pain, loss, and the unimaginable.

We first met at my client's office where Hawa greeted me as the receptionist. We packed a month's worth of conversation in our three-minute chat, and I left with Hawa's phone number scrawled on a yellow stickie note. For months, Hawa's contact info lay buried under a pile or two on my desk. I will be forever grateful that I made that call.

❧

Hawa nestles in an overstuffed leather chair at her favorite locally owned coffee shop and sips her triple berry smoothie. Her smile is quick, her Liberian-English accent is crisp. Hawa's vibrant West African attire reflects her peaceful beauty.

Over the next two hours, Hawa shares her personal account of nearly dying in her home country of Liberia, then escaping to America to find her life in danger yet again. Wise beyond her thirty-something years, Hawa has a message of courage and hope for every-one she meets.

"I never really had teenage years," Hawa tells me over the fruity drink. "Sometimes when I take my kids to the bounce house, I want to jump in there too because I missed play in Liberia. My grandparents did their best, but I never had a childlike life because my teenage years were during the civil war."

Liberia's first civil war from late 1989 through 1996 was brutal beyond words for the small nation founded in 1822 after the United States sent freed slaves back to West Africa. The 1990s infighting killed more than two hundred thousand and displaced a million citizens in refugee camps in neighboring countries.

In September 1990, as a twelve-year-old, Hawa catches sight of Liberia's tortured and mutilated president paraded on a stretcher in the streets of her hometown, Caldwell. The rebel faction then burn his body, cruelly mocking his remains in public.

"When the rebels killed the president, the fighting between the army and the rebels grew really intense. The army was really furious," Hawa explains, shifting in her comfy chair. "But neighbors were saying no fighting will affect us, like when we have hurricanes in the United States and people think they will always be okay."

As the brutality heightens, Hawa and her family flee their home in the middle of the night, fearing they will be slaughtered like other innocents. Trudging in the dark, Hawa and her grandparents head toward the capital Monrovia. Again and again they encounter and step over and around dead bodies.

The trio presses on all night and into the next day, hoping to stay with Aunt Maa-yon in the Sayon Town suburb of Monrovia, an Atlantic coastal port city. "We took nothing but the clothes on our backs," Hawa recalls. "No food or water."

When Hawa is just three, her unwed parents give Hawa and her eight-year-old sister, Maima, to their paternal grandparents to raise. Hawa always considers her grandparents as her parents and brushes off childhood friends who question why her parents are older with graying hair.

Her grandfather is a top notary public and a Sunday school teacher in the Episcopal church. On the opposite side of faith, Grandma Metzger is a Muslim and a local midwife who typically delivers people's babies without charge.

On Friday nights and religious holidays, Hawa and Maima go with their grandmother to Muslim services, and on Sunday the girls attend Episcopal services with their grandfather.

"My grandparents never talked about faith in depth. My grandmother would say, 'I do not believe that Jesus was the Son of God, but he was a prophet,'" Hawa shares. "Sometimes my grandfather would argue. It's disrespectful in Africa to question to your grandmother, so I never spoke up about her Muslim faith."

Just before the civil war breaks out, an aunt takes Maima to live in Nigeria. As is customary in African cultures, families share in caring for children whose parents can't care well for them. Maima, who is already seventeen, will most likely return in a few years, but the separation is a heartrending loss for Hawa. Much like the March girls in *Little Women*, good-byes between close sisters elicit heavier tears. When the civil war escalates, Hawa must shelter her emotions and attempt to soldier on.

When Hawa and her grandparents escape during the night, Hawa clings tighter to the God she believes is still on watch. Hawa and roughly forty of her extended family and friends jam into Aunt Maayon's house on the outskirts of Monrovia. Fear is rampant among the Liberian refugees. Hawa learns that some rebel soldiers cut open the stomachs of pregnant women or cut out people's hearts and eat them. Airdropped bombs and rockets explode on civilian houses.

During the day, the family tries to rest because when darkness descends they sit outside watching for planes dropping bombs in their direction. When the hordes of people spot the flash of an incoming bomb, they scatter for blocks. Untold numbers do not survive the blasts.

"Sometimes we'd be up until six in the morning, so most people slept during the day," Hawa remembers of the nationwide civil unrest. "Some people were killed when rockets dropped on their houses and that put such fear in people."

Even if the warfare weapons didn't kill Hawa and her loved ones, cholera and starvation took their own toll.

"We lived on just weak Lipton tea and buckwheat the first several months at my aunt's. There was looting at the port and someone sold us some buckwheat," Hawa explains. "When that ran out, we ate some wild-growing plant that looked like cabbage, but it made us really sick. My feet swelled up. With all the diseases around from dead animals and people, our well water was not always clean. The water killed a lot of people around us."

With the dozens of family members crammed in one house with only one bathroom, Hawa describes the sanitation without running water as "horrible." Water is limited and meagerly poured into a bucket to flush toilet waste. With all the unwashed cups and utensils everywhere, sickness enjoys a heyday.

Suddenly, Hawa stops and sets down her smoothie. She switches gears about the lack of cleanliness they faced. "Some of the men in the house were pedophiles," she reveals, the stark words tumbling out. "If that happened to me, it happened to others."

I cautiously answer back, trying not to show my internal grief over her declaration. "I didn't know you were abused. Are you okay with talking about this?"

"Oh, I remember it! These were family friends of my aunt. It was horrible for both girls and boys. Some of these girls are now married and telling me their story," Hawa quickly responds. "But at the time, I couldn't tell anyone because you fear something is going to happen to you. You're already in fear and danger because of the war and you're supposed to be in that house for a refuge, but instead it's a place where you are violated, and you can't escape. You're trying to find safety in the war, but you are still living in hell."

Words fall short at times like this when a newfound friend risks such vulnerability, zipping open her soul.

Hawa's revelation booms against my heart. Silence engulfs me. Words fall short at times like this when a newfound friend risks such vulnerability, zipping open her soul. I set down my latte, watching its swirly leaf design drift to the edge of the cup.

"I'm sorry, Hawa. I just feel for you," I get out before she bounces into her usual upbeat cadence. I hate that this vivacious go-getter has scrabbled her way through so many unthinkable battles and oppressive captivity. I know we are only partway through her recollections of bending to the point of breaking.

After about a year and a half of clandestine hiding in Aunt Maayon's home, the rebel soldiers invade Monrovia and raid the port to ransack food and supplies. In the chaos, Hawa and her family and friends leave behind the house and make it to a peacekeeping military barracks in the middle of Monrovia.

Hawa and her grandparents are racked with swollen stomachs and limbs, and the continual diarrhea and vomiting leaves them barely able to walk. The European and American relief workers nurse the Metzgers with thin porridge and salty water.

❧

Hawa playfully swirls her straw in her smoothie as if pushing aside those dreadful years of scarcity back in Liberia. She mentions how today hearing reports of civil wars, undocumented people, and refugees remind her of the struggle to stay alive in Liberia.

"What was the worst for you?" I pensively ask Hawa. Hawa sets her smoothie on the table in front of us and leans back in her chair. She closes her eyes and jostles her long-ago memories.

Photo by Beth Lueders

"I had a lot of dark moments, but my darkest moments were when we were living in the military barracks. It was terrifying to see the soldiers with guns," Hawa recounts. "I really didn't sleep there.

We laid on cold cement. I was always worried. We all thought we would die. It was terrifying."

Then comes the grim memory of the initial first night of escape.

"The rebels stopped us on the road and wanted to know if we were Muslims. My grandmother had brought along her whole hijab outfit. She got it in Mecca, and it was a treasure to her," Hawa shares, biting her lower lip. "Liberian women wear wrapped clothes, so my grandmother hid her hijab under her clothes. The rebels searched us, but did not find it. That was the first time in the chaos that I thought I was going to die."

Hawa continues with the time the rebels capture Monrovia's port and ransack house after house searching for boys and girls to recruit as child soldiers. "Usually, parents were already dead, so soldiers would give the kids drugs and influence them to join in as soldiers," Hawa haltingly reflects, grateful that she never faced this nightmare.

Hawa glances out the coffeehouse window, tilting her face to the sun warming the windowpanes. I sense there's another somber experience Hawa wants to bring to the light, so I let Hawa rest in her internal silence before she continues again.

❧

After the first cease-fire in 1995, Hawa and her family had not heard from a number of relatives who were holed up in another house on the northeast outskirts of Monrovia. Hawa joins her grandparents and several immediate family members on a daylight excursion to check on these relatives in Jallah Town.

"We found about thirty of them all dead in the house. It looked like they just stayed inside, and all died from starvation," Hawa explains. "I saw my Uncle George's skeleton still wearing his knee-high socks. We knew it was him because he always wore those socks."

Her voice still steady after recounting her family's bleakest moments, Hawa wants to focus on the intervention of other nations. After the barracks, the family moves to a relief center in Monrovia, where international relief workers including American Catholic nuns, American Red Cross volunteers, and Christian ministry workers step in with physical and spiritual aid. Samaritan's Purse gives Hawa a Bible and an Operation Christmas Child shoebox of goodies.

I'm curious about the practical difference her faith made in coming back from the civil war atrocities. I ask Hawa why she didn't give up, and I wonder what kept her going.

"I think we all thought we would die. It is terrifying to think that any day could be it. But people would pray for us. My grandfather read from his *Book of Common Prayer*, and we had family devotions every day and invited other refugee families to join us," Hawa remembers. "My grandfather would tell us to keep believing in God and that he will get us out of there."

Hawa's voice picks up strength and she steadies her eyes on mine.

"Hope kept us going," she assures me. "I promised God, 'If I ever get out of here, I promise you that I will serve you, I will tell people about you, and I will share my story.'"

One of the relief workers gives Hawa's family several psalms to pray through together. "For some reason, Psalm 46 was the one that stuck with me. 'God is our refuge and strength, a very present help in trouble,'" Hawa says, her smile growing wider. "No matter where I go, whether I'm covered in a building or outside, his refuge is with me and it's not about a building. I love this psalm."

Clutching her berry smoothie, Hawa savors every drop, thinking back to her teen years during the war rehydrating with salty water. She understands that life is both sweet and salty.

The sweetness of hope begins to unfold more for Hawa when humanitarian workers help her finish her high school education. At nineteen, Hawa moves to the United States on political asylum. In America, she settles in with an aunt who is already living in Maryland, and Hawa graduates from the University of Maryland in 2005 with a degree in business administration.

In 2009, Hawa marries a U.S. Marine and the next year he transfers to the Army and they move to Colorado. But a hidden side to her husband grows darker. He escalates in his anger outbursts and injures Hawa on a few occasions.

"Did you ever suspect his hostile behavior before you married?" I interject.

"I think every woman knows. We think we can fix people. We are born nurturers," Hawa elaborates. "He has a lot of good traits. He's very ambitious and very intelligent. You could meet him and have a long talk with him. But what you'd see is not the person I saw."

Hawa pauses. She glances back out the window as if searching for the tattered pieces in her puzzling marriage.

"He told me several times, 'If you ever call the police and if I ever lose my job because of this, I have guns and I can shoot you—and the military will back me up,'" Hawa voices, slowly revealing the manipulative power he held over her.

Hawa's last straw is the night he pins her against a wall, choking her until she passes out, right in front of their three crying children. Their divorce is final in 2015.

She glances back out the window as if searching for the tattered pieces in her puzzling marriage.

"I feel like I left from one captivity and entered another captivity. With every captivity, God always pulled me out of it. I lived through the atrocity of war and then I lived a different kind of war here," Hawa reflects. "I was basically in bondage because I couldn't speak about what happened with my husband. I was ashamed to tell people."

Hawa feared people would simply advise her to just work through her marital strife. "I thought some might say, 'Why should you complain, you have a nice house and you have military benefits?' But I was living with someone who was assaulting me physically, mentally, and emotionally," Hawa shares. "I began to wonder if I complained too much or was a whiner. Or, maybe I caused him to get too upset?"

Looking back now, Hawa knows she made the right choice to protect her life and her children's lives. And she again credits her Creator for carrying her through.

"God has his hand around me and he has brought me out of so many things," Hawa maintains. Her bondage of silence and shame continues to fall away as she now speaks to a variety of audiences about surviving civil war and an abusive war in her marriage.

Although she has never sought professional counseling for her traumatic experiences, Hawa says her Liberian upbringing taught her to view bending and facing down personal giants differently. "Africans deal with traumas differently," she says. "They see that life has a lot of things happening, and as time goes by, you get over the troubling times."

Hawa these days leans into her church family and prayer for the occasional civil war flashbacks like when July 4th rolls around.

"If I hear fireworks, I can freak out. So every July 4th, I am terrified because I think somebody is shooting," Hawa acknowledges. Near her former employer, local Air Force jets would put on an annual air show and all the company's employees were encouraged to sit outside for a picnic and watch the fighter jets soar overhead.

"Those jets going over remind me of the bombs in Liberia. Of the over a thousand employees in the building, I would be the only one not going outside," Hawa explains. "My boss even put earphones over my ears so I could join everyone outside. They tried so many times, and I couldn't do it."

Talking about the local jets reminds Hawa of her panic attack on the plane on her first return trip back to her homeland. Gratefully, on her occasional visits back to Liberia since, she has not been twisted into a fear knot.

Hawa also keeps in touch with her family back in Africa via social media and video calls. Before her ill father died from the effects of his decades of alcoholism, Hawa traveled back to Liberia in July 2017. She extended compassion and forgiveness to her long-absent father.

Today the single mother, who gained her dual Liberian-U.S. citizenship, works with disabled children at a local elementary school. Her own two daughters and son, Stephanie, eighteen, LJ, eleven, and Leila, eight, are her delight.

"I love my children deeply. I am living my childhood through the eyes of my children. I suffered a tough childhood with molestation and abandonment trauma, so now I work hard to protect my children," Hawa shares. "I talk to them about safety, something I wasn't taught, and I let them live a life of expression, which is something a lot of kids lack in Liberia. I smile knowing I am raising my children to grow up as decent people who understand a love for humanity."

In the future, the protective mother and human rights advocate plans to spend more time back in Liberia empowering her people to stand up for themselves and their loved ones.

Photo by Beth Lueders

I swear Hawa's smile gleams more when she talks about helping others still struggling in her homeland. Her words pick up a quickened pace as she reaches for her smoothie. But suddenly, Hawa stops. I see her tears pooling. Hawa blankly scans the ceiling.

Steadying her thoughts, Hawa returns to our conversation. I know she wants to share something deeply personal and painful. But what? Hasn't she already shown me the hidden closet of her soul?

Hawa coaxes out recollections of her beloved younger sister, Jackie, who was just a preschooler when the civil war erupted. Jackie was brutally gang raped and killed on the streets of Monrovia in December 2018. A single mother of five children ranging from a seven-month-old to teenagers, Jackie was only thirty years old when she died.

Ugh. Such senseless loss. It didn't have to be. I am touched by Hawa's do-not-break perseverance.

Hawa's impassioned voice for her home country and its disadvantaged and downtrodden people is catching the notice of advocacy groups and political leaders in America. In March 2020, Hawa was to speak before the United Nations in New York City about violence against women and children, but her talk was canceled when the Liberian women who invited her encountered red tape in Liberia and they were not granted visas. Hawa is confident this setback will not stop her and other Liberians from speaking up and speaking out. What about Hawa's takeaway message to the rest of us?

"I know what is to be hungry and so I take nothing for granted. In your pain, you have to realize there is some purpose that will come out of it if you don't give up," Hawa reflects. "I think Americans are not grateful and they complain about a lot of things. There are some people who just want to have food to eat and live. I am grateful when I see the sun in the morning and I'm grateful for peace."

Knowing what it is like to survive on scarcity and keep getting up when life wanted to break her spirit and her body, Hawa emulates a deep, inspiring resolve to never give up.

"You can't give up on God either. You have to believe that everything has been placed in your life and there is a purpose to it," Hawa adds with a final slurp of her berry smoothie. "I think somebody has to tell the story. Somebody has to say, 'Okay, I went through this. You can make it too.'"

I Wonder What qualities do some people possess to suffer so much and still manage to come back stronger than ever?

Dig deeper. *Bend.*
Additional insights and reflections on page 258.

Ten

More to the Story

*"Blessed are the hearts that can
bend; they shall never be broken."*
—Albert Camus

THERE IS MORE TO THE STORIES of these brave ones. There is more to your story. There is more to mine. There is more to every bending point.

The agonizing accounts of bending long stay with me. Beyond the resolute souls among these pages, I have talked with African polio patients who slither with lifeless legs along dusty roads. I have hunched inside the cardboard and chicken-wire shelters of prostitutes along filthy back alleys. I have writhed my way through my own pain and despair. Bend. Bend. Bend.

I can still see the grief contort Bob's face. I can still hear his uncontrollable sobs. Never have I encountered a man weep with such intensity, such searing lament. My long-time friend gripped in utter affliction.

When I edged to the doorway of the hospital room, a nurse was guiding Bob in bathing his just-born daughter in the bathroom sink. Baby Emma looked exquisitely beautiful with a delicate nose and dark, wispy hair. But, Emma had already left this Earth.

The obstetrician braced Bob and Kristi months before that their fourth child had a chromosomal irregularity and would most likely be stillborn or only live a month or two at best. Emma was gracefully formed on the outside, but inside her frail lungs lagged behind.

Emma took one breath outside the womb and could breathe no more.

I wonder how we view the days and years we have. The breaths we are given. Are we learning to bend or are we feeling stuck? Or, too worn out to even care right now?

As much as I'd like to soften it, none of us are immune to adversity and suffering. You are not immune. I am not immune. The harsh winds will blow and our spirits will dip like a newly planted tree in the spring.

But we are designed to bend. To stand firm. To press onward. To fight back. Bend. And bend again.

As I write to you today, I'm facing yet another round of intense neck stiffness. Changes in the weather's barometric pressure are my bane. Part of me feels like I want to crawl back in bed and scratch this day off the calendar. But from deep within I hear a whisper to: "Keep going. Don't stop now. Write another sentence and then another."

So here I am. Inching ahead, bending, as you read these final words of *Bend*. Thank you for coming along with me on my quest to find out what *really* keeps people bending and coming back . . . through the darkest of circumstances.

It's strangely ironic that I type these final words while the globe is tottering through the COVID-19 crisis. People are freaked out. People are dying. Jobs are pulverized, finances are decimated, medical teams are trampled. This is not the world we know, this is not the world we trusted.

Life is daring us all to break. To shatter. To crumble. To give up.

Yet, as I wrote in my introduction: "We are inherently designed to resist the curl, fold, and collapse when life dares to break us. We are created to stretch and buck against invasive pressures . . . no matter what."

Even without the belligerent threat of virulent pathogens, each us is learning to stretch and buck and bend. We bend every day— although we don't always realize it.

As you've read *Bend*, you have met a number of fellow sojourners who have wobbled, wiggled, and wended their way through hard knocks and knockdowns.

But you and I know that bending is not always lovely and gift-wrapped in dainty floral paper with a shimmery bow. Just ask any of the individuals in this book. Or me. Or yourself.

What is it that helps you bend? Is it working? Or are you curious about what many in *Bend* have discovered?

Cyndi is one of the most intriguing bending aficionados I met in my pursuit for answers. If you recall, Cyndi is a solo witch living in the shadows, hemmed in by a concrete and asphalt jungle. For decades, Cyndi has grappled and brawled her way through abusive relationships, job losses, and make-do living quarters.

Part of Cyndi's bending routine is to adhere to her god, Cernunnos, her goddess, Hecate, and Gaia, the Earth goddess. "I've got the earth, animals, the moon, and the sun, and the magic. That's all I need," Cyndi confidently states. "That serves my purpose."

That did. Until about seven months ago. Something unforeseen happened in Cyndi's life. Something I find mystifying. I'm not sure how to convey Cyndi's about-face. So I'll just tell you. Cyndi is no longer a witch.

On a day like any other, Cyndi was listening to YouTube videos on her phone. She stepped away to use the bathroom, and when she came back, a pastor was speaking about the origins of witchcraft denizens based on facts from the Bible and other historical writings including the Book of Enoch.

Cyndi kept listening and listening, huddled on her bed. She clutched her phone, pressing against the wall that is her headboard. It's the same double mattress flat on the floor where she invites me to sit next to her while she recounts tuning into the online pastor.

On the end of the bed, with my knees pressed almost up to my chin, and sinking and shifting on the swishy mattress, I don't care if I am awkwardly uncomfortable. Without realizing, I stop taking notes and let my digital recorder catch Cyndi's words.

Curiosity tumbles around in my head. Just how does a witch make a spiritual one-eighty?

"I just listened to the pastor talking about the fallen angels that left heaven and defiled themselves with human women," Cyndi fires off with excitement like a child supercharged on sugar. "From their offspring, the Nephilim, came incantations, curses, witchcraft, and the goddess Hecate. And I thought Holy sh*t!"

I stifle my chuckle and let Cyndi zip onward with what she calls "magical information" that messed up the human race. "Listening to several more of those YouTube messages was my wake-up call," Cyndi explains, locking her eyes on mine. "I realized that I don't want Hecate to be my queen. She's a piece of sh*t. I don't want her to be my goddess."

"Who wants to worship that kind of crap? I had enough of this."

Cyndi stands and darts around a jumbled pile of plastic grocery bags and canvas tote bags crammed with laundry. She grabs her phone to show me the proof of the YouTube videos that challenged her decades of defending witchcraft.

"Who wants to worship that kind of crap? I had enough of this. I'm a sensible person, if you give me sensible logical information," Cyndi adds, returning to sit next to me and recounting how she studied the Bible and theology at her Lutheran high school. Over the years, Cyndi says no one would really answer her questions, and some clergy told her, "Oh, the Bible is symbolic."

But in those hours online, cocooned in her one-room sanctuary, Cyndi wrestled with the divine. "I went over the pastor's other videos on everything to do with Jesus. I did this all on my phone," Cyndi continues, tapping her trusty communication device. "My eyes opened and I saw the truth. And I thought, *Maybe I better talk to Jesus about all this.* And I started talking to Renee, the pastor with Set Free."

Cyndi eases off the bed and faces me to describe her backstory of being a witch following earth religion. "When I was a Wiccan, I was all about saving Mother Earth and saving the trees and the wolves. And don't mess with the bees. And when I read that God gets upset about anyone messing with his creation, that gives me real hope,"

Cyndi explains, slowing her verbal pace. "I now know that someday God is going to put Earth back together again. I have hope in that security, so that takes care of my Wiccan stuff. Truthfully, I don't need it anymore."

Some might say, instead of living in the shadows, Cyndi has now found the light. As a reliable investigative reporter, I state the facts. Cyndi's life is on the upswing. When her landlord and ex-husband, Nick, ran into legal problems, he shut down his auto body shop, which forced Cyndi to move to the Set Free building next door. This bending landed her in a basement room three times the size of the cubbyhole at Nick's.

Now Cyndi's got a mini fridge, a microwave, and oodles of storage space. But it's not just Cyndi's physical surroundings that have changed. It's not just her finances that have started to improve. There is undeniably something different about how Cyndi views her bending points.

"I don't have any fear. I'm not a 'whatever will be will be' kind of person. I'm a military person of 'you've got a problem? Let's go take care of it,'" Cyndi explains. "But now I pray about these things. I don't like the feeling of being helpless or feeling I can't do anything, so I pray about things. I ask Jesus to put me in the direction that he wants me to go in."

And all this from the woman who called upon her gods while dancing naked in the moonlight and wanted to create a potion to stop her daughter's drinking. Cyndi notes that these days she's employing a different approach to the woes of her kids. She's talking to God.

"I know God's working on Merry. She quit drinking. It's going on five months that she hasn't had a drink or had any coke either," Cyndi says with a pleased smile.

Cyndi now regularly helps care for her own elderly mother (yes, the mom who used to press Cyndi's anger buttons). "I'm now older, wiser, more patient," Cyndi calmly reflects as she picks up her Bible and journal to show me her mini essays she's written on the first couple of chapters of the book of John.

Cyndi studies the Bible three times a day with other young Christians upstairs in the Set Free office when she's not working cleanup and cooking gigs at area event centers.

"At 9:00 we study Proverbs and Psalms and the armor of God from Ephesians 6. At 12:00 we're memorizing the names of the books of the Bible," she eagerly points out. "At 3:00 we're studying the Book of John and writing summaries of each chapter."

Something clearly has turned Cyndi around. She's still sassy. Still knows her way away around a few cuss words. She still respects Nature. But she's turned her back on the shadowy side of the supernatural.

And how is she learning to bend these days? I want to know.

"I have faith, and if I want something, I ask God for it," Cyndi adds as she walks me to her door. "It's important to be strong, to be steadfast, and to have faith. And whatever comes my way I'll deal with it when it comes."

I have to ask if feisty Cyndi is still, well, her feisty self. "So is God rounding off your rough edges?"

"Nah. Not really," she quickly responds. "I think God just shoves me and says, 'Go, for it.'"

Now that earns a full chortle from me. Yet I'm kind of speechless at this point taking in the changes that Cyndi is describing. There's a spark in her countenance now. An uptick in her smile framing her new dentures.

After Cyndi turns on a flashlight to show me that boa constrictor Paul is coiled asleep in his aquarium (sorry, still not a snake lover), I eye the pink lettering on Cyndi's black sweatshirt "This Girl Can" with "Philippians 4:13" printed below.

"Walmart. Twenty bucks," Cyndi simply states. "Philippians 4:13, 'for I can do all things through Christ who strengthens me.'"

"What does that message mean to you?" I pose as we stop in front of Cyndi's stash of chunky peanut butter, oatmeal, and soup.

"I'm a country girl," Cyndi responds. "If you fall off the horse, do you run away and cry or do you get back on the horse?"

"That's bending," I reply.

"A mountain can't move in the wind, it gets eroded, but a tree bends in the wind. Right?"

"You're exactly right," I voice back to the woman who is more like me than I ever expected.

A former witch who is now avidly studying the Bible? Cyndi reminds us we can all bend and change. And bend and change for the better.

Perhaps you're wondering if in writing *Bend*, I found my answer to what helps people like Cyndi make a comeback. Did I discover how others find something of promise in the toughest of days? Did my interviewees solve if we *really* need God to right ourselves again?

I will let the rest of baby Emma's story answer that. Perhaps the most tender experience of sweet Emma's life was what the doctors discovered while Emma was still growing inside her mama. Near the end of Emma's gestation, sonogram photos revealed the tiny babe was reaching out her hand and curling her fingers tightly. The medical team thought Emma's hand was folded in deformity. But upon birth, both of Emma's hands were open and relaxed.

After Emma passed, Bob and Kristi shared that they believed that God was bending down from heaven and holding onto Emma's hand in the womb. Her bitty fingers rested in his steady palm.

Countless family, friends, neighbors, and even strangers, prayed and hoped that the wee one would find a way to beat the odds of the doctors' prognosis.

And in the end, without opening her eyes or speaking a word, Emma taught us all an indomitable lesson: God bends too.

I wonder if the Creator of the universe is doing the same for us this very day. I wonder. Does God have his hand firmly clasped around ours, even when we don't realize it? Even when we shake our fists heavenward? Even when our life dares us to break?

Is he bending toward us as he kneels down in prayer on our behalf? Is he bending his head in tears because he wants so much more for us? Is he bending, extending his hands in loving help?

I wonder. Do you think he's bending toward you?

Dig deeper. *Bend.*
Additional insights and reflections on page 260.

Bending Points

Chapter One

*"I don't think of all the misery
but of the beauty that still remains."*
—Anne Frank

Jewish teen Anne Frank recorded indelible wisdom beyond her years in her diary. The German-born Anne and her family hid from the Nazis in an Amsterdam warehouse for two years. In August 1944, the German secret police discovered the Franks in their Secret Annex about the same time Walter and his family crammed in the abandoned farmhouse attic. Even when life grew darkest, the young diarist expressed her profound perspective, "I don't think of all the misery but of the beauty that still remains."[1]

Life pivots on our perspective. We can hyper-focus on our misery or widen our eyes to "the beauty that still remains." Were Walter's Holocaust years entirely bleak misery? Or were there slivers of beauty piercing the pitch-black atrocities?

Walter faced serendipitous bending again and again, but this stalwart boy refused to let the Nazis break him. But there is more to Walter's bending points. Through it all, Walter vows that he never relied on God's help. God, however, offered help anyway from which beauty emerged.

---

[1] Anne Frank, Good Reads, https://www.goodreads.com/quotes/803286-i-don-t-think-of-all-the-misery-but-of-the.

From his initial days of captivity in the Jewish ghetto, Walter leaned closer to his parents and William. Aunt Felicja sneaked Walter and William into her orphanage to nourish them with extra food. Twice Polish workers freed Walter from Dr. Mengele's barbaric experiments. The American GIs rescued and safeguarded young Walter and William.

The Holocaust was a juxtaposition of terror and kindness. Did you catch the beautiful kindness extended to Walter? Were all these happenstances random coincidences or did the sovereign God of the universe oversee each one? Was the Judeo-Christian *Jehovah Elohim*, the God Most High, totally absent in the Nazi-crazed years or was his presence just harder to detect at times?

In my Holocaust research, I ran across a tender story of Swiss-American psychiatrist Dr. Elisabeth Kübler-Ross, who is best known for her breakthrough work with dying patients and the five stages of grief. In 1946, a year after Walter and William freed themselves from Dachau II, Kübler-Ross visited Germany's Majdaneck concentration camp. In surveying the children's barracks amid its tossed-about toys and shoes, Kübler-Ross was taken back by a number of etchings on the barracks' walls.

The children sensed they were going to die, so they used pebbles and their fingernails to scratch hundreds of butterflies into the wooden walls on their cells. The butterflies represented beauty and hope in transitioning from the little ones' earthly bodies.

The Holocaust children recognized something beyond the gloom of their present turmoil. We face a similar challenge to look beyond our today. Kübler-Ross later wrote, "Should you shield the canyons from the windstorms you would never see the true beauty of their carvings."[2]

We need windstorms in our lives to chip away at the externals so we can appreciate the true beauty underneath.

---

[2] Elisabeth Kübler-Ross, Reddit, https://www.reddit.com/r/quotes/comments/69u57e/should_you_shield_the_canyons_from_the_windstorms/.

I believe everything points to God orchestrating the compassionate help in sparing Walter's life. God never took his eyes off Walter. At times in Walter's life and even in our own, it can *feel* as if God has turned his eyes away from us.

Yet when I feel I'm bending beyond what I can handle, my steady plumb line comes back to: what does God say? What can we absolutely know to be true about him?

I take the insightful words in Proverbs 15:3 as comforting truth. "The eyes of the Lord are everywhere, keeping watch on the wicked and the good" (New International Version). I also find solace when the Old Testament's patriarch Job, languishing in his own unthinkable loss and sorrow, declared that God "views the ends of the earth and sees everything under the heavens" (Job 28:24, NIV). That includes you and me.

In our struggles, it may appear as if God is blind. Or, we'd at least like him to get his vision checked. But you know, ahem, I have to admit. When it comes to seeing who God really is, I am the one with the limited eyesight.

Walter's distant relatives, the Israeli Jews, called the Creator of the universe, *El Roi*, the God who sees. *El Roi* is always on watch. You and I are never farther than God's perfectly sighted eyes can see. He sees the good, the bad, and the real ugly on this earth. And someday, in the blink of an eye, when God fully renews Earth, he will restore the death and destruction of Hitler and his lackeys to complete loveliness. There will be no more misery, but only beauty that still remains.

❧

Bending Points

Chapter Two

"I can be angry about not having limbs, or I can be thankful that I have a purpose. I chose gratitude."

—Nick Vujicic

In the movie *Still Alice,* cognitive psychology and linguistics professor Alice Howland finds her steel-edged mind slowly rusting from early-onset Alzheimer's disease. In a sweet scene with fifty-year-old Alice and her youngest daughter, Lydia, the two are meandering on a boardwalk, talking about the future. Alice shares her wish for Lydia to go to college to study drama rather than continue to struggle as a wannabe actress.

"Life's tough," Alice slowly voices to Lydia. "It is tougher than you know. I want you to have some sort of security before I go."[1]

That's how I feel about you, my reader. Life is tough and tougher than I want you to know. And I also want you to have some security in this world before we part ways for now. So let's skip to the tough, yet still beautiful, realities.

Not everyone arrives in this world in mint condition. Some babies like Sarah, Katie, and Hadley, arrive with physical challenges. But is their life any less valuable than those of us born in full health? The answer lies in what God says about all his handcrafted children.

---

[1] Richard Glatzer and Wash Westmoreland, directors and screenwriters, adapted from the Lisa Genova novel, *Still Alice* (Sony Classics, 2014).

Psalm 139:13–17 (New International Version) gives us one of the most descriptive assessments of how the Creator views his human creations. The psalmist reflects on the wonder of his own prenatal development:

> For you created my inmost being; you knit me together in my mother's womb. I praise you because I am fearfully and wonderfully made; your works are wonderful, I know that full well. My frame was not hidden from you when I was made in the secret place, when I was woven together in the depths of the earth. Your eyes saw my unformed body; all the days ordained for me were written in your book before one of them came to be. How precious to me are your thoughts, God! How vast is the sum of them!

Each of us was knit together under God's watchful guidance. To the divine Artist, even birth irregularities are not a mistake. Not an oops.

Most of my grade-school years I felt a big oops because I was continually teased for being "too tall" and "too fat." By fifth grade, I reached my full height of five feet ten inches, fitting in with my dad's towering side of the family. But among my slower-growing peers, I felt like a giant. A misfit who inwardly grumbled at God.

Thankfully, those grumblings have lessened over the years. I've learned to be grateful for all that I do have and not hyper-focus on what I lack or might like to see different in my life.

The families of Sarah, Katie, and Hadley are living proof of choosing to cherish the beautiful in the tough and unexpected. I'm glad that in spite of distressing raw emotions at times, they continue to walk in shoes of gratitude.

❦

Bending Points

Chapter Three

*"Kind words do not cost much.
Yet they can accomplish much."*
—Blaise Pascal

Matthew shuffles cautiously toward the woman holding out her hand. He dips his head at her questions. Wringing his bony hands, the seven-year-old mumbles about why the principal sent him home from school. Matthew punched his teacher in the stomach.

But the lad needn't feel afraid of Marisa Blay. She's Matthew's loyal advocate and director of Puerto Rico's Proyecto Amor (Project Love), a home for Matthew and nearly thirty other abandoned or abused children—all inflicted with HIV or AIDS. Besides, Marisa understands school suspensions. She once tripped a nun down the stairs in high school.

Marisa is more worried about her normally amicable Matthew's recent fits of aggression. Marisa wonders, *Is Matthew's disease affecting his brain?* I watch Matthew and the other orphans play and roughhouse and find it hard to fathom that they carry an invisible virus. They giggle, screech, wobble, and slide. But drawing closer, you notice their skin blotches and scrawny legs that betray their failing immune systems. Most of them probably will not make it to their teen years.

"I want the children nobody wants. I want the ones who are the worst off," Marisa shares with me. "If you really like children, you don't care what they have."

Yet not everyone in the outskirts of metro San Juan feels the same way. Many people on the lush island have shunned the Blays and the children. When the first Proyecto Amor children entered kindergarten, ten of their classmates transferred to other schools.

"A lot of parents raised hell. Many threw papers and rocks at me and would say all the bad words you can think of from A to Z," recalls Marisa. So Marisa simply passed these bully parents and said, "*Que Dios te bendiga*," which means, "God bless you."

Marisa's philosophy is these people are just uninformed about HIV/AIDS. "I used to be ignorant myself," she says with a tender smile, "and it took me a time to learn."

The Brown Bombers confronted similar spiteful bantering and callous mistreatment of opponents and everyday citizens back in the 1940s and 1950s—and years beyond. But they, like Marisa, never let the verbal sticks and stones stop them from taking the high road and stepping up to the plate.

The Brown Bombers garnered disrespect for the color of their skin. The Puerto Rican children garnered disrespect for an illness underneath their skin. You and I no doubt have faced our own experiences with not quite fitting in.

This is why I appreciate uplifting words like, "Be devoted to one another in love. Honor one another above yourselves" (Romans 12:10, New International Version). Loving and honoring other individuals above us takes finesse and class like turning the other cheek at judgmental parents or mean-spirited baseball fans.

✼

Bending Points

Chapter Four

> *"To refuse [forgiveness] means to refuse*
> *God's mercy for ourselves."*
> —C. S. Lewis

Near the end of my interview time with Josh and Nina, I sense I need to interject. Josh seems heavy-hearted over the enormity of the lives he took during the Iraq war. It's hard to imagine the oppressive crush of Josh's angst. It is beyond my life experience to comprehend pulling the trigger that ended the life of thirty-one human beings.

Heavens, I'm the girl who grew up with an avid hunter dad and two older brothers, but to this day, I still wince just thinking about the time I aimed my brother's BB gun at a sparrow and actually hit it.

Josh knows intellectually that he was following military orders and that God extends forgiveness for this wartime loss of life, but in his inner soul, Josh still lugs around an overstuffed footlocker of guilt. So I pause our conversation to share the story of another person I once interviewed. Someone else who dragged around insurmountable remorse for the death of others.

Her name is Norma McCorvey, but she was known by most as simply Miss Norma. Miss Norma never went by the assumed name of Jane Doe on the piece of paper she signed in 1973 in the landmark U.S. Supreme Court case, *Roe v. Wade*. Pregnant and just twenty-one at the time, Miss Norma scrawled "Jane Roe" on the historic document that ushered in America's legalized abortion and the deaths so far of more than 61.6 million babies.

For almost five decades, many individuals and groups vehemently blamed Miss Norma for these lives cut short before they could even take a breath. But Miss Norma shared more to the story with me.

"I never really was Jane Roe. No such person existed, except on paper. She was fictitious," Miss Norma explained when I ask her about the people who essentially used her to be their poster girl for abortion rights. "I basically just signed on the dotted line. I never went to any of the court proceedings."

Miss Norma's legal counsel at the time insisted "Jane Roe" remain pregnant to bolster their case that so many unfortunate women like Jane are legally denied choosing what's right for their own bodies. The young woman had no idea her signature would light a flame to an intensifying hell storm across our nation.

So how did Miss Norma, who never had an abortion herself, cope with the burden of guilt over her association with *Roe v. Wade*? How did Miss Norma find peace when she was often a target in the pro-life versus pro-death combat? And what does forgiveness look like to this woman forever thrust into U.S. history books?

Miss Norma turned her life over to God in 1995 and became one of the most outspoken pro-life champions on the planet. Yet still she encountered malicious accusations.

"People will say to me, 'You should be ashamed!' But I don't have shame anymore because when I crawled out of my gin bottle and looked around, I realized I was wrong. I made a mistake," said the Texan who drowned her guilt and remorse for years in alcohol and drugs. "I was ashamed of what I had done, but when Jesus forgave me for my role—that just made all the difference in the world. I don't really care if mankind ever forgives me. As long as I'm in tune with the Lord, that's all that counts."

As I retell my Miss Norma phone conversation to Josh, I want to make sure he hears the next part of Miss Norma's journey. Once living with deep regrets for her association with Jane Roe, Miss Norma shared with me another kind of forgiveness.

"Forgiving yourself is the hardest part. To not forgive oneself is probably the worst addiction in the whole world," Miss Norma explained. "I lived mainly from 1969 to 1995 on regrets. Being healed around forgiving myself was a process."

That process for the gregarious grandmother included letting others remind her of the truth. A number of years ago, a woman from a crisis pregnancy center gave Miss Norma a tiny blackboard. Miss Norma asked the giver why the slate lacked words.

"She told me, 'It's blank, Miss Norma, because your slate has been wiped clean.' How cool is that? God has forgotten all of my sins. Then once you forgive yourself, that's when you start really living. That's what I found in the sense of being joyous, happy, and secure with myself," Miss Norma adds. "Once you go through the Refiner's fire and come out pure as gold, and you do forgive yourself, a whole new world opens up to you. For me, it's now a much better world to be in."

I see both Josh's and Nina's eyes sparkle with a fresh glimmer of hope. The New Testament's Romans 8:1 (The Passion Translation) reminds us, "So now the case is closed. There remains no accusing voice of condemnation against those who are joined in life-union with Jesus, the Anointed One."

When we come to God and dump our failures and burdensome guilt at his feet, he, the Righteous Judge, informs us that he already swung the gavel in the courtroom of life and boomed, "The case is closed. There remains no accusing voice of condemnation. Your slate is wiped clean."

Miss Norma entered the presence of her Forgiving God in February 2017. Even after her death, her intentions and actions on turning pro life are still questioned. Despite Miss Norma's complexities, I sometimes wonder if she confidently marched into heaven carrying a blank, tiny blackboard.

❧

Bending Points

Chapter Five

*"Everything that we see is a shadow
cast by that which we do not see."*
—Martin Luther King Jr.

Sunday's paper delivers news I do not want to hear, but news that I need to hear. Over the past year and half, eighty-seven homeless people died in my city. Some were discovered dying or dead inside a drainage pipe, under a bridge, or on train tracks. Robin shimmied up a tree and died like a stretched-out scarecrow, straddling a gap in the tree's trunk. At age forty-seven, Robin died alone.

To many of us, homeless folks are faceless and nameless living in *that* part of town. Before I met Cyndi, I had never really met a displaced person. Handing an occasional bill out of my car window or buying a destitute stranger some fast food is not the same as putting a name to a face and liking the face you get to know.

Robin called her mama monthly. Robin checked in here and there at a homeless shelter. But Robin's fake friend, methamphetamine, turned on Robin real bad. Meth stole Robin's depleted hope and final breath. Two teen boys found Robin motionless, her blond hair fluttering in the biting breeze. A syringe lay among the autumn leaves in the shadow of the tree.

Robin lived and died among the shadow of her addiction. In a sense, we all have a choice of what we allow to shadow us. Our past can loom over us. Our present stressors can darken our perspective. Our unknown future can appear gloomy.

Maybe this is why the psalmist spells out the best place to live, whether we scrape it together on the street, reside comfortably in a palatial mansion, or dwell somewhere in between. "Those who live in the shelter of the Most High will find rest in the shadow of the Almighty" (Psalm 91:1, New Living Translation).

The original Hebrew word translated "live in" in this verse means to stop, lodge, and stay. We were not created to be relentless lone rangers. God invites us to nestle under the shadow of his protection and shade—and make this our permanent home. And when we do, we'll find rest. Plus, comfort, strength, and a reason to stand up to any detractors that hiss at us to numb ourselves up and deal with disappointment, pain, and loneliness by ourselves.

I so wish Robin had chosen God's shadow instead of meth's.

Bending Points

Chapter Six

> *"The marvelous richness of human experience would lose something of rewarding joy if there were no limitations to overcome."*
> —Helen Keller

Rhidale's chronicle of captivity reminds me of famed Russian artist Nikolai Yaroshenko's 1888 classic painting, *Life Goes On Everywhere*. Known for painting about Russia's social contradictions of his day, Yaroshenko in *Life Goes On* depicts the tenderness of humanity amid the turmoil of inhumanity.

Yaroshenko's piece portrays prisoners feeding a flock of pigeons from the barred window of a convict railcar. A mother and three men surround a young child who is dropping morsels to the birds on the railway platform. In their own uncertainty and angst, these five captives are creating their own helping of joy.

Yet, if you look closely, you see a contrast on the other side of the railcar. You catch a glimpse of a man staring out the opposite window. He appears somber and alone in his thoughts, detached from the merriment just feet away. Yaroshenko, whom Soviet leader Vladimir Lenin, called "a marvelous artist and wonderful psychologist of real life,"[1] shows us the tension we all face.

Are our most heart-wrenching challenges marked by despair or is there another point of view to consider? Is there a way to create our own helping of joy in times when we feel imprisoned by pain, disappointment, and a posse of other concerns?

Rhidale models this every day he wakes up inside his prison cell. In a sense, Rhidale can find purpose and joy feeding birds on the railway platform or he can stay aloof and depressed on the other side of the railcar.

We are granted this choice too in our own lives. Find joy in our confining circumstances or wallow alone in a self-imposed pity party. But, trust me, I understand from a myriad of personal angst, that finding joy is almost humanly impossible. You and I are not meant to just suck it up, move on, and pretend we have joy. Nope. That is above our pay grade. Joy is an integral part of God's character, and it is up to him to download joy into our here and now.

Let me tell you a little secret. My parents gifted me with the middle name Joy. As a kid, I never liked my name. Beth Joy. I really don't know why, but maybe my name sounded so short and plain-sounding to me. And, no one else around in my rural community had my name. But you know what? Today, I LOVE my name. And here's mainly why. *Joy* shows up everywhere in the Bible and just when people like you and me need it most.

King David is one of these people. Right in the thick of the fallout from his adultery-murder cover-up, he cries out to God in Psalm 51:8 (New American Standard Bible), "Make me to hear joy and gladness, Let the bones which You have broken rejoice." David is comparing his sinful condition to feeling like he's battered and crushed physically.

[1] Nikolai Alexandrovich Yaroshenko, Great Russian Artists, Rusartist.org, http://www. rusartist.org/nikolai-alexandrovich-yaroshenko-1846-1898/#.Xmcehi2ZPUI.

In the ancient Hebrew language, the *bones* here represent the center of emotional strength. David felt the weight of his wrongdoing deep into his bones.

The New English Translation (NET Bible) puts this verse another way, "Grant me the ultimate joy of being forgiven. May the bones you crushed rejoice." There is ultimate joy in knowing that God truly forgives us.

This heaven-sent joy is what fuels Rhidale to flourish in his imprisonment. It's what Nikolai Yaroshenko painted in his *Life Goes On Everywhere* classic. You can view your confining situations with a helping of God's joy or you can detach yourself and stare out the window alone.

I'm glad day after day, Rhidale lives out the better choice.

❧

Bending Points

Chapter Seven

"Tears at times have the weight of speech."
—Ovid

Tears do not flow readily for me. Growing up, I had two older brothers who advised me not to be a cry baby. In journalism school, the professors stressed that as reporters, we should not enter into our stories. We were directed to check our emotions at the door.

So for decades I did.

No hint of grief when holding the hand of dying AIDS patients. No hint of an impending sob when visiting radiation-poisoned children of Chernobyl. None when interviewing families devastated by murder, disasters, or disturbing crimes.

Some editors nicknamed me the "Tragedy Queen" because I could interview hurting people, and they would pour out their hearts. All without shedding a tear myself.

Call it focus. Call it pride in my craft. Call it unusual.

But on that March Saturday sitting at the dining room table with Wayne and Gwen Wrich, my decades of steely interviewing resolve cracked. The dam to my stored-up emotions crumbled in a floodgate. Whoosh. My sobs mingled with theirs. Whoosh. Pass the tissue box, please.

And it was okay.

No one prepares you to stand at the side of your lifeless child—especially not a second time. It pains me to think about the wrenching losses that the Wrich family faced. Two daughters with disabilities and then a tragic accident that ended their son's life.

In those sacred hours of talking candidly about life, love, and loss, and dabbing our eyes freely, I believe God was wiping his own eyes. Years ago a friend shared this verse with me from Psalm 56:8. I especially appreciate *The Living Bible's* translation, "You have seen me tossing and turning through the night. You have collected all my tears and preserved them in your bottle! You have recorded every one in your book."

Our tender-hearted God actually collects every one of our tears. He also records each tear from our wanderings and sorrows in his own private record book. Archeologists have uncovered ancient tear bottles from Israel and other Middle Eastern locations. People owned these cherished vessels to catch and preserve their own tears during times of immense grief and pressure.

God may not have many of these tear bottles collected for me, but he knows the inward grief of my soul. He is intimately aware of every one of my heartaches and tears—and yours too. Having an aware and personal God lessens the sting of our anguishes.

I find uplifting hope in reading God's plans for our tears in eternity. "'He will wipe every tear from their eyes. There will be no more death' or mourning or crying or pain, for the old order of things has passed away" (Revelation 21:4, New International Version).

The Wrich children, Laura and Lee, revel, already assured of this tear-free elation.

Bending Points

Chapter Eight

*"Hope is the word which God has
written on the brow of every man."*
—Victor Hugo

I love comeback stories. Something inside me stands and cheers when I learn of underdogs refusing to buckle and break. One such comeback was the Jewish captives in Ilana's hometown who defied the Nazis and won a cunning battle of wit and willpower.

No one could stop the music, the photography, the art, and the beauty in the Kovno ghetto. No swastika, no gun, no flame could eradicate a centuries-deep passion of Kovno's Hebrew people to rise above the dismal and dank to preserve their stories and their lineage.

When Germany stormed across Lithuania in June 1941 and inflicted killing rampages over the next three years, the Nazis did not expect the cunning bravery of Kovno's creative finest.

Determined to resist the Nazi eradication of Jewish culture and personhood, nearly all the ghetto's prisoners, from artists, painters, and photographers to doctors, lawyers, and students worked in secret to preserve their life narratives.

Ghetto prisoner George Kadish, a local high school science teacher with knowledge of photography, snapped images of his fellow Jews through a buttonhole on his overcoat. Click. Click. Click. Kadish captured the rawness, the reality of living fenced in by sadistic enemies yet coming alive in the misery.

Kadish crafted a camera himself and bartered for and smuggled film into the ghetto by hiding it in a hollowed-out crutch. The Germans assigned Kadish to repair X-ray machines at the city's local hospital, and he secretly developed his film in the hospital's lab. Kadish took thousands of photographs to chronicle the day-to-day life in the ghetto. And the Nazis never knew.

Other Kovno Jews sketched maps of their confined space and created pen-and-ink and watercolor paintings of their surroundings. Still others penned accounts or collected these ghetto images and documents—some thirty thousand pages—and hurriedly buried them in tin boxes inside the ghetto at the height of the March 1944 *Kinder Aktion.*

The diary pages, photographs, song lyrics, and precious artifacts of Kovno's hidden-from-the world Jews were concealed in a desolate grave. Hidden from the viciousness, hidden from those who wanted to fully eradicate *die Juden* from the planet.

But *Yahuah-Yahweh,* God of the Hebrews, designed other plans. In 1964, during excavations for a new building on the former ghetto site, workers discovered the tin boxes. Among the archived treasures are a number of Kadish's black-and-white photos, particularly of the ghetto's semi-secret orchestra.

In one close-up image, a half dozen playing violinists are seated and leaning forward to get in Kadish's viewfinder frame. The woman in the foreground with the bobbed haircut and bangs held back by a bobby pin is ever-so-slightly smiling. In another photograph, two men in double-breasted suit jackets are playing a clarinet and a trumpet.

All were members of the Jewish ghetto police orchestra organized in the summer of 1942 under the direction of the Jewish Council of Elders, the ghetto's leadership committee sanctioned by the Nazis themselves. On paper, the musicians were ghetto police, but their ultimate role was to play concerts in the police station, which on occasion even some of the German authorities attended. At dire risk, the orchestra also at times performed at underground locations throughout the ghetto.

Hearing Hebrew melodies and Hebrew readings of God's faithfulness to his people lifted the weary souls of the ghetto prisoners. At one fully packed concert performed all in Hebrew, the audience stood at the end of the recital in exuberant unity singing *Hatikva,* the nineteenth-century Jewish poem and national anthem of Israel.

The secretary of the Jewish Council, Avraham Tory, described the emotional event in his diary. "Everyone's heart was filled with rejoicing and tears poured from their eyes," Tory wrote. "Hope flowed from the depths of the soul, courage and a cry out loud: 'We have not yet lost our hope.'"[1]

"We have not yet lost our hope" is similar to "Let no one lose hope" echoed from the lips of the revered leader of these Jewish sojourners long before they were born. Around 980 BC, youthful shepherd David, the future king of Israel, stared at the behemoth Goliath and refused to cower. In the face of his own Nazi-like enemy, David declared, "Don't let anyone lose hope because of that Philistine" (1 Samuel 17:32, New International Reader's Version).

Hope is empowering. Hope is liberating. Hope inscribes a melody upon the heart. The Jews of Kovno understood this. Do we?

In whom or in what do we place our hope? Where do we hide when our world caves in and we feel imprisoned in fear and despair?

As the orchestra ghetto struck a chord with their fellow Jewish captives, they played songs and hymns written and performed by noble King David. King David's Psalm 32:7 (New American Standard Bible) bursts forth with, "You are my hiding place; You preserve me from trouble; You surround me with songs of deliverance."

The Hebrew word for "hiding place" is *mis•tor,* which is essentially the English word for *mystery.* Mystery implies something hidden or secretive. *Mis•tor* also refers to a place of refuge or safety.

No matter what we face in this life, God is always our safe place to hide. He composes songs of deliverance to resonate within our soul.

[1] Ofer Aderet, "The Secret of the Kovno Ghetto Orchestra Discovered," Haaretz, January 28, 2016, https://www.haaretz.com/jewish/.premium-the-secret-of-the-kovno-ghetto-orchestra-discovered-1.5396608.

And for the men and women of the Kovno ghetto orchestra, when the rest of the Jewish police were arrested at the end of March 1944, these stalwart musicians were spared. Once the entire ghetto was destroyed, the Nazis sent the orchestra members to Germany's Dachau concentration camp to play there. For all these instrumentalists who survived the Holocaust, many continued to play in concerts in Germany's post-war displaced persons camps.

No one can stop the music that honors *Yahuah-Yahweh*, our forever secure hiding place.

Bending Points

Chapter Nine

> *"Brokenness is often the road to*
> *a breakthrough. Be encouraged."*
> —Tony Evans

Everybody has scrapes and scars and dings and dents. Yes, no one escapes life without obstacles that crack the façade of perfection. Hawa has certainly endured trials that threatened to compress and splinter her faith in humanity and in God. Yet Hawa refuses to let her pain and suffering mar her optimism and her hope.

In many ways, Hawa resembles the gorgeous ceramic pieces created by the traditional Japanese art of *kintsgui,* which literally means golden ("kin") and repair ("tsugi"). Also called *kintsukuroi,* this Japanese golden repair practice transforms broken pieces of pottery into refined masterpieces. Each shattered fragment of a bowl, vase, teapot, or other cherished stoneware is reconnected with a precious metal such as liquid gold or lacquer dusted with powdered gold.

Because each original object breaks in a different way, unique, random patterns are featured across each restored piece. The gold lacquer draws the shards together to enhance the breaks with their own one-of-a-kind beauty. And now considered literally better than new, the restyled pottery is regarded as more beautiful and valuable. Each striking piece earns praise because it also comes with an exclusive history and a brand-new story.

In much the same way as the *kintsgui* restoration, our struggles and wounds create different marks on each of us. Our broken efforts and broken relationships and broken dreams may feel like they are nothing but a useless pile of remnants, but there is more to each of our stories.

If we ever feel life is crashing down and we're beyond repair. Or we want to hide our brokenness and our scars. We can dare to leave all those jagged edges in the gentle hands of the Master Potter. The prophet Isaiah writes of the Potter's accomplished handiwork, "But now, O Lord, You are our Father, We are the clay, and You our potter; And all of us are the work of Your hand" (Isaiah 64:8, New American Standard Bible).

We are all clay. We are all in-process works in his hands. Some of us doubt anything can really be done with our clumps of dried-out clay. Others of us might think we are more capable than God at reconstructing our lives. But regardless of our feelings or mental miscalculations, the truth is, God wants to turn us and our imperfections into exquisite works of art far beyond our wildest comprehension.

God doesn't just patch us up with some celestial super glue. He doesn't scrimp on repair materials or scurry through our mending with haphazard care. Ecclesiastes 3:11 (New International Version) advises us, "He has made everything beautiful in its time. He has also set eternity in the human heart; yet no one can fathom what God has done from beginning to end."

The Master Potter is mending and restoring us right now, and most likely behind the scenes. Our gold-filled chinks and fractures are making us even more resiliently strong and captivatingly beautiful. And he declares each of us forever priceless.

🌿

Bending Points

Chapter Ten

*"When all the routines and details and the human
bores get on our nerves, we just yearn to go
away from here to somewhere else."*
—Herbert Hoover

French *Elle* magazine editor-in-chief Jean-Dominique Bauby suffered a massive stroke at age forty-three that left him paralyzed with a neurological condition known as locked-in syndrome. Bauby was unable to move except for blinking his left eyelid.

Trapped in his motionless body, Jean-Dominique refused to break. Instead, with the aid of his speech and language therapist and a tight circle of friends, Jean-Dominique learned to blink his left eyelid to spell out words.

Blink. Blink-blink. Blink. With the painstaking communication code, Jean-Dominique wrote his book *The Diving Bell and the Butterfly*. He spelled out the entire eloquent memoir with some two hundred thousand blinks.

Jean-Dominique died two days after the book was published and had no hint that his blink-after-blink efforts would become an international bestseller and movie. But because of his dogged determination to not die in spirit, Jean-Dominique is now an inspiration to all who learn of his story.

Halfway through his book, Jean-Dominique writes of his two trips outside the hospital facility to meet with Paris medical specialists. On the first ambulance excursion, Jean-Dominique spots the high-rise that hosts the sixth-floor *Elle* office.

> I shed a few tears as we passed the corner café where I used to drop in for a bite. I can weep quite discreetly. People think my eye is watering. The second time I went to Paris, four months later, I was unmoved by it. . . . My own crossing of Paris left me indifferent. Yet nothing was missing—housewives in flowered dresses and youths on roller skates, revving buses, messengers cursing on their scooters. The Place de l'Opéra, straight out of a Dufy canvas. The treetops foaming like surf against glass building fronts, wisps of cloud in the sky. Nothing was missing, except me. I was elsewhere.[1]

"I was elsewhere," Jean-Dominique concludes. I've been there to elsewhere, particularly during times I find unfavorable. And sometimes I feel I'm elsewhere with God.

Our bending points have a way of whisking us away from our normal life, from our hoped-for plans of living. We face off with our latest round of trials. We bend.

Our mind and heart can drift elsewhere. Most anywhere we do not have to confront the reality that life is daring us to break. Cyndi has scuffled with a number of wanting-to-be-elsewhere moments—escaping from abusive marriages, enduring homelessness, encountering falsehoods in her faith.

What elsewhere moments coax you into slipping away into your own world where you reign supreme? Where you call the shots. Where you think you have little need for the tenderness of God. May I suggest another place to park your weariness? A place to relax your

---

[1] Jean-Dominique Bauby, *The Diving Bell and the Butterfly*, (New York: Vintage Books, 1997), 78-79.

grip on your personal compass? Because, honestly, God is already there before you reach your elsewhere. That is worth repeating. There is no elsewhere that God is not already there. Don't take my word for it. Listen to the ancient Hebrew psalmist explain.

"Where can I go from your Spirit? Where can I flee from your presence? If I go up to the heavens, you are there; if I make my bed in the depths, you are there. If I rise on the wings of the dawn, if I settle on the far side of the sea, even there your hand will guide me, your right hand will hold me fast" (Psalm 139:7–10, New International Version).

At times you may feel like Jean-Dominique Bauby did—perpetually locked in. As you bend your way through difficulties, do not despair. No matter how steep the uphill gets, the present-everywhere Creator will be right beside you. God's nearness is the antidote to your breaking. His faithful love for you can cure your mistrust. His compassionate understanding can heal the complacency of your soul.

If you're camped out in elsewhere right now, pause and look around. Lean in and listen. Inch a step toward the All-Present One as you bend. He's already in full stride toward you.

❧

Throughout the pages of *Bend,* you met courageous everyday sojourners like you who have faced their own brink of, "I just can't do this anymore," and they hung on. They dug deep. They refused to quit. They bent. And beauty surprised them in the bending.

So how are you doing lately? I mean really doing? Just remember: you are stronger than you think.

Keep bending, my friend. Keep bending.

Notes

Chapter 1

1. Markus Zusak, *The Book Thief,* (New York: Knopf, 2007), 401.
2. Andrea Jacobs, "What is a burned house compared to a burned and gassed family?" *Intermountain Jewish News,* January 6, 2011, https://www.ijn.com/walter-plywaski/.

Chapter 2

1. David Lindsay-Abaire, playwright, screenwriter, *Rabbit Hole,* (Blossom Films, 2010).
2. Martin Pistorius, *Ghost Boy,* (Nashville: Nelson Books, 2013), 63.

Chapter 3

1. Bill Vogrin, "Hdyhdyhdyhdy," *The Gazette,* Colorado Springs, Colo., October 13, 2013, https://gazette.com/sports/hdyhdyh-dyhdy/article_cecdca08-c2a2-5b34-96ce-53c448c4f0c6.html.

Chapter 4

1. Patricia Kime, "Active-Duty Military Suicides at Record Highs in 2018," Military.com, https://www.military.com/daily-news/2019/01/30/active-duty-military-suicides-near-record-highs-2018.html.

Chapter 6

1. "Hickenlooper Announces Clemency," *Valley Courier,* May 15, 2019, https://alamosanews.com/article/hickenlooper-announces-clemency.
2. Prison Culture, "A Prisoner's Words Describing the 'Hole'," USPrisonCulture.com, http://www.usprisonculture.com/blog/2011/07/18/a-prisoners-words-describing-the-hole/.

3. Robert Green Ingersoll, Brainyquote.com, https://www.brainyquote.com/quotes/robert_green_ingersoll_135548.

Chapter 7

1. Henri Nouwen, BrainyQuote.com, https://www.brainyquote.com/quotes/henri_nouwen_131151.

Chapter 8

1. C. Peter Chen, World War II Database, "Annexation of the Baltic States," https://ww2db.com/battle_spec.php?battle_id=283.
2. Encyclopedia Britannica, "Lithuania, Independence Lost," https://www.britannica.com/place/Lithuania/Russian-rule.
3. VilNews, Kaunas Ghetto (1941-1944), "An entire urban district turned into a merciless death camp," http://vilnews.com/2012-12-18271.
4. Jono David, Jewish Virtual Library, "Virtual Jewish World: Kovno (Kaunas), Lithuania," https://www.jewishvirtuallibrary.org/kovno-kaunas-lithuania-jewish-history-tour.
5. Task Force for International Cooperation on Holocaust Education Remembrance and Research, "Report: Mass Graves and Killing Sites in the Eastern Part of Europe," p. 6. https://www.holocaustremembrance.com/sites/default/files/MMWG_Killing_Sites.pdf.
6. VilNews, "The largest mass murder of Lithuanian Jews," http://vilnews.com/2012-12-18261.
7. VilNews, "Kaunas Ghetto (1941-1944)."
8. Ibid., "The Underground School."
9. Jono David, Jewish Virtual Library.
10. Holocaust Education & Archive Research Team, "The Kovno Ghetto (Kaunas)," http://www.holocaustresearchproject.org/ghettos/kovno.html.

11. Museum of Jewish Heritage, Jewishgen.org, "Stuffhof – Sztutowo (Poland)," https://www.jewishgen.org/ForgottenCamps/Camps/StutthofEng.html.
12. History.com, "U.S. Army liberates Dachau concentration camp," https://www.history.com/this-day-in-history/dachau-liberated.
13. History.com, "Germany surrenders unconditionally to the Allies at Reims," https://www.history.com/this-day-in-history/germany-surrenders-unconditionally-to-the-allies-at-reims.
14. Holocaust Encyclopedia, "Lithuania," https://encyclopedia.ushmm.org/content/en/article/lithuania.
15. Kimberly McDowell, *West Seneca Bee,* "Do you remember?", (West Seneca, New York, April 14, 2011), https://www.westsenecabee.com/articles/do-you-remember/.

Acknowledgments

I am deeply grateful to God for giving me the creativity and perseverance to see this book through from initial concept to you now reading these pages. When Jeanette Thomason and I brainstormed over coffee and dessert that chilly February 2013 afternoon, she encouraged me to dig deep to find the best possible remarkable stories of remarkable people. We found them, Jeanette. How can I ever thank you enough? Even though you've now got the best view ever to read *Bend,* we all miss you here dearly.

I wish I could list every person who has inspired me to keep going with this book. My sincerest praise to each brave soul I interviewed for these chapters. Thank you, thank you for entrusting me with your life journeys.

My family—Dan, Linda, Christine, Doug, Becky, Stephanie, Kurt, Erica, Dan, Adam, Laney, Addison, Maddox, Haidyn, and Maura—thank you for carrying on Dad's and Mom's heritage of resiliency through anything.

To my advisory team, you gals kick it: Angie Boyd, Terry Cornuke, Blythe Daniel, Karen DeLorenzo, Shelly Johnson, Deb Krumland, Kathy Parham, and Kristi Phipps. Laura Lisle, thank you for always being there as a steady voice of reason. Your countless hours editing and proofing and your deciphering and typing my lengthy interviews are the bedrock of this book.

Sara Plott, words fall short in thanking you for keeping me energized and focused. Your writing, social media, and marketing expertise nudge me to a higher standard.

Everyone should be blessed with such a supportive editorial, design, photography, and marketing team. My thanks to each of you for excelling above and beyond: Stephanie Alton, Candace Andrews, Karen Bouchard, Nancy Brummett, Jerry Daniel, Lisa Dorman,

Anne Emmons, Sara Ewbank, Sylke Lacy, Joy Miller, Ray Moore, Karen Morgan, Tracy Nolton, Jane O'Gorman, Rob Parham, Dorease Rioux, Bryndi Schult, Karen Sherry, Edie Snyder, Lindsay Weatherford, and Olivia Wheelock.

To my freelancers group, bless you for all your counsel, laughter and prayers: Karen Scalf Bouchard, Tez Brooks, Neal Browne, Catherine DeVries, Marianne Hering, Mike Klassen, Andy Sloan, Danny Summers, and Gaylyn Williams. My hugs and gratitude to my Bible study women, WVC community group, and faithful friends who continually uplift me with your encouragement and prayers. Because of your investment in me, I am one of the richest women in the world.

And to you, my dear readers, thank you for joining me in this quest to explore how any of us make a comeback. May none of us ever lose hope.

I'd love to hear how you are bending.

Connect with me:

Website: BethLueders.com

Blog: BethLueders.com/blog

Facebook: facebook.com/BethLuedersAuthor/

LinkedIn: https://www.linkedin.com/in/BethLueders

About the Author

Many people describe Beth as lively, soulful, and humorous, and she would agree. She'd also add in curious and a champion of the underdog. Crisscrossing the planet to document stories in nearly twenty countries, Beth is an award-winning journalist whose exposés include the plight of Chernobyl's radiation-poisoned children and at-risk prostitutes in the Philippines.

Photo by Robert Parham

Beth has authored and co-authored several books, including *Lifting Our Eyes*: Finding God's Grace through the Virginia Tech Tragedy (2007, Berkeley Trade), *Two Days Longer*: Discovering More of God as You Wait for Him (2006, Howard), and reflective commentary and practical study tools for the *Women of Faith Study* Bible.

Beth is also a Cru alumni staff member and former editor of *Worldwide Challenge* and *Clarity* magazines. As founder and director of MacBeth Communications, Beth writes and edits for several companies, ministries, and nonprofits. Beth speaks about faith and resiliency and is a comeback coach and pet therapy volunteer.

A Nebraska native now living in Colorado, Beth admires the simple things in life: nature's beauty, fresh coffee, deep conversations, and long walks with her collie.

CPSIA information can be obtained
at www.ICGtesting.com
Printed in the USA
FSHW021618190820
73112FS